What Would You Do?

An Ethical Case Workbook for Human Service Professionals

Patricia Kenyon

Arizona Western College

National Organization for Human Service Education
Education Committee

Brooks/Cole Publishing Company

I(T)P® An International Thomson Publishing Company

Pacific Grove ▪ Albany ▪ Belmont ▪ Bonn ▪ Boston ▪ Cincinnati ▪ Detroit ▪ Johannesburg ▪ London
Madrid ▪ Melbourne ▪ Mexico City ▪ New York ▪ Paris ▪ Singapore ▪ Tokyo ▪ Toronto ▪ Washington

Sponsoring Editor: *Eileen Murphy*
Marketing Team: *Michael Campbell/Christine Davis*
Editorial Assistant: *Susan Carlson*
Production Editor: *Tessa A. McGlasson*
Manuscript Editor: *Lorraine Anderson*
Permissions Editor: *Connie Dowcett*

Cover Design: *Cheryl Carrington*
Cover Photo: *Hideki Kuwajima/Photonica*
Interior Design: *Scratchgravel Publishing Services*
Typesetting: *Scratchgravel Publishing Services*
Printing and Binding: *Patterson Printing*

For more information, contact:

BROOKS/COLE PUBLISHING COMPANY
511 Forest Lodge Road
Pacific Grove, CA 93950
USA

International Thomson Publishing Europe
Berkshire House 168-173
High Holborn
London WC1V 7AA
England

Thomas Nelson Australia
102 Dodds Street
South Melbourne, 3205
Victoria, Australia

Nelson Canada
1120 Birchmount Road
Scarborough, Ontario
Canada M1K 5G4

International Thomson Editores
Seneca 53, Col. Polanco
México, D. F., México
C. P. 11560

International Thomson Publishing GmbH
Königswinterer Strasse 418
53227 Bonn
Germany

International Thomson Publishing Asia
60 Albert Street
#15-01 Albert Complex
Singapore 189969

International Thomson Publishing Japan
Hirakawacho Kyowa Building, 3F
2-2-1 Hirakawacho
Chiyoda-ku, Tokyo 102
Japan

Printed in the United States of America

10 9 8 7 6 5 4 3 2 1

Library of Congress Cataloging-in-Publication Data
Kenyon, Patricia, [date]–
      What would you do? : an ethical case workbook for human service
   professionals / Patricia Kenyon.
         p.   cm.
      Includes bibliographic references and index.
      ISBN 0-534-34938-2
      1. Human services—Moral and ethical aspects.   I. Title.
   HV41.K45   1998
   174'.9362—dc21   98-10279
                                                                    CIP

Upon entering a profession each person inherits a measure of both the responsibility and the trust that have accrued to that profession over the years, as well as the corresponding obligation to adhere to the profession's code of conduct for ethical practice.
—Adapted from American Nurses Association, 1985

Foreword

In the more than thirty years since the human service movement began, it has continued its evolution toward becoming a recognized profession. This workbook represents a milestone in that evolution because of its focus on understanding and applying ethical principles that are a foundation of responsible human service practice.

Virtually all of our beliefs and actions are based on values we hold, acquired from multiple influences such as family, church, peers, teachers, and so forth. The human service profession attracts persons from varying backgrounds and varying value systems, yet the profession itself has identified its own values and ethical guidelines to which all practitioners must adhere. These guidelines are essential for responsible practice in that they provide everyone, regardless of personal values, general guidelines to use in making decisions, without dictating precisely what *must* be done in any individual situation or when ethical principles conflict. Understanding and implementing these guidelines is critical for several reasons: They help with responsible, reasoned decision making; they help the practitioner avoid litigation; and they are more likely to result in effective, high-quality service to clients.

It is not surprising that ethical guidelines of virtually all helping professions have striking similarities. A general consensus exists about workers' obligations to self, client, agency, and society. All workers in helping professions must understand their own values, know the expectations of their specific profession, and have a useful model for applying ethical guidelines to practical situations. The model presented here is unique in that it utilizes the specific ethical guidelines of the human service profession, yet can easily be applied to any helping profession's code of ethics. It is a model that demands critical thinking, and helps a worker make *reasoned* choices about behaviors and actions. Its major strengths are that it (1) bridges the gap between theory and practice, (2) provides a framework for dealing with difficult issues, and (3) does this in relation to many different stages and situations in a career.

By illustrating how ethical principles apply to all stages and aspects of human service work, this text brings these issues to the forefront of every worker's mind in a consistent and continual manner. The result can only be a practitioner in whom ethical reasoning has become imbedded—so much so that ethical thinking is continuous and automatic, rather than compartmentalized to be applied only when specifically called upon to do so, such as in a case conference or workshop.

Because the material presented here focuses on the very heart of human service practice, this is a text that should be required for every student in every human service program. All workers should become thoroughly familiar with its concepts. To do so will ensure the continued professionalism of the human service movement and its practitioners.

Miriam Clubok
Associate Professor of Social Work, Ohio University
Founding member, National Organization for Human Service Education (NOHSE)
NOHSE President, 1981–1985

Foreword

The knowledge, skills, and competencies required by human service professionals are the same knowledge, skills, and competencies required by Nazi Gestapo agents who sought to demean and destroy their victims. The difference between a human service professional and a member of the Gestapo lies in completely different sets of values, attitudes, and ethics.

Most academic programs stress traditional knowledge and skills with relatively little attention to values, attitudes, and ethics. While human service programs have given greater attention to identifying and teaching about appropriate values and attitudes in students, even they have focused in only limited ways on the ethical development and decision-making of students who will soon be entry-level human service professionals.

Because ethics and ethical development are difficult and often murky areas, they are too often simply ignored in educational programs for the helping professions. The professional codes of ethics then seem like just so many platitudinous ideals. In these days of reduced funds for human service programs and managed care for health care programs, many professionals seem to be compromising on their ethics—the fraud in Medicare and Medicaid programs, physical and personal abuse in criminal justice programs, and so forth.

The author has designed this workbook to help faculty and students in human service education programs to better understand ethical standards and to apply the critical thinking necessary to practice ethical behavior with clients, professional colleagues, agencies, and communities in which they work. She has skillfully woven in issues of personal values, community values and attitudes, and some legal and regulatory areas where workers are especially likely to encounter ethical conflicts.

A profession is sometimes defined as an occupation that follows a written code of ethics, and so the National Organization for Human Service Education and the Council for Standards in Human Service Education adopted a code of ethics, the *Ethical Standards for Human Service Professionals*. What remains is for each student and worker to grasp these ethical standards and make them an integral part of his or her professional conduct. In this way each worker will establish his or her own self-concept as a professional and also a reputation among clients and colleagues as a professional. I find this workbook impressive in helping students and faculty deal with issues of ethical decision making, personal values, and attitudes.

Harold L. McPheeters, MD
Director, Commission on Mental Health and Human Services,
Southern Regional Education Board, 1965–1987

Preface

In the 1980s a book called *All I Really Need to Know I Learned in Kindergarten* (Fulghum, 1988) became a bestseller. In his title essay, Fulghum focused on values and ethics in our everyday lives: "Play fair. . . . Don't take things that aren't yours. Say you're sorry when you hurt somebody." As this book's popularity demonstrated, people seek to do the right things and treat others well, but find it difficult to know just what is right—so they hunt for simple and clear rules to follow. And yet, unethical behavior of politicians, law enforcement officers, businesspeople, diplomats, clergy, physicians, lawyers—and, yes, of human service professionals—is highlighted in our daily news. *What Would* You *Do?* helps entry-level human service professionals connect ethical guidelines with professional behavior: In a complex world, apparently clear and specific rules will guide actions only when the professional adds reflection, practice, and experience.

Teaching professional ethics is difficult—doing it well involves not only information about values and ethical guidelines, but also instructional activities that promote the learners' awareness of their own attitudes, foster attitude changes when appropriate, and build their decision-making skills in response to ethical issues. Compounding the difficulty for those of us who work with entry-level human service professionals and students is their wide variety of personal, social, and cultural backgrounds and the limited periods of time during which we work with them.

In human services, unethical behavior by entry-level professionals often goes unremarked by the public and the popular media. But those of us who in the course of our teaching or practice responsibilities are in human service agencies on a daily basis know that unethical behavior is relatively common. We cringe when we overhear a worker on the phone betray confidential information about the caller in front of a full waiting room. We wonder if we should reprimand staff members who are gossiping about clients on their lunch break—or would this endanger yet another field placement site and our students' educational options? What should we do when we see sexually evocative behavior among staff members and between staff members and clients? How should we advise entry-level workers who do not report workplace harassment because they fear losing their jobs? Through this all we ask ourselves and each other, "How can I teach entry-level professionals to recognize the differences between ethical and unethical behavior? How can I help them figure out how to respond to unethical behavior in others? How do I encourage them to consider their own professional behavior through an ethical frame of reference?"

To do this, we need more than a desire to teach ethics to our students. Over many years of teaching, I have found it invaluable to use real-life examples of ethical issues faced by students and by entry-level professionals who have graduated from human service programs. The many textbooks available on professional ethics give students an excellent theoretical understanding of ethical issues, but they use examples from advanced practice and administrative settings. Entry-level professionals or students preparing for entry-level careers frequently do not connect these examples to themselves. Their comment, "I would never do that!" may be more reflective of lack of relevance than it is reflective of highly developed ethical decision-making abilities.

Central to *What Would You Do?* is the use of real experiences reported by human service students and professionals from across the United States. Collected in a national survey and also at regional conferences, these experiences have been developed into anecdotes that provide the focus for exercises promoting individual reflection and group discussion. The anecdotes are arranged topically, starting with issues that are familiar to beginning students and progressing to issues that are more familiar to those in field practicums or already employed. The issues also increase in complexity: In the earliest chapters students apply their own values and the profession's ethical standards to fairly clear-cut issues, while in the later chapters students encounter issues that are more complex and involve ethical dilemmas. An additional chapter is devoted to exercises that can be used to help students expand their self-awareness in relation to their own values and how they affect their choices and behavior.

This workbook is intended to supplement current textbooks in ethical decision making, not to supplant them. It can be used as a resource in introductory, seminar, field practicum, and ethics courses, and in workshops. It can help you weave ethical decision making developmentally into your curriculum. Students in their first term will benefit particularly from the exercises in chapters 2, 5, and 6, which assist them to explore their own values and look at ethical issues that commonly occur in their academic and personal lives. Students in the introduction to human services course will use the exercises in chapter 3 to help them analyze the guidelines of their profession and relate these standards to themselves as entry-level professionals, rather than simply recognize or memorize the standards. (In this section I even ask students to find terms that are new to them, write definitions for them, and discuss them—activities that promote mastery of the many essential concepts.) If you teach an introductory course in another human service profession, you can easily adapt this chapter by substituting professional guidelines you select for the *Ethical Standards of Human Service Professionals.* Ethical codes and standards of other selected professions are included in Appendix A.

In field practicum and seminar courses and in workshops for professionals, you will use the anecdotes and exercises in chapters 7–14 to sensitize entry-level professionals to issues and dilemmas that occur in agency settings. These exercises provide them many opportunities to examine their own personal values and the ethical standards of the profession in relation to the well-being of themselves and others. Some exercises provide good starting points for in-depth consideration of ethical issues related to particular populations, such as the aged or those with HIV or disabilities. If your course is devoted to the examination of ethical issues related to human services, you will probably pick and choose relevant anecdotes and exercises from all chapters in this workbook.

Entry-level human service professionals need to make informed ethical decisions in the course of their work. If we teach them how to make those decisions in the relative safety of the classroom rather than on their own at work, we minimize the potential harm that could occur to themselves and others and increase their comfort with the process. As they learn, they need to think through their own beliefs and values, not simply accept someone else's beliefs and values. They need to explore the possible consequences of action, not simply read an expert's list of possible consequences. They need to decide what action they would take and defend their decision to others. They need to change their minds when challenged by preferable ethical thinking, not stick to decisions based on their emotional reactions. They need to understand and evaluate their profession's ethical standards and decide whether they are willing to support these standards.

In the exercises I do not recommend any particular action that the human service professional might take. You, as the faculty member in direct contact with your students—not me, removed by time, distance, and the printed word—have the opportunity and the responsibility to assist students in their own ethical development. I believe that suggesting preferred behaviors would hamper you in your teaching efforts.

The goals of this workbook are the following:

1. To acquaint practitioners, students, and faculty with the variety of ethical and related issues that are being faced by entry-level professionals.
2. To assist practitioners, students, and faculty to integrate ethical decision-making practice in introductory, field practicum, seminar, and ethics and law courses.
3. To stimulate reflection, discussion, and questions regarding ethical issues and standards.
4. To inform current and prospective entry-level professionals of the ethical standards of the human service fields.
5. To stimulate human service professionals' self-awareness concerning ethical decision making.

I have written this workbook at a level that should challenge—but not overwhelm—your students. *What Would You Do?* uses language at the level of most lower-division college students, with examples and brief definitions to encourage their understanding. Because ethics is a complex subject demanding some use of terminology that is new to most readers, I have included a glossary.

ACKNOWLEDGMENTS

I am grateful to a great many people who contributed to the creation of this workbook. The National Organization for Human Service Education (NOHSE) and its board provided leadership and direction in the development of written ethical standards; many members of NOHSE and the Council for Standards in Human Service Education (CSHSE) contributed suggestions for the standards. When the statement on the *Ethical Standards of Human Service Professionals* was first adopted, it was Gerald Corey who planted the idea of writing a case manual for human service professionals; he has continued throughout to provide me with resources and ideas.

Arizona Western College and its District Governing Board provide an environment that promotes professional development. They granted me a sabbatical during which to begin this project. My particular thanks go to James R. Carruthers, Past President; Millicent Valek, Past Vice-President; and Kathryn Watson, Human Services Division Chair. All the library staff, especially Rickley Prewitt and Alan Schuck, assisted with the research. Kathleen "Sam" Robinson and Terry Loether helped in the preparation of different stages of the manuscript.

Five colleagues served as prepublication reviewers, contributing their time and energy to reading and reacting to the workbook: I appreciate the helpful comments made by Mary H. Davidson, Columbia Greene Community College; Kraig L. Kurtz, Lindenwood University; Lenore Parker, Creative Community Solutions; Barbara Peterson, Tacoma Community College; and Judith Slater, Kennesaw State College. At Brooks/Cole, Eileen Murphy, Tessa McGlasson, Vernon Boes, Carline Haga, Lorraine Anderson, and Connie Dowcett have been consistently helpful to me as a novice author, answering my questions, providing their expertise, and encouraging me.

I am particularly grateful to the students, practitioners, and faculty who contributed anecdotes anonymously and to those who gave me their names: Rose Badroe, Suzanne Bautista, Clemintene Benjamin, J. Bennett, Nayshom Bland, Rhonda Boisvert, Armada Buhlinger, George Buttles, Evelyn Cherichetti, Mollie Davidson, Mary DiGiovanni, Helen

Lieberman Fenske, Ann Frisch, Kimberley Gardner, Lynn Gaulin, Daniel Gonzales, Elizabeth Harris, Mark Homan, Kathy Howes, Robert E. Keim, Mary King, Cheryl Kinney, Matt Kirkley, Mary Kay Kreider, Marilyn Lairsey, Pat Lamanna, Robert MacDonald, Michael Madora, Scott Metcalfe, Tommie Miller, Maryann Moldoff, Colleen Morin, Donahue Mortein, Karen E. Muench, Jackie Nace, Cyndie Piehler, Sue Pike, Liz Prendergast, Pamela Sapaugh, Michele Scordato, Caroline A. Sullivan, Carol Mielo Swerzenski, Walter Swett, Brenda Underwood, Stephen A. Weaver, and Charles R. Whittingstall.

Wesley N. Rather, my husband and friend, has been a vital part of this project. His patience, support, and encouragement have been invaluable. He has certainly done more than his share of what we, with our tongues in our cheeks, refer to as "woman's work"!

Patricia Kenyon

Contents

Chapter Three
ETHICAL STANDARDS OF
HUMAN SERVICE PROFESSIONALS   60

Chapter Four

WELFARE REFORM IMPACTS A STUDENT: A CASE STUDY   78

Chapter Five

ETHICAL ISSUES FOR STUDENTS IN
THE ACADEMIC ENVIRONMENT   86

Chapter Six

PERSONAL ISSUES AND RELATIONSHIPS   104

Chapter Seven

THE FIELD PRACTICUM: CREATING AND MAINTAINING A LEARNING ENVIRONMENT   113

Chapter Eight

CONFIDENTIALITY

Chapter Eleven
DUAL RELATIONSHIPS AND SELF-DISCLOSURE   175

Chapter Twelve
RELATIONSHIPS WITH COLLEAGUES AND SUPERVISORS IN THE WORK SETTING   191

Chapter Thirteen
PROFESSIONALS, AGENCIES, AND OTHER ENTITIES   206

Chapter Fourteen
APPLYING ETHICAL THINKING
IN YOUR OWN EXPERIENCE   215

Appendix A
ETHICAL CODES AND STANDARDS
OF OTHER HELPING PROFESSIONS

Appendix B
PROFESSIONAL ORGANIZATIONS IN HUMAN SERVICES

Appendix C
ORGANIZATIONS IN HUMAN SERVICES
AND SELECTED RELATED PROFESSIONS:
CONTACT INFORMATION

Appendix D
QUESTIONNAIRES USED IN COLLECTING REPORTS
OF ETHICAL EXPERIENCES

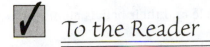

To the Reader

Ethical decision making. Many years ago I observed an entry-level human service professional answer a telephone, address the caller by name, then give the caller confidential information about his health status—in a voice clear enough to be understood by me and some ten other people present in the waiting room. At the time I thought, "She doesn't even realize that what she just did was break her client's confidentiality and, as a result, possibly cause him harm in this community."

This workbook is designed to help you recognize and respond ethically to such issues as you encounter them daily. It combines short anecdotes describing real issues with questions to guide your decision making. The anecdotes were submitted by human service students, entry-level professionals, and faculty. Each anecdote describes an actual situation and has no ending. As happens in real life, the anecdotes don't contain all the facts we would like to have, but they do create problems or dilemmas for us to resolve.

Despite the brevity of most of these anecdotes, they are not simple. Many involve not only ethical issues and conflicts, but also clinical, legal, and other aspects. It is likely that one response will initially seem to be the most correct, but after reflection and discussion, other options may become preferable.

Many students approach the study of values, ethics, and professional ethical standards with a lot of doubt. "I'm in human services because i want to learn how to help people—that's good enough. Look at all those people out there who don't care what happens to others. I care! What's wrong with my ethics? Why do I need to study philosophy and ethics?"

And you are right. Our values, acquired along with our basic language and socialized behaviors when we were young children, come from some very old traditions, often religious, that are part of our societies and our cultures. A great number of people live long and useful lives without ever consciously defining the values that guide their social, personal, and work lives.

Before picking up this workbook you've done a lot of living and decision making that involved your values—your beliefs about good and bad, right and wrong. You decided how to respond when someone offered you an illegal drug. You figured out what to do when you were a victim of abuse at the hands of a parent, sibling, or spouse whose well-being was important to you. You knew the right way to respond when you saw other students in school cheating on tests. You reacted when one acquaintance was receiving undeserved welfare payments—or when another couldn't get the welfare assistance he needed. You decided what was *right* and you did it. That is the core of ethical decision making and you have already mastered it.

Sometimes, however, we have difficulty deciding what's right and what's wrong. Perhaps our own experience and knowledge is not enough. Perhaps we don't recognize issues as being ethical in nature. Sometimes we recognize ethical issues, but we don't understand that different sets of personal or professional values might lead to different decisions. Sometimes we have conflicting values and have difficulty deciding which is more important. And as difficult as it can be when we're trying to define right and wrong for ourselves, it becomes more difficult when other people and their beliefs about right and wrong are involved.

Start discussing the concepts of right and wrong with another person and you will quickly discover that different people have different beliefs. Add differences in their backgrounds and experiences—ethnic, social, cultural, gender-related, economic, geographic, or whatever—and the variety of beliefs and values becomes infinite.

But isn't there a true *right*—a right that pertains to everyone? Perhaps in some situations there is. The human service professions attempt to define a true right when they write their codes of ethics and standards for ethical behavior. Yet even these are not absolute: They can't cover every possible combination of circumstances that we might face as professionals, so the written guidelines leave room for reflection and interpretation.

The majority of ethical decisions made by human service workers aren't dramatic. They aren't: "Who lives, who dies?" or "Shall I have sex with this former client?" Most are ordinary, everyday, garden-variety issues: "What happens if I refuse to do what this professional has asked me to do because I think it is unprofessional?" "Should I report this family for neglect or refer it for more assistance?" "Should I keep teaching this resident to wash the dishes or save time and effort by doing it myself?"

The ethical anecdotes you encounter in this workbook describe issues actually faced by students and entry-level professionals in human services. They introduce you to ordinary issues faced somewhere every day. I hope that your learning, as you read the anecdotes and complete the exercises, prepares you for the situations you will face throughout your career in human services. And I hope your mastery of ethical decision making contributes to a long and fulfilling career for you in the human services.

Patricia Kenyon

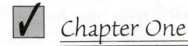

Chapter One

Ethical Decision Making in Human Services

And what More [Sir Thomas] wanted to be, what Erasmus wanted to be, what
every strong intellect wants to be, is a guardian of integrity.

—Jacob Bronowski, 1973

What should I do? What can I say? How do I decide? What's right? Who decides what's right? What if my client thinks differently from me about what he or she should do? What if my boss or my agency wants me to do something and I think it is wrong? What if my parents taught me the right way to behave, but most other people don't do it that way? What if I think I know the right thing to do, but it's illegal? Sometimes I'm caught in a situation where, no matter what I do, someone will probably get hurt. What if I'm the person who will be hurt?

Difficult questions frequently arise for entry-level human service practitioners. This workbook is designed to help you learn how to find answers, first in reaction to specific exercises, and then in response to the ethical issues you encounter. To do this, I'm using a workbook approach—instead of giving you extensive theory about ethics and ethical decision making or an expert's point of view about what is the best approach in response to various professional **dilemmas,** I have used as the core of the workbook more than 80 **anecdotes** (short descriptions of actual occurrences) written by students, faculty, and entry-level practitioners when I asked them to describe ethical issues and dilemmas they had encountered.[1]

These true stories differ from many of the cases you find in ethics textbooks: They are often quite short. Information you'd like to have is missing. They deal with ordinary events and experiences. Sometimes it's not clear whether the ethical aspects are very important. Sometimes the correct answers seem simple and obvious. Most will engage you, because they are so believable and because the incidents described are likely to happen to you in a field practicum, a job, or in your own personal life.

To build your ethical decision-making skills, I have expanded the ethical decision-making process into a detailed step-by-step model. You will use this model in the exercises, and by the time you have completed the workbook, you will be ready to adapt it to your own needs and ways of thinking.

In this chapter I introduce you to some concepts pertinent to a study of ethical decision making: ethical choices in human services, values and value development, ethics, and professional ethical guidelines. I then explore why you can benefit from study and practice in ethical decision making and present the ethical decision-making model used in this workbook.

ETHICAL CHOICES: DO WE USE CONVENTIONAL OR REFLECTIVE MORALITY?

> *When possible make the decisions now, even if action is in the future. A reviewed decision usually is better than one reached at the last moment.*
>
> —William B. Given, Jr.

In the human services we deal with the needs, wants, and preferences of people who are our clients. Not only is there often conflict as to what is best for the **client,** but also what is best for the client can be in conflict with the needs, wants, and preferences of others who are involved, including ourselves. As we respond to people with conflicting needs, wants, and preferences, we make **ethical** choices—choices that can be made using conventional **morality** or reflective morality (Callahan, 1988, p. 10).

In everyday personal decisions, most of us use conventional morality: We base our decisions on customary practice without examining or criticizing those customs or practices. Conventional morality lends itself to spontaneous **decisions**. In a professional capacity, if we make ethical choices spontaneously, we risk being inconsistent in the way we treat practitioners, clients, and society: Choices based on the feelings of the moment are affected by such things as our temporary emotional states, current topics in the media, and our judgments of others. Spontaneous choices also risk unforeseen, and potentially harmful, consequences.

Reflective morality, on the other hand, requires a deliberate and thoughtful approach. This limits the impact of temporary influences on the process and anticipates possible consequences. Its goals are to ensure that we are consistent in the decisions we make—treating practitioners, clients, and society the same regardless of unrelated but influential factors—and that we consider all possible outcomes of our decisions.

As human service practitioners we need to make ethical decisions based on reflective morality, especially when those actions involve the rights and interests of other people or our own integrity.

VALUES: HOW DO THEY DEVELOP AND HOW DO THEY AFFECT US?

> *Values are the tools we use in making decisions. What we build, in the process, is our own character. And it is our character . . . that ultimately determines the course of our lives.*
>
> —Jim Lichtman, 1996

Our **values** (beliefs about what is good or desirable) guide our choices and motivate our actions. "Any belief, **attitude,** or other value indicator that is chosen freely [and] thoughtfully, prized, and acted upon consistently is defined as a value" (Uustal, 1993, p. 16). Values may be based on knowledge, aesthetic considerations, moral grounds, or on a combination of these.

- Knowledge-based value: I value handwashing because it prevents colds and other infections.
- Aesthetics-based value: I prefer classical music because it sounds much better than country music.
- Morals-based value: I believe it is wrong to lie because lying shows disrespect for other people.

Values are influenced by culture and society, but, because of differences among people and experiences, are interpreted by each of us in our own way (Uustal, 1993, pp. 12–13).

We begin to develop our values very early in life: As infants and toddlers we start to accept values as a result of the rules, punishments, and rewards given us by others. Sharing, respect for others, personal cleanliness, and not hurting others are examples of values that are taught to children in their earliest years. This is an important aspect of the preparation of young children for their roles and responsibilities in society.

Values persist over time. After childhood, we continue to develop our values, now influenced as much or more by peers and other adults in our lives as by our parents. We build new values upon earlier ones. Unless we make deliberate efforts to examine our own values, internal and external values conflicts, and their consequences, most of us don't radically revise our values over our lifetimes.

Entering a profession like human services presents an opportunity for examining and evaluating those values that we have adopted. Students and professionals will find many values worth retaining, some that should be modified, and a few that need to be discarded. Consider the following anecdote, contributed by a human service professional:

Racial Slur

One time, while I was serving at a soup kitchen, a client—without any aggravation on my part—made a racial slur involving people of my color. He recommended that they all (including me, he implied) should be killed.

A person who valued highly the protection of his own racial group from derogatory comments by others would probably have responded to the racial slur by challenging the client who made the slur. A person who valued the rights of all to express their beliefs would probably have responded by accepting the comment as the client's own belief. A human service professional or volunteer—as the contributor was—might hold both values as important and, at the same time, recognize that the individual may also be communicating something else—a meaning below the surface. This practitioner reported it as an ethical dilemma: He experienced conflict about how he should understand the communication, what values he should apply, and how he should respond to the person in the line at the soup kitchen.

HUMAN SERVICE VALUES: WHAT ARE THEY?

Some values are especially important if you are to be successful in a human service career. Here are three lists from well-known human service professionals for you to consider. Corey and Corey (1993, p. 87) list the following values as basic to the process of helping others:

- assuming responsibility for one's actions
- developing effective strategies for coping with stress

- developing the ability to give and receive affection
- being sensitive to the feelings of others
- practicing self-control
- having a sense of purpose for living
- being open, honest, and genuine
- finding satisfaction in one's work
- having a sense of identity and feelings of worth
- being skilled in interpersonal relationships, sensitivity, and nurturance
- being committed in marriage, family, and other relationships
- having deepened self-awareness and motivation for growth
- practicing good habits of physical health

Woodside and McClam (1994, p. 155) identify the following as commonly held values in human services:

- acceptance
- tolerance
- individuality
- self-determination
- confidentiality

Egan (1994, p. 49) addresses five groups of helping values:

- pragmatism
- competence
- respect
- genuineness
- client self-responsibility

As you complete the exercises in this workbook and as you enter your career in human services, you will discover that you will be more effective if you have chosen most of the values above as your own. If you have not, you and your clients will probably be dissatisfied and your decisions will not be supported by your colleagues. After you complete the exercises in chapter 2, it may be useful for you to review these three lists of values and consider whether your preferred values seem to indicate you will be content in human services. If you consider most of these values to be important, you will probably be content and successful.

ETHICS

[Ethics] is not about what we say. It's about what we do. It's a code of conduct based on certain universal, moral duties and obligations that indicate how one should behave. It deals with the ability to distinguish good from evil, right from wrong and what is proper from what is improper.

—Jim Lichtman, 1996

Values are usually shared by the members of groups (families, communities, religious organizations, sociocultural groups). **Ethics** (the rules, standards, or moral principles adopted by an individual or group to govern conduct) extend our values into sets of guidelines that tell us what we should and should not do.

Our first contact with systems of ethics and ethical decision making comes for many of us as part of our religion. One of the simplest ethical statements is familiar to most of us: "So whatever you wish that men would do to you, do so to them" (Matthew 7:12, Holy Bible, Revised Standard Version). By itself, this Golden Rule can—and does—govern many peoples' behavioral choices.

ETHICAL THEORIES

Ethical theories are concerned with understanding systems of ethics. A premise of ethical thinking is that there is no absolute right or wrong that fits all humans in all situations. Therefore, to develop ourselves as ethical beings, each of us must understand ethical decision making, select among acceptable principles and ways of thinking, and arrive at our own decisions. The following very brief comments are intended only to highlight aspects of ethical theories that underlie some of the issues addressed in this workbook. For more complete coverage of ethical theories, see the bibliography in the back of this workbook and consult the works of relevant ethicists.

Loewenberg and Dolgoff (1996, pp. 43–45) describe two aspects of ethical theories: relativism and absolutism. Ethical relativists believe there are no definite ethical rules. Ethical decisions must be based on the context in which they are made (that is, on cultural practices, political climates, contemporary norms, moral standards, and other contextual considerations) or on the consequences that the ethical decisions create. Loewenberg and Dolgoff describe two types of teleologists (relativists who base their ethical reasoning on the consequences of action): utilitarians (who believe one should maximize the greatest good for the largest number of people) and egoists (who believe one should maximize the good for oneself, regardless of the consequences for others). Utilitarianism is commonly accepted by human service professionals; egoism is not.

Ethical absolutists believe it is essential to establish universal rules on which to base ethical decision making and practice. Known as deontologists, ethical absolutists claim that certain actions are right or wrong regardless of their consequences.

> Practitioners may not be aware of these efforts by professional philosophers. Neither do they always know which of the two ethical theories they follow in making ethical decisions. . . . the differences between the major theories frequently are not as clear in practice as they are on the printed page. The two theoretical approaches often seem to merge in practice, but it does make a difference in ethical decision making whether a social worker follows one or the other theory. (Loewenberg & Dolgoff, 1996, p. 45)

As you approach the exercises in this workbook, you will find anecdotes and questions that ask you to use both absolutist and relativist approaches. You are challenged to consider whether—and when—one or the other approach is preferred. To select the preferred action, do you consider contextual features and consequences or do you base your decision on generally accepted ethical guidelines? Understanding and applying theories and principles will help you make and justify those ethical decisions that are a necessary part of being a human service professional.

ETHICAL PRINCIPLES

Ethical principles (statements of humans' obligations or duties that are generally accepted) are the expression of ethical systems. Ethical principles are one aspect of the decision-making process for ethical relativists; they are central to the considerations of ethical absolutists. Following is a list of some of the commonly recognized ethical principles, with their definitions. These principles, although generally accepted, may be ranked differently in their relative importance by various people and groups—thus contributing to internal and external conflict in reaching ethical decisions.

autonomy—the duty to maximize the individual's right to make his or her own decisions

beneficence—the duty to do good

confidentiality—the duty to respect privacy of information

fidelity—the duty to keep one's promise or word

finality—the duty to take action that may override the demands of law and social customs

gratitude—the duty to make up for (or repay) a good

justice—the duty to treat all fairly, distributing risks and benefits equitably

nonmaleficence—the duty to cause no harm

ordering—the duty to rank the ethical principles that one follows in order of priority and to follow that ranking in resolving all ethical issues

publicity—the duty to take actions based on ethical standards that must be known and recognized by all who are involved

reparation—the duty to make up for a wrong

respect for persons—the duty to honor others, their rights, and their responsibilities

universality—the duty to take actions that hold for everyone, regardless of time, place, or people involved

utility—the duty to provide the greatest good or least harm for the greatest number of people

veracity—the duty to tell the truth

ETHICAL GUIDELINES FOR PROFESSIONALS: HOW DO THEY GUIDE AND WHAT ARE THEIR LIMITS?

Deviations [from the profession's standards of practice] on the part of members taint a profession as a whole.

—Charles S. Levy, 1993

Based on the generally accepted ethical principles, members of professions develop specialized **codes of ethics** and statements of **ethical standards.** Created to provide timely and relevant help to students and practitioners, such guidelines focus on professionals' responsibilities and give directions for actual behavior. They are revised periodically to keep up with changes in the **profession** and in society. Professional guidelines serve three primary functions: (1) They guide ethical practice, (2) they provide **criteria** for evaluating the ethics of a professional's practice, and (3) they serve as benchmarks in the enforcement of ethical standards (Levy, 1993, p. 37).

Guiding Ethical Practice

Professional guidelines "reflect our state of knowledge and general consensus on ethical issues at the time they are written" (Herlihy & Corey, 1997). Sometimes the guidelines address issues that seem timeless and sometimes they reflect currently evolving issues that are affecting the practice of the profession.

One issue that seems timeless is confidentiality. One of the oldest professional codes of ethics is the Oath of Hippocrates, developed in early Greece to guide the actions of physicians. It reads, in part, "What I may see or hear in the course of the treatment or even outside of the treatment in regard to the life of men, which on no account one must spread abroad, I will keep to myself holding such things shameful to be spoken about" (Edelstein, 1943/1987, p. 6). Another is the Florence Nightingale Pledge, written in 1893 for the emerging profession of nursing. It reads, in part, "[I] will hold in confidence all personal matters committed to my keeping and all family matters coming to my knowledge in the practice of my calling" (Kalisch & Kalisch, 1986, p. 171). The *Ethical Standards of Human Service Professionals*, adopted in 1995, says, "Human service professionals protect the client's right to privacy and confidentiality . . ." (Statement 3). The language that expresses the idea has changed over the years, yet maintenance of confidentiality is an ethical principle that endures in the helping professions.

An example of a guideline that responds to currently evolving issues is Statement 17 of the *Ethical Standards of Human Service Professionals:* "Human service professionals provide services without discrimination or preference based on age, ethnicity, culture, race, disability, gender, religion, sexual orientation, or socioeconomic status." This standard has as its background some 200 years of social change in the United States, dating from the beginning of public debate about the ethical and legal aspects of slavery and deliberate racial discrimination. It is a currently evolving ethical guideline.

Providing Criteria for Evaluating a Professional's Practice

Despite efforts by practitioners, educators, and students in the profession to model and teach ethical practice, not all members of a profession will meet that profession's standards. Professional guidelines set expectations and standards for practice, but they do not "assure the virtues required for professional practice within the character of each [practitioner]" (American Nurses Association, 1985, p. iii). Occasionally an individual's professional behavior must be judged against the expectations of colleagues and clients. Such a review and evaluation is frequently based on the standard provided by the profession's ethical guidelines.

Serving as Benchmarks for Enforcement

When members fail to follow the profession's guidelines, other members must be committed to taking constructive action rather than ignoring the unethical behavior. One professional's unethical behavior reflects badly on the profession, but the failure of other professionals to take action in response to the unethical behavior reflects even more badly on the profession. Therefore, professions develop mechanisms, usually within the professional organization, through which they enforce the ethical standards.

Students are often surprised that the ethical guidelines of different professions and in different societies sometimes vary significantly. There is significant variation in the duties of lawyers, journalists, human service professionals, and educators.[2] Students can review the ethical guidelines of professions they are considering; the closer the match between the student's personal values and standards and those of the profession, the better will be his or her fit with the career. The *Ethical Standards of Human Service Professionals* are shown in Table 1.1. Codes and standards of other human service professions are included in Appendix A.

Table 1.1   *Ethical Standards of Human Service Professionals*

National Organization for Human Service Education
and Council for Standards in Human Service Education (1995)

Preamble

Human services is a profession developing in response to and in anticipation of the direction of human needs and human problems in the late twentieth century. Characterized particularly by an appreciation of human beings in all of their diversity, human services offers assistance to its clients within the context of their community and environment. Human service professionals, regardless of whether they are students, faculty, or practitioners, promote and encourage the unique values and characteristics of human services. In so doing human service professionals uphold the integrity and ethics of the profession, partake in constructive criticism of the profession, promote client and community well-being, and enhance their own professional growth.

The ethical guidelines presented are a set of standards of conduct which the human service professional considers in ethical and professional decision making. It is hoped that these guidelines will be of assistance when the human service professional is challenged by difficult ethical dilemmas. Although ethical codes are not legal documents, they may be used to assist in the adjudication of issues related to ethical human service behavior.

Human service professionals function in many ways and carry out many roles. They enter into professional-client relationships with individuals, families, groups, and communities who are all referred to as "clients" in these standards. Among their roles are caregiver, case manager, broker, teacher/educator, behavior changer, consultant, outreach professional, mobilizer, advocate, community planner, community change organizer, evaluator, and administrator.* The following standards are written with these multi-faceted roles in mind.

The Human Service Professional's Responsibility to Clients

Statement 1. Human service professionals negotiate with clients the purpose, goals, and nature of the helping relationship prior to its onset, as well as inform clients of the limitations of the proposed relationship.

Statement 2. Human service professionals respect the integrity and welfare of the client at all times. Each client is treated with respect, acceptance, and dignity.

Statement 3. Human service professionals protect the client's right to privacy and confidentiality except when such confidentiality would cause harm to the client or others, when agency guidelines state otherwise, or under other stated conditions (e.g., local, state, or federal laws). Professionals inform clients of the limits of confidentiality prior to the onset of the helping relationship.

Statement 4. If it is suspected that danger or harm may occur to the client or to others as a result of a client's behavior, the human service professional acts in an appropriate and professional manner to protect the safety of those individuals. This may involve seeking consultation, supervision, and/or breaking the confidentiality of the relationship.

Statement 5. Human service professionals protect the integrity, safety, and security of client records. All written client information that is shared with other professionals, except in the course of professional supervision, must have the client's prior written consent.

Statement 6. Human service professionals are aware that in their relationships with clients power and status are unequal. Therefore they recognize that dual or multiple relationships may increase the risk of harm to, or exploitation of, clients, and may impair their professional judgment. However, in some communities and situations it may not be feasible to avoid social or other nonprofessional contact with clients. Human service professionals support the trust implicit in the helping relationship by avoiding dual relationships that may impair professional judgment, increase the risk of harm to clients, or lead to exploitation.

*Southern Regional Education Board. (1967). *Roles and functions for mental health workers: A report of a symposium.* Atlanta, GA: Community Mental Health Worker Project.

Table 1.1 *Ethical Standards of Human Service Professionals (continued)*

Statement 7. Sexual relationships with current clients are not considered to be in the best interest of the client and are prohibited. Sexual relationships with previous clients are considered dual relationships and are addressed in Statement 6 (above).

Statement 8. The client's right to self-determination is protected by human service professionals. They recognize the client's right to receive or refuse services.

Statement 9. Human service professionals recognize and build on client strengths.

The Human Service Professional's Responsibility to the Community and Society

Statement 10. Human service professionals are aware of local, state, and federal laws. They advocate for change in regulations and statutes when such legislation conflicts with ethical guidelines and/or client rights. Where laws are harmful to individuals, groups, or communities, human service professionals consider the conflict between the values of obeying the law and the values of serving people and may decide to initiate social action.

Statement 11. Human service professionals keep informed about current social issues as they affect the client and the community. They share that information with clients, groups, and community as part of their work.

Statement 12. Human service professionals understand the complex interaction between individuals, their families, the communities in which they live, and society.

Statement 13. Human service professionals act as advocates in addressing unmet client and community needs. Human service professionals provide a mechanism for identifying unmet client needs, calling attention to these needs, and assisting in planning and mobilizing to advocate for those needs at the local community level.

Statement 14. Human service professionals represent their qualifications to the public accurately.

Statement 15. Human service professionals describe the effectiveness of programs, treatments, and/or techniques accurately.

Statement 16. Human service professionals advocate for the rights of all members of society, particularly those who are members of minorities and groups at which discriminatory practices have historically been directed.

Statement 17. Human service professionals provide services without discrimination or preference based on age, ethnicity, culture, race, disability, gender, religion, sexual orientation, or socioeconomic status.

Statement 18. Human service professionals are knowledgeable about the cultures and communities within which they practice. They are aware of multiculturalism in society and its impact on the community as well as individuals within the community. They respect individuals and groups, their cultures and beliefs.

Statement 19. Human service professionals are aware of their own cultural backgrounds, beliefs, and values, recognizing the potential for impact on their relationships with others.

Statement 20. Human service professionals are aware of sociopolitical issues that differentially affect clients from diverse backgrounds.

Statement 21. Human service professionals seek the training, experience, education, and supervision necessary to ensure their effectiveness in working with culturally diverse client populations.

The Human Service Professional's Responsibility to Colleagues

Statement 22. Human service professionals avoid duplicating another professional's helping relationship with a client. They consult with other professionals who are assisting the client in a different type of relationship when it is in the best interest of the client to do so.

Statement 23. When a human service professional has a conflict with a colleague, he or she first seeks out the colleague in an attempt to manage the problem. If necessary, the professional then seeks the assistance of supervisors, consultants, or other professionals in efforts to manage the problem.

(continued on next page)

Table 1.1 *Ethical Standards of Human Service Professionals (continued)*

Statement 24. Human service professionals respond appropriately to unethical behavior of colleagues. Usually this means initially talking directly with the colleague and, if no resolution is forthcoming, reporting the colleague's behavior to supervisory or administrative staff and/or to the professional organization(s) to which the colleague belongs.

Statement 25. All consultations between human service professionals are kept confidential unless to do so would result in harm to clients or communities.

The Human Service Professional's Responsibility to the Profession

Statement 26. Human service professionals know the limit and scope of their professional knowledge and offer services only within their knowledge and skill base.

Statement 27. Human service professionals seek appropriate consultation and supervision to assist in decision making when there are legal, ethical, or other dilemmas.

Statement 28. Human service professionals act with integrity, honesty, genuineness, and objectivity.

Statement 29. Human service professionals promote cooperation among related disciplines (e.g., psychology, counseling, social work, nursing, family and consumer sciences, medicine, education) to foster professional growth and interests within the various fields.

Statement 30. Human service professionals promote the continuing development of their profession. They encourage membership in professional associations, support research endeavors, foster educational advancement, advocate for appropriate legislative actions, and participate in other related professional activities.

Statement 31. Human service professionals continually seek out new and effective approaches to enhance their professional abilities.

The Human Service Professional's Responsibility to Employers

Statement 32. Human service professionals adhere to commitments made to their employers.

Statement 33. Human service professionals participate in efforts to establish and maintain employment conditions which are conducive to high-quality client services. They assist in evaluating the effectiveness of the agency through reliable and valid assessment measures.

Statement 34. When a conflict arises between fulfilling the responsibility to the employer and the responsibility to the client, human service professionals advise both of the conflict and work conjointly with all involved to manage the conflict.

The Human Service Professional's Responsibility to Self

Statement 35. Human service professionals strive to personify those characteristics typically associated with the profession (e.g., accountability, respect for others, genuineness, empathy, pragmatism).

Statement 36. Human service professionals foster self-awareness and personal growth in themselves. They recognize that when professionals are aware of their own values, attitudes, cultural background, and personal needs, the process of helping others is less likely to be negatively impacted by those factors.

Statement 37. Human service professionals recognize a commitment to lifelong learning and continually upgrade knowledge and skills to serve the populations better.
April 1995

THE DIFFERENCE BETWEEN LAW AND ETHICS

To no man will we sell, or deny, or delay, right or justice.

—Magna Carta, 1215

It can become very difficult for the student or practitioner to understand the differences between actions required by the law and actions required by ethics. Legal mandates and ethical obligations are often congruent, because law usually expresses the values and beliefs of the society. Yet law and ethics do sometimes approach the same issue differently, and the ethical person must balance conflicting demands and occasionally decide whether legal mandates or **ethical duties** take priority.

Let's take as an example a situation that arises frequently in my own state, Arizona. The immigration laws of the United States permit and even encourage citizens to report the names of people known or suspected of being in the U.S. illegally—undocumented aliens. Many citizens within and outside the law enforcement communities believe it is their duty to report suspected undocumented aliens. In human service agencies many practitioners and students work with clients who are undocumented. It is legal for those human service practitioners and students to report these undocumented aliens to law enforcement authorities. Is it ethical?

The contract between the professional or student and the client, whether written or unwritten, is based on such ethical principles as beneficence, confidentiality, fidelity, finality, and nonmaleficence. To report the client to law enforcement authorities without his or her knowledge and concurrence would not only hurt the client but would also hurt the agency and the profession—if clients cannot trust us, they will not seek and use our services. The answer, then, is that it is not ethical to report a human service client to the law enforcement authorities: A greater harm would result from reporting than from not reporting.

One human service agency with which I am familiar learned that several employees had reported clients as undocumented aliens to the U. S. Border Patrol. The Border Patrol had subsequently arrested and deported the clients. In addition to a concern about potential legal **liability** based on invasion of privacy, the agency also became concerned about the impact on potential clients and on the agency's ability to continue to provide services. This agency wrote a policy forbidding such reports: If an employee reports a client as an undocumented alien, it is grounds for disciplinary action, including dismissal. The agency made confidentiality (an ethical principle) into a particular agency policy (a legally binding regulation that applies to agency employees).

The law uses a right/wrong, white/black approach to decision making—one is either not guilty or guilty. Whether you are talking about written laws, rules, regulations, agency policies and procedures, or court decisions that interpret the law, the meaning and intent seem precise and specific. Legal approaches to decision making also involve mechanisms through which one can ask others to review and reverse a decision. (An example of this in human services is the appeal process mandated in agencies funded by federal tax dollars: If the client does not accept or agree with a decision about whether he or she should receive services, the client has the right to request an official review of the decision.)

Ethics does not use a white/black, right/wrong approach. Ethical decisions are usually seen in shades of gray—what is more right or less wrong? In addition, there are seldom any others who will officially review or reverse our decisions.[3] Practitioners who want to make the best ethical decisions use a **decision-making process** that helps them protect the rights of all involved and ensures that they don't neglect any of their duties or responsibilities. Faced with an ethical issue in which there is a relevant law, the practitioner may tell himself, "I didn't want to do it, but I had to." Faced with an ethical dilemma in which there is no relevant law, the practitioner can only strive to make the best decision and tell himself, "I made the best decision I could." Corey summarizes, "It is a mistake to confuse legal behavior with being ethical. Although following the law is part of ethical behavior, being an ethical practitioner involves far more" (1996, p. 56).

Laws and ethics alike respond to societal trends and values. Sometimes legal changes seem to precede societal consensus, and sometimes the opposite is true. The human service professional, as a member of society and of a helping profession, has a responsibility to keep abreast of changes in law, ethics, and social policy. In his or her work he or she must understand and balance the sometimes conflicting demands. And sometimes he or she must also take responsibility for assisting to create change in laws, social policy, and societal values.

ETHICAL DILEMMAS

Whenever two good people argue over principles, they are both right.

—Marie von Ebner Eschenbach, 1905

Some **ethical issues** are clear and relatively simple for the practitioner to resolve. Some, however, are complex and involve situations in which it is not possible to avoid some sort of harm (physical, social, ethical, emotional, psychological, or such) to one or more of the participants. These are **ethical dilemmas.** "An ethical dilemma is a situation where professional duties and obligations, rooted in core values, clash. These are the instances when social workers must decide which values—as expressed in various duties and obligations—will take precedence" (Reamer, 1995, p. 4).

In an ethical dilemma, the professional must consider conflicting duties and the consequences of possible actions, and then select the best course of action. This is a difficult process, requiring **critical thinking.** As an example of a potential dilemma, consider the following from a human service student preparing for his field practicum: "I don't believe in abortions. What will I do when a pregnant client asks me for references to have an abortion?"

He knows he's not supposed to hurt another person. The fetus will certainly be harmed by an elective abortion. The mother may be harmed by not being allowed to have an abortion. The mother's values may be different in this matter than the student's. And, to top it all off, the law says it is legal to have an elective abortion. Suddenly (and it often *is* suddenly) the simple value "Don't harm others" isn't enough. Multiple ethical standards apply. The student is facing a dilemma in which, no matter what choice he makes, someone's values will not be honored because other values will take precedence.

THE IMPORTANCE OF PRACTICE WITH ETHICAL DECISION MAKING

Our own values provide us guidance with ethical decision making. Societal values provide us guidance with ethical decision making. Ethical principles provide us with guidance with ethical decision making. Professional ethical guidelines provide us guidance with ethical decision making. And legal mandates influence our ethical decision making. Despite all these guidelines—and, sometimes, because of disagreements among them—**conflicts** occur.

Some conflicts are internal: My personal values support my doing one thing, but my professional values say I should do something else. I'd be comfortable doing one thing, but ethically I think I should do something else. The values I learned at an early age direct me to make this decision, but my newly forming values push me to another decision.

Some conflicts are external: I know what I think is right, but my agency policies require me to do something different. What I think is right, my client thinks is wrong. My profession has an ethical standard, but I disagree with it.

We need experience with ethical decision making. As with any new skill, mastery takes practice. All of us need to start with relatively simple ethical issues and, after we have mastered the basic steps in the process of ethical decision making, gradually increase the complexity of the issues and the conflicts inherent in them. Becoming knowledgeable and skilled takes time, experience, and feedback from others.

The ethical issues noticed on the job by human service professionals are more often complicated than simple. Yet the work settings of entry-level practitioners don't encourage them to spend time and effort on such issues as skill building in ethical decision making. Instead, either ethical issues may be ignored or agency policies may determine what the professional is to do. For example, at the Desert View Human Service Agency, women who request elective abortions are referred to one of three clinics. And that's that. Done. Finished. Ended. Go on to the next client.

But wait! What happens to the **internal conflict** experienced by the practitioner who isn't really certain that it is right to send women off for abortions? Does it simply disappear? No, it doesn't. Is there anyone for him to talk with about his feelings, thoughts, and values? No, there usually isn't. In a human service agency today, there's seldom enough time to meet the clients' needs, let alone deal with workers' feelings and ethical conflicts.

We know that humans who don't resolve conflicts are often haunted by those conflicts at a later date. Ethical conflicts encountered by entry-level practitioners, in my experience, are often not expressed in values-related terms. More often, after six months or a year of doing things that she was brought up to believe were wrong while working in a professional climate where those same things are considered to be right, the entry-level practitioner may begin to lose her enthusiasm for the career, may put less effort into figuring out the best way to help the clients, may consider the other employees to be deficient, may have personality conflicts with coworkers or clients, and may have learned to cope by not investing herself emotionally in the lives and problems of her clients.

This pattern of responses has been described as **burnout** (a state of mental and physical exhaustion experienced in all of the helping professions). Without some form of assistance, burned-out human service professionals become ineffective helpers—they quit, get fired, or resign on the job (continuing employment but producing little). The agency and the profession lose practitioners in whom they have invested significant effort and resources.

One aspect of protecting yourself—preventing unresolved ethical dilemmas and the resulting personal and professional difficulties—is to master the basic elements of ethical decision making.

DEVELOPING YOUR ETHICAL THINKING

The aim of ethics education is not to change students' behavior but to give them an understanding of the nature of ethics so that they can develop approaches to analyzing ethical dilemmas.

—Norman Linzer, 1990

Although many of our personal values seem to have come naturally, the processes by which we become aware of our values, ethics, and ethical decision making do not come automatically. Nor does the process of ethical decision making come in isolation from other people. You need to explore your own values and thinking, share and compare your ideas with those of others (colleagues, consultants, and ethicists), and evaluate your decision-making process. Because there is no "one right answer" to an ethical dilemma and because you will find your ethical thinking develops with practice, you need to know that you are not ever going to arrive at a point where you can say, "Ah! Now I can make the best ethical decisions!" You will, however, become more comfortable when facing ethical issues. You will learn to explain your reasoning to others. You will become more secure with your choices. And you will become adept at seeking assistance with decisions that are too complex for your experience.

This workbook is intended to help you begin the learning process. It presents you with anecdotes (short descriptions of incidents) submitted by students, entry-level practitioners, and faculty in human services, then asks you reflective questions designed to promote your ethical thinking and decision making. Discussion questions are also included for you to use in your class or workshop group to stimulate sharing, feedback, and thoughtful consideration of each other's ideas.

AN ETHICAL DECISION-MAKING MODEL

The exercises in this workbook are built on a detailed step-by-step model of ethical decision making. This model is adapted from those used by many ethicists in the human services (Bond, 1993; Corey, Corey, & Callanan, 1998; Herlihy & Corey, 1996; Kentsmith, Salladay, & Miya, 1986; Levy, 1993; Loewenberg & Dolgoff, 1996; Uustal, 1993). It is extensive and detailed, designed to help you not only approach each exercise deliberately, but also master the process, so you can use it as you encounter your own ethical issues.

The entire model has 10 steps, as summarized in Table 1.2. As you read the steps for the first time, concentrate on getting an overview of the process—don't try to memorize the steps. As you progress through the workbook exercises, mastery will come.

Step 1: Describe the Issue

Describe the ethical difficulty or dilemma. This first step ensures that we understand the issue fully before we make decisions or take action. We consider the participants: Who is involved? How are they related? What is their involvement? We decide just whose issue it is: Who has the right and/or responsibility to make the decision? Who bears the highest risk from the decision? Is it the human service professional's issue? Is it the client's issue? Is it the faculty's issue? Is it the agency's issue? Is it a shared issue? If possible, the person who is making the decision should be the person whose issue it is.

We also look at the other aspects of the issue: What is involved? What is at risk? What are the relevant situational features (agency, family, job, community)? What type of issue is it (ethical, legal, personal, clinical, or a combination of these)?

Step 2: Consider Ethical Guidelines

Consider all available ethical guidelines and legal standards. In this second step we seek to understand and apply values, relevant ethical principles, and legal mandates. It is important to identify our own personal values in relation to the issue. Then we consider whether there are any relevant societal or community values. We review the professional standards to see if any are pertinent. We consider whether there are relevant laws and regulations.

Having reviewed applicable ethical and legal guidelines, we apply these guidelines. In an uncomplicated ethical issue, it may be clear at this point what action we should take.

Table 1.2 An Ethical Decision-Making Model

Step	Considerations to be addressed
1. Describe the issue	Describe the ethical issue or dilemma. Who is involved? What is their involvement? How are they related? Whose dilemma is it? What is involved? What is at risk? What are the relevant situational features? What type of issue is it?
2. Consider ethical guidelines	Consider all available ethical guidelines and legal standards. Identify your own personal values relevant to the issue. Identify societal or community values relevant to the issue. Identify relevant professional standards. Identify relevant laws and regulations. Apply these guidelines.
3. Examine the conflicts	Examine any conflicts. Describe the conflicts you are experiencing internally. Describe the conflicts you are experiencing that are external. Decide whether you can minimize any of these conflicts.
4. Resolve the conflicts	Seek assistance with your decision if needed. Consult with colleagues, faculty, or supervisors. Review relevant professional literature. Seek consultation from professional organizations or available ethics committees.
5. Generate action alternatives	Generate all possible courses of action.
6. Examine and evaluate the action alternatives	Consider the client's and all other participants' preferences based on a full understanding of their values and ethical beliefs. Eliminate alternatives that are inconsistent with the client's and significant others' values and beliefs. Eliminate alternatives that are inconsistent with other relevant guidelines. Eliminate alternatives for which there are no resources or support. Eliminate remaining action alternatives that don't pass tests based on the ethical principles of universality, publicity, and justice. Predict the possible consequences of the remaining acceptable action alternatives. Prioritize (rank) the remaining acceptable action alternatives.
7. Select and evaluate the preferred action	Select the best course of action. Evaluate your decision.
8. Plan the action	Develop an action plan and implement the action.
9. Evaluate the outcome	Evaluate the action taken and the outcome.
10. Examine the implications	What have you learned? Are there implications for future ethical decision making?

Step 3: Examine the Conflicts

If the various guidelines don't address the specific issue or provide conflicting guidance, or if there is conflict among the participants involved in the issue, then we need to examine the conflicts.

First, we examine and describe the conflicts we are experiencing internally—inside ourselves. These conflicts may involve competition and conflict in any combination of personal values, societal values, professional guidelines, legal mandates, personal preferences and well-being, and other practical considerations. Then we describe the **external conflicts.** These may involve ourselves, colleagues, clients, faculty, supervisors, the profession, the community, society, our agency, or any combination of these.

Having fully described the conflicts, it is sometimes possible to make a decision; for example, in one particularly difficult **scenario,** if there is conflict between our personal values and applicable professional guidelines, we may recognize it is best to set aside our personal values and apply the professional guidelines directly.

Most ethicists and professionals say professional guidelines should take precedence over our own personal value system and societal values (Loewenberg & Dolgoff, 1996, p. 62). Corey, Corey, and Callanan (1998) comment that community standards—as reflected in the actions professionals *actually* take—are usually more permissive than are ethical standards—as reflected in beliefs about the actions professionals *should* take (p. 8). We may respond more to personal values and practical considerations than to formal codes of ethics and legal guidelines in deciding what we actually will do (Corey, Corey, and Callanan, 1993, p. 7). Such conflicts between the demands of our personal values and those of our profession must be addressed directly and openly. This is one of the times when all human service professionals need colleagues who can and will help them examine the conflicts and the possible repercussions of their decision.

Step 4: Resolve the Conflicts

If, on our own, we cannot resolve the conflict or dilemma, then we need to seek assistance. It is often helpful to rank the relevant ethical principles and guidelines. Much of the time we will consult with colleagues, faculty, or supervisors. Additional points of view may clarify or reduce the apparent conflicts. We may also review relevant professional literature. And we can seek consultation from professional organizations and ethics committees in our agencies and academic institutions.

Step 5: Generate Action Alternatives

Once we've developed a pretty thorough understanding of the issue, the ethical guidelines involved, and the ethical conflicts or dilemma, we can start generating all possible alternative actions. This can be done even if the conflicts are not yet resolved, though it is important that we don't lose sight of these conflicts and their implications for us.

Step 6: Examine and Evaluate the Action Alternatives

In this step we decide which action alternatives are acceptable and prioritize them. First, we consider the client's and other participants' preferences based on a full understanding of their values and/or ethical beliefs. Because autonomy is valued highly in human services, we eliminate alternatives that are inconsistent with the client's and significant others' values and beliefs. With other participants (for example, colleagues) we may decide to discuss the alternative, rather than automatically eliminate it: We do not impose our values and principles on our clients, but we certainly can and should engage in serious review of conflicting positions with colleagues. Sometimes we also need to challenge clients about their values, but only very carefully—this must be dealt with as an ethical decision in and of itself to ensure we are not imposing our values in the very act of challenging theirs.

Being realistic, we then eliminate any action alternatives for which there are no resources or support.

Stadler (1986, p. 9) recommends we evaluate the remaining action alternatives using the ethical principles of universality, publicity, and justice:

- Universality: Is the action applicable to all people in similar situations, including yourself? Would you recommend the action to other professionals? Would you approve it if a colleague did it?
- Publicity: Is the action based on ethical standards that are recognized by all who might be involved? Would you be willing to explain your action to colleagues or the public? Would they accept your explanation?
- Justice: Does the action treat people fairly? Would you take the same action for other clients in similar situations? Would you do the same if the client were well known or influential?

We eliminate alternatives that don't pass these three tests.

We then predict the possible short-term and long-term consequences of the remaining acceptable action alternatives. It's also important to consider whether the consequences are certain, probable, possible, or unlikely.

Now we've got a clear understanding of the issue, the relevant guidelines, conflicts among the guidelines and among the participants, and the predictable consequences of all acceptable action alternatives. So we prioritize (rank) the acceptable action alternatives. We must consider to what extent the alternative actions will be efficient, effective, and ethical. Loewenberg and Dolgoff (1996, p. 61) offer the following questions, which may help with ranking the action alternatives:

- Which of the alternative ethical actions will protect to the greatest extent possible your client's rights and welfare as well as the rights and welfare of others?
- Which alternative action will protect to the greatest extent possible society's rights and interests?
- What can you do to minimize any conflicts between protecting the rights and welfare of clients, others, and society?
- Which alternative action will result in your doing the "least harm" possible?

Step 7: Select and Evaluate the Preferred Action

After selecting the best course of action, we need to reflect a bit more. Particularly if we have not chosen the action that ranked as the highest one, we need to evaluate our decision. Were we influenced by a factor we hadn't recognized? Should we reconsider?

Step 8: Plan the Action

Once we've decided on a preferred action, it is important to do it!

Step 9: Evaluate the Outcome

What happened? Was the action we selected actually implemented? Were the results what we expected? Do we still think this was the best decision?

Step 10: Examine the Implications

We periodically need to ask ourselves what we've learned from the process and outcome. What implications are there for future ethical decision making?

PREVIEW OF THE WORKBOOK

In the next chapter you will find a series of exercises designed to help you explore your values and their influence on your behavior; then in chapter 3 you'll find exercises to expand your understanding of the *Ethical Standards of Human Service Professionals*. Chapter 4 presents an example in which a faculty member and a student used the ethical decision-making process. Starting in chapter 5 and continuing through the remainder of the workbook, exercises will use anecdotes to focus your attention on actual personal, academic, and professional ethical issues encountered by other human service students and professionals.

NOTES

1. To protect the confidentiality of the human service practitioners, students, and faculty who submitted these anecdotes, all identifying information has been removed or changed. Some anecdotes were submitted anonymously.
2. Each profession's ethical guidelines are published by its professional organization(s). These guidelines are often included in relevant textbooks.
3. There are ethical review boards in many professional organizations that consider ethics charges brought against their members, but they don't act as general resources for all members and their individual decisions. There also are ethics committees in many educational and human service organizations that review the ethics of proposed human research and advise practitioners, as requested, about ethical dilemmas in providing services.

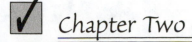 *Chapter Two*

Exploring Your Own Values

. . .we have to work to be good people, . . . goodness always involves the choice to be good.

—Liv Ullman

Your values and your **value system** (the ways you organize, rank, and make decisions based on your values) provide the foundation from which you make your personal and professional choices. Your success at working within your chosen profession's ethical standards is strongly influenced by the congruence between your own values and those of the profession. In this chapter we start by focusing on your own personal values: Where did they come from? How do they influence you and your behavior?

These exercises ask you to explore some aspects of who you are. They ask you to identify, clarify, and understand your values. They challenge you to choose among competing values, show how you make value judgments, and ask you to evaluate your own process of making judgments. They give you the opportunity to practice and evaluate value-based decision making. The last exercise in this chapter asks you to anticipate how your values will influence you as a human service professional.

These are only a few of many exercises that are available. To continue your own process of personal values exploration, review the bibliography in this workbook and search resources listed under "values education" at your library, bookstore, or on the Internet.

HOW DO I VIEW MYSELF AND MY LIFE RIGHT NOW?[1]

All personal adventures have their beginning points. The following exercise will help you assess your current state of growth and adjustment. Use the outline below to explore the factors that you believe have significantly contributed to your life and who you are right now. Use your personal journal to record and reflect on your responses.

I. How I became who I am
- A. Influences from childhood
    1. Relationships with parents, siblings, and other significant family members
    2. Family values, cultural expectations, and community beliefs and standards
    3. Socioeconomic status
- B. Influences from adolescence
    1. Relationships with friends
    2. School performance
    3. Important role models
    4. Accomplishments and risk taking
- C. Influences of chance
    1. Unusual childhood experiences
    2. Traumatic events
    3. Illnesses/injuries
    4. How others saw me as a child

II. How I describe my present position
- A. What type of person I am
- B. How others would describe me
- C. How well I get along with others; what type of friends I prefer
- D. Which values are most important to me
- E. How I view manhood /womanhood, and my attitude toward the opposite sex
- F. How I view my sexuality
- G. My dating experiences
- H. My career aspirations
- I. My academic abilities

III. What I would like to see happen
- A. What my ideal life would be like
- B. How I am currently working toward my ideal
- C. What role others (friends, spouse, children, partners, employers, mentors) might play in my future
- D. What obstacles can keep me from my ideal
- E. Where I see the most room for future personal growth

CHILDHOOD VALUE MESSAGES[2]

By the time we are about 10 years old, most of our values have already been "programmed." Values are taught to us by family members and friends, through the media, in churches and schools, and by watching other people. What are the value messages you learned as a child? Recall as many values as you can remember hearing as a child and write them in the space provided.

Here are a few examples to get you thinking:

"Nothing worthwhile ever comes easy."

"Life is fatal—you're eternal."

"You can accomplish almost anything you want to if you persevere."

"Clean your plate, there are starving children in China!"

"You are your brother's keeper—reach out to others."

"Tell me the truth and I won't punish you!"

"Get your work done first, then you can play."

Now, write some of the messages you heard as a child that taught you your values:

1. _____

2. _____

3. _____

4. _____

5. _____

6. _____

7. _____

8. _____

9. _____

10. _____

1. Next to each of the messages or values you identified, write the person's name who taught or modeled that value.
2. Put a star next to those messages that are still your values today.
3. Put a check next to those messages you need to alter.
4. Consider how some of these values are still influencing you today. Is this a positive or negative influence? Explain your thinking.

RATE YOUR VALUES[3]

Individual Work

Below is a list of values. You are going to rate these values twice. First, rate them according to how important they are to you according to the following scale:

1 = not at all important
2 = a little important
3 = important
4 = very important
5 = extremely important

Value	Rating 1	Rating 2
Having a lot of money	2	13
World peace	4	11
A life filled with excitement	3	2
Family	5	1
A job you enjoy	3	3
Feeling good about yourself	4	4
A healthy love relationship	3	10
Wisdom	3	7
Respected/known by others	2	
Honesty	5	6
Personal salvation	4	5
Contributing to society		9
Accomplishing/achieving	3	8

For the second rating, rank order these 13 values in order of most important to least important. In other words, mark the most important one "1," next most important "2," and so on.

Small Group Work

Respond to the following questions. Write your personal reflections in the space provided.

1. How are your rankings similar to other group members' rankings?

2. How are they different?

3. What dilemmas did you see yourself sorting out when you were required to rank order these values?

SELF-ESTEEM RATING SCALE[4]

This questionnaire is designed to measure how you feel about yourself. It is not a test, so there are no right or wrong answers. Please answer each item as carefully and accurately as you can by placing a number by each one as follows:

1 = never
2 = rarely
3 = a little of the time
4 = some of the time
5 = a good part of the time
6 = most of the time
7 = always

_____ 1. I feel that people would NOT like me if they really knew me well.
_____ 2. I feel that others do things much better than I do.
_____ 3. I feel that I am an attractive person.
_____ 4. I feel confident in my ability to deal with other people.
_____ 5. I feel that I am likely to fail at things I do.
_____ 6. I feel that people really like to talk with me.
_____ 7. I feel that I am a very competent person.
_____ 8. When I am with other people I feel that they are glad I am with them.
_____ 9. I feel that I make a good impression on others.
_____ 10. I feel confident that I can begin new relationships if I want to.
_____ 11. I feel that I am ugly.
_____ 12. I feel that I am a boring person.
_____ 13. I feel very nervous when I am with strangers.
_____ 14. I feel confident in my ability to learn new things.
_____ 15. I feel good about myself
_____ 16. I feel ashamed about myself.
_____ 17. I feel inferior to other people.
_____ 18. I feel that my friends find me interesting.
_____ 19. I feel that I have a good sense of humor.
_____ 20. I get angry at myself over the way I am.
_____ 21. I feel relaxed meeting new people.
_____ 22. I feel that other people are smarter than I am.
_____ 23. I do NOT like myself.
_____ 24. I feel confident in my ability to cope with difficult situations.
_____ 25. I feel that I am NOT very likable.
_____ 26. My friends value me a lot.
_____ 27. I am afraid I will appear stupid to others.
_____ 28. I feel that I am an okay person.
_____ 29. I feel that I can count on myself to manage things well.
_____ 30. I wish I could just disappear when I am around other people.

- − _____5_ 31. I feel embarrassed to let others hear my ideas.
- + _____5_ 32. I feel that I am a nice person.
- − _____7_ 33. I feel that if I could be more like other people I would feel better about myself.
- − _____7_ 34. I feel that I get pushed around more than others.
- + _____4_ 35. I feel that people like me.
- + _____3_ 36. I feel that people have a good time when they are with me.
- + _____2_ 37. I feel confident that I can do well in whatever I do.
- − _____3_ 38. I trust the competence of others more than I trust my own abilities.
- − _____5_ 39. I feel that I mess things up.
- − _____6_ 40. I wish that I were someone else.

−56

Neg.   Pos.
−112   56

Scoring and Interpretation

Put a "+" or "−" in front of each score, depending on the item number:

+: 3, 4, 6, 7, 8, 9, 10, 14, 15, 18, 19, 21, 24, 26, 28, 29, 32, 35, 36, 37

−: 1, 2, 5, 11, 12, 13, 16, 17, 20, 22, 23, 25, 27, 30, 31, 33, 34, 38, 39, 40

Sum the positive and negative scores. Your total will fall between +120 and −120. A positive score indicates a more positive self-esteem; a negative score represents self-esteem that is more negative.

BELIEF IN PERSONAL CONTROL SCALE: REVISED[5]

Individual Work

This questionnaire consists of items describing perceptions you have of yourself, others, and life in general. Please respond to each item by using the following rating scale. In the blank space write the rating scale number (1–5) that best describes how you feel about the statement.

1 always true for you
2 often true for you
3 sometimes true for you
4 rarely true for you
5 never true for you

_____ 1. I can make things happen easily.

_____ 2. Getting what you want is a matter of knowing the right people.

_____ 3. My behavior is dictated by the demands of society.

_____ 4. If I just keep trying, I can overcome any obstacle.

_____ 5. I can succeed with God's help.

_____ 6. I find that luck plays a bigger role in my life than my ability.

_____ 7. If nothing is happening, I go out and make it happen.

_____ 8. I am solely responsible for the outcomes in my life.

_____ 9. I rely on God to help me control my life.

_____ 10. Regardless of the obstacles, I refuse to quit trying.

_____ 11. My success is a matter of good luck.

_____ 12. Getting what you want is a matter of being in the right place at the right time.

_____ 13. I am able to control effectively the behavior of others.

_____ 14. If I need help, I know that God is there for me.

_____ 15. My behavior is governed by the demands of others.

_____ 16. There is little that I can do to change my destiny.

_____ 17. I feel that I control my life as much as is humanly possible.

_____ 18. God rewards me if I obey his laws.

_____ 19. I am not the master of my own fate.

_____ 20. I continue to strive for a goal long after others would have given up.

_____ 21. There are some things in my life that I just can't control.

_____ 22. God helps me to live an effective life.

_____ 23. I have more control over my life than other people.

_____ 24. I actively strive to make things happen for myself.

_____ 25. Older people hinder my ability to direct my life.

_____ 26. What happens to me is a matter of good or bad fortune.

_____ 27. When something stands in my way, I go around it.

_____ 28. I can be whatever I want to be.

_____ 29. I know how to get what I want from others.

_____ 30. Fate can be blamed for my failures.

_____ 31. With God's help, I can be whatever I want to be.

_____ 32. I am the victim of circumstances beyond my control.

_____ 33. I can control my own thoughts.

_____ 34. There is nothing that happens to me that I don't control.

_____ 35. Whenever I run up against some obstacle, I strive even harder to overcome it and reach my goal.

_____ 36. By placing my life in God's hands, all things are possible.

_____ 37. I am at the mercy of my physical impulses.

_____ 38. In this life, what happens to me is determined by fate.

_____ 39. My actions are the result of God working through me.

_____ 40. I am the victim of social forces.

_____ 41. Controlling my life involves mind over matter.

_____ 42. When I want something, I assert myself in order to get it.

_____ 43. The unconscious mind, over which I have no control, directs my course in life.

_____ 44. If I really want something, I pray to God to bring it to me.

_____ 45. I am not very good at controlling my life.

Scoring

This scale is made up of three subscales: A, B, and C. They are scored separately. Following is a breakdown of the scales. For each subscale you will first copy down the scores you assigned to those items, then total your score. For Subscale B, you put down the opposite score from what you originally assigned (in other words, if you put down 5, you enter 1; if you put down 2, you enter 4, and so on).

Subscale A
2. ____
3. ____
6. ____
11. ____
12. ____
15. ____
16. ____

Subscale B
(reverse scored)
1. ____
4. ____
7. ____
8. ____
10. ____
13. ____

Subscale C
5. ____
9. ____
14. ____
18. ____
22. ____
31. ____
36. ____

Subscale A
19. ____
21. ____
25. ____
26. ____
30. ____
32. ____
33. ____
37. ____
38. ____
40. ____
43. ____
45. ____
____Total A

Subscale B
17. ____
20. ____
23. ____
24. ____
27. ____
28. ____
29. ____
34. ____
35. ____
41. ____
42. ____
____Total B

Subscale C
39. ____
44. ____
____Total C

Interpretation

Each subscale illustrates a different style of internal/external locus of control. Following is a description of what each scale measures, and how to interpret your score.

Subscale A: Internality/Externality

This scale measures the extent to which you believe the outcomes in your life are produced by you (internal locus of control) or by fate or others (external locus of control). If you score 60 or lower, you score similarly to individuals who have an external locus of control. If you score between 60 and 77, you place somewhere in between internal and external locus of control. If you score 77 or higher, you score more like individuals with an internal locus of control.

Subscale B: Exaggerated Sense of Control

This scale measures the possibility that you think you have more control over what goes on around you than you really do. So if **Subscale A** suggests that you have an internal locus of control and **Subscale B** suggests that your sense of internal control is unrealistic, you may still need to do some work on your sense of internality. A score below 48 suggests that your sense of control is probably realistic. A score between 48 and 63 suggests that you have some realistic and some unrealistic beliefs about your ability to control your environment. A score above 63 suggests that your sense of personal control may be unrealistically high.

Subscale C: Control Through God

Belief in God's assistance as we influence the world around us does not necessarily represent an external locus of control. This subscale helps you assess whether your belief in God's assistance has evolved as internality or externality. In other words, to what extent do you view God as an asset to internality, helping you gain internal control? If your score is above 40, you most likely have a more internalized concept of God's influence in your life. If you scored on **Subscale A** as having an external locus of control yet believe in God as a mediator of your life outcomes, your religious beliefs may be providing you with a buffer against the depression, anxiety, and other problems that may crop up in association with an external locus of control.

Small Group Discussion

1. Discuss what is meant by locus of control. How might your locus of control affect you in your academic and career aspirations and activities?
2. The results of a single psychological assessment tool only suggest possibilities of what you might be like. Do you agree or disagree with the findings of these subscales? Why or why not?
3. Describe a few personal situations that either supported or refuted the findings of the subscales.

TIME SCHEDULING EXERCISE[6]

Individual Work

On the next page is a chart representing the days of the week and the hours of the day. Design a time schedule for this term that takes into account:

1. Activities that must happen at a certain time, such as classes, meetings, sports practices, your children's schedules, scheduled social events, and inflexible work hours.
2. Activities that must happen but have some flexibility in when they occur, such as flexible work hours, homework, self-care, and housekeeping activities.
3. Activities you would like to do that are not crucial or time-restricted events, such as socializing, playing games, watching TV, and hanging out with friends and family. However, make sure that you do include time in your schedule somewhere for leisure!
4. Room for flexibility, in the event that something comes up that interferes with a priority.

Reflection

Look at the schedule you have made. Consider these questions: Is it realistic? Does it reflect your values? Will it be useful to you this term in helping you accomplish those things that are important to you? Will you use it or will you ignore it?

Modify the schedule and post it where it will catch your eye frequently if you want to make it useful.

Time	SUN	MON	TUE	WED	THU	FRI	SAT
6–7 am							
7–8 am							
8–9 am							
9–10 am							
10–11 am							
11–12 noon							
12–1 pm							
1–2 pm							
2–3 pm							
3–4 pm							
4–5 pm							
5–6 pm							
6–7 pm							
7–8 pm							
8–9 pm							
9–10 pm							
10–11 pm							
11–12 midnight							

THE SOCIAL READJUSTMENT SCALE[7]

Individual Work

Circle the number value preceding each stressful life event that you have experienced in the last 12 months.

100	Death of spouse
73	Divorce
65	Marital separation
63	Jail term
63	Death of a close family member
53	Personal injury or illness
50	Marriage
47	Fired from job
45	Marital reconciliation
45	Retirement
44	Change in health of family member
40	Pregnancy
39	Sex difficulties
39	Gain of new family member
39	Business readjustment
38	Change in financial state
37	Death of a close friend
36	Change to a different line of work
35	Change in number of arguments with significant other
31	Mortgage over $47,000
30	Foreclosure of mortgage or loan
29	Change in responsibilities at work
29	Son or daughter leaving home
29	Trouble with in-laws
28	Outstanding personal achievement
26	Wife (husband) begins or stops work
26	Begin or end school
25	Change in living conditions
25	Revision of personal habits
23	Trouble with boss
20	Change in work hours or conditions
20	Change in residence
20	Change in schools
19	Change in recreation
19	Change in church activities
18	Change in social activities

17 Mortgage or loan less than $47,000

16 Change in sleeping habits

15 Change in number of family get-togethers

15 Change in eating habits

13 Vacation

12 Christmas

11 Minor violations of the law

Scoring and Interpretation

Based on research with this scale (Holmes & Masuda, 1973; Rahe, 1968, 1974), an individual's likelihood of experiencing a major health change within two years increases as the total score rises. This chance of experiencing a health change has been expressed as follows:

0–150 points: 1 in 3 chance

150–300 points: 50:50 chance

Over 300 points: almost a 90 percent chance

Total the values you have circled:

Total ___258___

Compare your total with the guidelines. What are *your* chances of experiencing a major health change in the next two years?

Individual Work or Group Discussion

1. Did some of the events on this checklist surprise you? If so, which ones? What reasons can you think of that would explain why they contribute to health negatively?
2. How can knowing that such stressors add up to health problems help you limit the effect of stressors on your health? In other words, how can being forewarned result in your becoming forearmed?
3. How do our responses to stressors affect our values?

Alternative Exercise

While the Holmes-Rahe test applies to everyone, there are a number of stressors that are specific to college students.

Small Group Work

Generate a list of at least 20 typical college stressful events, then rank order them according to which your group thinks are the most catastrophic and which are of the least significance. Assign values between 1 and 100 to these items according to how stressful your group thinks they are. This may result in some changes in ranking.

Our group's items:

PLEASANT EVENTS LIST[8]

Here is your chance to develop your own personalized remedy for feeling down in the dumps. When we feel bad, we sometimes continue to feel bad, or even worse, because we conjure up more and more unpleasant thoughts and memories. If you retrieve pleasant thoughts and memories instead, you are more likely to reduce your unpleasant feelings.

On the next page, write out your own list of pleasant events. A list of sample pleasant events is included below, from which you can choose events for yourself or consider as examples only. Then the next time you are feeling down, try reading your pleasant events list. Close your eyes and imagine that you are experiencing these events. You may be surprised at the positive results!

Spending time with a significant other
Having a meaningful heart-to-heart conversation
Going for a drive in the country
Having friends over for a lively evening
Performing a job exceptionally well
Observing a beautiful sunset
Telling a good joke and having others laugh
Hearing a really good joke
Having someone indicate they think I'm attractive
Feeling completely relaxed and at ease
Going to a party
Taking a leisurely, hot bubble bath
Being in the middle of a really good book
Feeling joined with God
Having a fun vacation
Receiving compliments from others
Having others express a desire to get together with me
Having someone say "I love you"
Sunbathing
Skiing
Snorkeling
Being the center of attention
Having a whole day entirely to myself
Kissing
Feeling close to nature
Successfully learning a new skill
Getting a raise or promotion
Getting a letter from an old friend
Finding something important that I thought I had lost

My Pleasant Events List

RATE YOUR GOAL-SETTING ABILITY[9]

For the following statements, select the answer that best describes your behavior.

1. Whenever I am faced with some small task that needs to be attended to, I attend to it right away.
   - a. nearly always
   - b. most of the time
   - c. sometimes
   - d. hardly ever

2. Whenever I am about to go into a situation that is important to me, I take a few minutes to clarify my objectives.
   - a. nearly always
   - b. most of the time
   - c. sometimes
   - d. hardly ever

3. Often when I am involved with a project that I know I am fully capable of handling, I get "bogged down" with inconsequential details.
   - a. hardly ever
   - b. sometimes
   - c. most of the time
   - d. nearly always

4. I say things that I regret afterward.
   - a. hardly ever
   - b. sometimes
   - c. most of the time
   - d. nearly always

5. When I write down a list of things to do on a given day, I manage to get everything finished that I've written down.
   - a. nearly always
   - b. most of the time
   - c. sometimes
   - d. hardly ever

6. If I am involved in a large-scale project, I can accurately project when it will be completed.
   - a. nearly always
   - b. most of the time
   - c. sometimes
   - d. hardly ever

7. When I am under a lot of pressure, it is easy for me to plan my day in a logical manner.
   - a. nearly always
   - b. most of the time
   - c. sometimes
   - d. hardly ever

8. When I am faced with a number of responsibilities, I feel a sense of being overwhelmed.
   - a. hardly ever
   - b. sometimes
   - c. most of the time
   - d. nearly always

9. Give me a deadline and I'll meet it without trouble.
   - a. nearly always
   - b. most of the time
   - c. sometimes
   - d. hardly ever

10. When I have a lot of things to do I have trouble getting started on any of them.
    - a. hardly ever
    - b. sometimes
    - c. most of the time
    - d. nearly always

Scoring

Give yourself a score of 4 points for every time you marked "a," 3 points for "b," 2 points for "c," and 1 point for "d." Total your scores, and analyze them thus:

- *35–40:* You are no doubt an extremely focused and goal-oriented person. You are well organized, and probably feel reasonably content and fulfilled as well. You might want to assess, however, whether or not you are successfully goal-oriented or actually goal-obsessed.

- *25–34:* You are above average in your ability to orient yourself toward your goals. You are probably better at it for some activities and situations than for others.

- *15–24:* This is a relatively average score. You are probably successful in applying goal-directed behavior in some areas of your life, but there are many areas where you have difficulty becoming focused and organized.

- *14 or below:* Goal-directed behavior does not play a great role in your life. You probably do not realize your full potential, and you may have difficulty meeting those few goals that are important to you.

VALUES LIST

Group Discussion

In your group discuss values. Write down as many values as you can think of. List any and all values that occur to you—even if you believe they are unimportant or even harmful to people. Use a brainstorming approach: Strive for quantity, listing as many as you can think of, and don't judge anyone's ideas while you're making the list.

1. Our group's list of values:

2. Discuss the values you've listed. Give examples of each.

Individual Work

1. Review the list of values your group created. As you read, consider:
   - Which ones are important to you?
   - Which ones seem to guide your decisions and actions?
2. Circle five or six values that seem most important to you, and that are already influential in your life.
3. Describe how your choices and activities are consistent with these circled values.
4. Star four or five values that seem most important to you and that don't really seem to be guiding your decisions and actions yet.
5. What might you do to start taking action that would be more consistent with these starred values? What activities would you have to stop doing? What would you need to start doing?

VALUES CONFLICT RESOLUTION ASSESSMENT (VCRA)[10]

Conflict Description

Read the following definitions of values and values conflicts and then describe a values conflict in your life.

Values

A person's values are his or her *beliefs about what is important in life*. Some values refer to how one should act (for example, to be honest, altruistic, competitive, self-disciplined, courageous, kind). Other values refer to what one wants to accomplish or obtain in life (for example, to want a lot of money, security, fame, a large family, meaningful friendships, world peace, equality, peace of mind, physical health, salvation, wisdom). Your values exist as a complex set of interweaving personal policies or priorities that serve as a guide for decision making. Some examples of personal value statements are "My family always comes first," "I would rather be honest and unpopular than dishonest and popular," "I do not need to be wealthy—just comfortable," "My physical health is relatively important to me but maintaining my ideal weight is not a priority at all," "The most meaningful thing I can do with my life is to help others."

Values Conflicts

A person cannot "have it all" or "be all things." Priorities must be established and choices made. An *intra*personal values conflict occurs when an individual experiences uncertainty about what *he or she really believes or wants* and/or when two or more *priorities or beliefs conflict or seem incompatible* to the person. The following are examples:

- I want to be very successful in my career, but I also want a more relaxing lifestyle and more time to spend with my family and friends.
- On the one hand, I don't believe in being materialistic and don't want to be. Yet, on the other hand, I am attracted to and want expensive things. I do want a bigger house, a high-quality car, and such.
- Generally, I want a comfortable and secure life—I want a secure job and a permanent home in a close-knit community. Yet part of me is attracted to the excitement of change, new challenges, and risk.

These are just a few general examples. Of course, there are numerous idiosyncratic values conflicts. In the space provided below please describe an *important values conflict issue that you are experiencing in your life right now*.

Conflict Resolution

You described a values conflict in your life. Pretend that you have to resolve that conflict or make a clear decision right now. In the space provided below write the best resolution that you can see *at this particular point in time.* Avoid vague responses like "I would compromise." Rather, write a concise decision or resolution so that it is clear what you would do if you were to carry it out.

Questionnaire

The following questions refer to the specific conflict you just described and resolution you wrote. Do not change what you wrote. Evaluate *that particular resolution* exactly as written and as objectively as you can. Please respond honestly to each question by circling one number for each continuum.

1. How satisfied are you with the resolution you just wrote?

0	1	2	3	4
completely dissatisfied		moderately		very satisfied

2. To what extent is this resolution compatible with your basic ethical, spiritual, or moral standards and principles?

0	1	2	3	4
not at all compatible		somewhat compatible		very compatible

3. To what extent has your actual behavior been consistent with this resolution during the past few months?

0	1	2	3	4
not consistent at all		somewhat consistent		very consistent

4. Resolving conflicts or making decisions usually involves gathering information, considering various alternatives, and critically thinking about options. During your life to what extent do you think you have carefully analyzed and thought about your alternatives or options for this conflict?

0	1	2	3	4
I need to do much more thinking.		I need to do some more thinking.		I have thought sufficiently.

5. All decisions carry consequences. During your life, to what extent have you carefully considered possible positive and negative consequences of living in accordance with this resolution?

0	1	2	3	4
I have not thought about possible consequences.		I have thought about possible consequences to some extent.		I have carefully considered possible consequences.

6. Assuming that every act or decision has a beneficial, neutral, or negative effect on society and the improvement of humankind—in your opinion what effect (no matter how small) would this resolution have on society?

0	1	2	3	4
more negative		neutral (equally positive and negative)		more positive

7. To what extent does the thought of carrying out this resolution make you feel bad about yourself?

0	1	2	3	4
very		somewhat		not at all

8. Imagine, however unlikely it may seem, being in a public meeting and hearing this resolution criticized as being selfish and unhumanitarian. To what extent could you defend the resolution in good conscience?

0	1	2	3	4
not defend it at all		defend it to some extent		defend it wholeheartedly

9. To what extent have you thought about or made plans regarding what you need to do in order to carry out this resolution?

0	1	2	3	4
I have not made any plans or thought ahead about it.		I have done some planning and thinking.		I have planned or thought about it sufficiently.

10. If most people lived in accordance with the values implied in this resolution, how do you think the world would be changed?

0	1	2	3	4
a worse world		no better or worse		a better world

11. To what extent would you experience feelings of guilt if you actually carried out this resolution?

0	1	2	3	4
very guilty		somewhat guilty		not guilty at all

12. To what extent would you feel embarrassed if people you cared about knew you wrote this particular resolution? Overall, how embarrassed would you feel?

0	1	2	3	4
very embarrassed		somewhat embarrassed		not embarrassed at all

13. In general, how do you think people who know you well would judge how consistent your behavior has been with this resolution?

0	1	2	3	4
not consistent at all		somewhat consistent		very consistent

14. Sometimes people make certain decisions because they feel pressured, influenced, or manipulated by others. In such cases the decisions are not really theirs. To what extent do you think that the resolution you wrote is truly what you want or believe?

0	1	2	3	4
not at all		somewhat		very much

15. To what extent do you feel committed to carrying out this resolution during the next year?

0	1	2	3	4
not committed at all		somewhat committed		very committed

16. People often tell themselves that a certain decision is better than it really is in order to avoid feeling bad about having made a mistake. To what extent do you think you are being honest with yourself about your evaluation of this resolution?

0	1	2	3	4
not at all honest		somewhat honest		very honest

17. Try to imagine the following situation. It is sometime in the future and you have only a few months to live. Pretend that you have lived in accordance with this resolution and are thinking about your decision and your impending death. In that context to what extent do you believe you will regret having lived in accordance with the resolution?

0	1	2	3	4
much regret		some regret		no regret

Scoring and Interpreting the VCRA

Total the values selected for all 17 items. A mean score would be about 36. Higher scores indicate better conflict resolution. If you are not satisfied with your score, consider repeating the exercise with an alternative solution.

SELF-ASSESSMENT: AN INVENTORY OF YOUR ATTITUDES AND BELIEFS ABOUT PROFESSIONAL AND ETHICAL ISSUES[11]

Individual Work

This inventory surveys your thoughts on various professional and ethical issues in the helping professions. Most of the items relate directly to topics that are explored in detail later in the workbook. The inventory is designed to introduce you to these issues and to stimulate your thoughts and interest. You may want to complete the inventory in more than one sitting, so that you can give each question your full concentration.

This is *not* a traditional multiple-choice test in which you must select the "one right answer." Rather, it is a survey of your basic beliefs, attitudes, and values on specific topics related to a career in human services. For each question, write in the letter of the response that most clearly reflects your viewpoint at this time. In many cases the answers are not mutually exclusive, and you may choose more than one response if you wish. In addition, a blank line is included for each item. You may want to use this line to provide another response more suited to your thinking or to qualify a chosen response.

Notice that there are two spaces before each item. Use the spaces on the left for your answers as you begin your exploration of values and ethics in the human service professions. After completing much of your coursework, field placements, and this workbook, you can retake this inventory using the spaces on the right and covering your initial answers so that you won't be influenced by how you originally responded. Then you can see how your attitudes have changed as a result of your development and experiences.

____ ____ 1. The personal characteristics of human service practitioners are
  a. not really that relevant to the helping process.
  b. the most important variable in determining the quality of the helping process.
  c. shaped and molded by those who teach human service practitioners.
  d. not as important as the skills and knowledge the human service practitioners possess.
  e. _____

____ ____ 2. Which of the following do you consider to be the most important personal characteristic of a good human service practitioner?
  a. willingness to serve as a model for clients
  b. courage
  c. openness and honesty
  d. a sense of being "centered" as a person
  e. _____

____ ____ 3. Concerning human service practitioners' self-disclosure to their clients, I believe that
  a. it is essential for establishing a relationship.
  b. it is inappropriate and merely burdens the client.
  c. it should be done rarely and only when the practitioner feels like sharing.
  d. it is useful for human service practitioners to reveal how they feel toward their clients in the context of helping.
  e. _____

___ . A 4. A client-professional relationship characterized by warmth, acceptance, caring, empathy, and respect is
   a. a necessary and sufficient condition of positive change in clients.
   b. a necessary but not sufficient condition of positive change in clients.
   c. neither a necessary nor a sufficient condition of positive change in clients.
   d. _____

___ ___ 5. Of the following factors, which is the most important in determining whether helping will result in change?
   a. the kind of person the human service practitioner is
   b. the skills and techniques the human service practitioner uses
   c. the motivation of the client to change
   d. the theoretical orientation of the therapist
   e. _____

___ ___ 6. Of the following, which do you consider to be the most important attribute of an effective human service professional?
   a. knowledge of the theories of helping
   b. skill in using techniques appropriately
   c. genuineness and openness
   d. ability to specify a treatment plan and evaluate the results
   e. _____

___ ___ 7. I believe that, for those who wish to become helpers, personal psychotherapy
   a. should be required for licensure.
   b. is not an important factor in developing the capacity to work with others.
   c. should be encouraged but not required.
   d. is needed only when the practitioner has serious problems.
   e. _____

___ ___ 8. I believe that, in order to help a client, a human service professional
   a. must like the client personally.
   b. must be free of any personal conflicts in the area in which the client is working.
   c. needs to have experienced the same problem as the client.
   d. needs to have experienced feelings similar to those being experienced by the client.
   e. _____

___ ___ 9. In regard to the client-practitioner relationship, I think that
   a. the practitioner should remain objective and anonymous.
   b. the practitioner should be a friend to the client.
   c. a personal relationship, but not friendship, is essential.
   d. a personal and warm relationship is not essential.
   e. _____

___ ___ 10. I should be open, honest, and transparent with my clients
   a. when I like and value them.
   b. when I have negative feelings toward them.
   c. rarely, if ever, so that I will avoid negatively influencing the client-helper relationship.
   d. only when it intuitively feels like the right thing to do.
   e. _____

_____ _____ 11. I expect that I will experience professional burnout if
  a. I get involved in too many demanding projects.
  b. I must do things in my work that aren't personally meaningful.
  c. my personal life is characterized by conflict and struggle.
  d. my clients complain a lot and fail to change for the better.
  e. _____

_____ _____ 12. I think that professional burnout
  a. can be avoided if I'm involved in personal therapy while working as a professional.
  b. is inevitable and that I must learn to live with it.
  c. can be lessened if I find ways to replenish and nourish myself.
  d. may or may not occur, depending on the type of client I work with.
  e. _____

_____ _____ 13. If I were an intern and were convinced that my supervisor was encouraging trainees to participate in unethical behavior in an agency setting, I would
  a. first discuss the matter with the supervisor.
  b. report the supervisor to the director of the agency.
  c. ignore the situation for fear of negative consequences.
  d. report the situation to the ethics committee of the state professional association.
  e. _____

_____ _____ 14. Practitioners who work with culturally diverse groups without having cross-cultural knowledge and skills
  a. are violating the civil rights of their clients.
  b. are probably guilty of unethical behavior.
  c. should realize the need for specialized training.
  d. can be said to be practicing ethically.
  e. _____

_____ _____ 15. If I had strong feelings, positive or negative, toward a client, I think that I would most likely
  a. discuss my feelings with my client.
  b. keep them to myself and hope they would eventually disappear.
  c. discuss them with a supervisor or colleague.
  d. accept them as natural unless they began to interfere with the helping relationship.
  e. _____

_____ _____ 16. I won't feel ready to help others until
  a. my own life is free of problems.
  b. I've experienced helping as a client.
  c. I feel very confident and know I'll be effective.
  d. I've become a self-aware person and developed the ability to continually reexamine my own life and relationships.
  e. _____

_____ _____ 17. If a client evidenced strong feelings of attraction or dislike for me, I think that I would
  a. help the client work through these feelings and understand them.
  b. enjoy these feelings if they were positive.
  c. refer my client to another human service practitioner.
  d. direct the sessions into less emotional areas.
  e. _____

___ _B_ 18. Practitioners who help clients whose sex, race, age, social class, or sexual orientation is different from their own
    a. will most likely not understand these clients fully.
    b. need to understand the differences between their clients and themselves.
    c. can practice unethically if they do not consider cross-cultural factors.
    d. are probably not going to be effective with such clients because of these differences.
    e. _____

___ _D_ 19. When I consider being involved in the helping professions, I value most
    a. the money I expect to earn.
    b. the security I imagine I will have in the job.
    c. the knowledge that I will be intimately involved with people who are searching for a better life.
    d. the personal growth I expect to experience through my work.
    e. _____

___ _C_ 20. If I were faced with a helping situation where it appeared that there was a conflict between ethical and legal courses to follow, I would
    a. Immediately consult with an attorney.
    b. always choose the legal path first and foremost.
    c. strive to do what I believe to be ethical, even if it meant challenging a law.
    d. refer my client to another professional.
    e. _____

___ _E_ 21. With respect to value judgments in helping, professionals should
    a. feel free to make value judgments about their clients' behavior.
    b. actively teach their own values when they think that clients need a different set of values.
    c. remain neutral and keep their values out of the therapeutic process.
    d. encourage clients to question their own values and decide on the quality of their own behavior.
    e. _____

___ _C_ 22. Human service practitioners should
    a. teach desirable behavior and values by modeling them for clients.
    b. encourage clients to look within themselves to discover values that are meaningful to them.
    c. reinforce the dominant values of society.
    d. very delicately, if at all, challenge clients' value systems.
    e. _____

___ _D_ 23. In terms of appreciating and understanding the value systems of clients who are culturally different from me,
    a. I see it as my responsibility to learn about their values and not impose mine on them.
    b. I would encourage them to accept the values of the dominant culture for survival purposes.
    c. I would attempt to modify my helping procedures to fit their cultural values.
    d. I think it is imperative that I learn about the specific cultural values my clients hold.
    e. _____

____ ____ 24. If a client came to me with a problem and I could see that I would not be objective because of my values, I would
    a. accept the client because of the challenge to become more tolerant of diversity.
    b. tell the client at the outset about my fears concerning our conflicting values.
    c. refer the client to someone else.
    d. attempt to influence the client to adopt my way of thinking.
    e. _____

____ ____ 25. I believe that the real reason for professional licensing and certification is
    a. to provide information to the public services.
    b. to protect the public by setting minimum levels of competence for professionals.
    c. to upgrade the helping professions by ensuring that the highest standards of excellence are promoted.
    d. to protect the interests of various helping professions and to reduce competition.
    e. _____

____ ____ 26. I would tend to refer a client to another professional
    a. if I had a strong dislike for the client.
    b. if I didn't have much experience working with the kind of problem the client presented.
    c. if I saw my own needs and problems getting in the way of helping the client.
    d. if the client seemed to distrust me.
    e. _____

____ ____ 27. My ethical position regarding the role of values in helping is that, as a professional, I should
    a. never impose my values on a client.
    b. expose my values, without imposing them on the client.
    c. teach my clients what I consider to be proper values.
    d. keep my values out of the helping relationship.
    e. _____

____ ____ 28. If I were to counsel lesbian and gay clients, a major concern of mine would be
    a. maintaining objectivity.
    b. not knowing and understanding enough about this lifestyle.
    c. establishing a positive therapeutic relationship.
    d. pushing my own values.
    e. _____

____ ____ 29. Of the following, I consider the most unethical form of helper behavior to be
    a. promoting dependence in the client.
    b. becoming sexually involved with clients.
    c. breaking confidentiality without a good reason to do so.
    d. accepting a client who has a problem that goes beyond one's competence.
    e. _____

_____ _____ 30. Regarding the issue of helping friends, I think that
  a. it is seldom wise to accept a friend as a client.
  b. it should be done rarely, and only if it is clear that the friendship will not interfere with the therapeutic relationship.
  c. friendship and professional helping should not be mixed.
  d. it should be done only if it seems appropriate to both the client and the human service practitioner.
  e. _____

_____ _____ 31. Regarding confidentiality, I believe that
  a. it is ethical to break confidence when there is reason to believe that clients may do serious harm to themselves.
  b. it is ethical to break confidence when there is reason to believe that a client will do harm to someone else.
  c. it is ethical to break confidence when the parents of a client ask for certain information.
  d. it is ethical to inform the authorities when a client is breaking the law.
  e. _____

_____ _____ 32. Therapists should terminate therapy with a client when
  a. the client decides to do so and not before.
  b. they judge that it is time to terminate.
  c. it is clear that the client is not benefiting from the therapy.
  d. the client reaches an impasse.
  e. _____

_____ _____ 33. A sexual relationship between a former client and helper is
  a. ethical if the client initiates it.
  b. ethical only two years after termination of therapy.
  c. ethical only when client and practitioner discuss the issue and agree to the relationship.
  d. never ethical, regardless of the time that has elapsed.
  e. _____

_____ _____ 34. Concerning the issue of physically touching a client, I think that touching
  a. is unwise, because it could be misinterpreted by the client.
  b. should be done only when the practitioner genuinely feels like doing it.
  c. is an important part of the helping process.
  d. is ethical when the client requests it.
  e. _____

_____ _____ 35. A clinical supervisor has initiated sexual relationships with former students. He maintains that, because he no longer has any professional responsibility to them, this practice is acceptable. In my view, this behavior is
  a. clearly unethical, because he is using his position to initiate contacts with former students.
  b. not unethical, because the professional relationship has ended.
  c. not unethical but is unwise and inappropriate.
  d. somewhat unethical, because the supervisory relationship is similar to the therapeutic relationship.
  e. _____

_____ _____ 36. Regarding the role of spiritual and religious values, as a professional I would be inclined to
  a. ignore such values for fear that I would impose my own beliefs on my clients.

b. actively strive to get my clients to think about how spirituality or religion could enhance their lives.
   c. avoid bringing up the topic unless my client initiated such a discussion.
   d. conduct an assessment of my client's spiritual and religious beliefs during the intake session.
   e. _____

37. In working with a family, I think that the human service practitioner
   a. is primarily responsible to the family as a unit.
   b. should focus primarily on the needs of individual members of the family.
   c. should attend to the family's needs and try to hold the amount of sacrifice by any one member to a minimum.
   d. has an ethical obligation to state his or her bias and approach at the outset.
   e. _____

38. The practice of limiting the number of therapy sessions a client is entitled to under a managed care plan is
   a. unethical as it can work against a client's best interests.
   b. a reality that I expect I'll have to accept.
   c. an example of exploitation of a client's rights.
   d. wrong because it takes away the professional's judgment in many cases.
   e. _____

39. Regarding the issue of who should select the goals of helping, I believe that
   a. it is primarily the practitioner's responsibility to select goals.
   b. it is primarily the client's responsibility to select goals.
   c. the responsibility for selecting goals should be shared equally by the client and the practitioner.
   d. the question of who selects the goals depends on what kind of client is being seen.
   e. _____

40. Concerning the role of diagnosis in helping, I believe that
   a. diagnosis is essential for the planning of a treatment program.
   b. diagnosis is counterproductive for therapy, since it is based on an external view of the client.
   c. diagnosis is dangerous in that it tends to label people, who then are limited by the label.
   d. whether to use diagnosis depends on one's theoretical orientation and the kind of helping one does.
   e. _____

41. Concerning the place of testing in mental health treatment, I think that
   a. tests generally interfere with the treatment process.
   b. tests can be valuable tools if they are used as adjuncts to treatment.
   c. tests are essential for people who are seriously disturbed.
   d. tests can be either used or abused in treatment.
   e. _____

42. Regarding the issue of psychological risks associated with participation in group therapy, my position is that
   a. clients should be informed at the outset of possible risks.
   b. these risks should be minimized by careful screening.

c. this issue is exaggerated, since there are no real risks.

d. careful supervision will offset some of these risks.

e. _____

43. Concerning the human service practitioner's responsibility to the community, I believe that

a. the human service practitioner should educate the community concerning the nature of possible services.

b. the human service practitioner should attempt to change patterns that need changing.

c. community involvement falls outside the proper scope of helping.

d. human service practitioners should become involved in helping clients use the resources available in the community.

e. _____

44. If I were working as a human service professional in the community, the major role I would expect to play would be that of

a. a change agent.

b. an advisor.

c. an educator or a consultant.

d. an advocate.

e. _____

45. As an intern, if I thought my supervision was inadequate, I would

a. talk to my supervisor about it.

b. continue to work without complaining.

c. seek supervision elsewhere.

d. feel let down by the agency I worked for.

e. _____

46. My view of supervision is that it is

a. a place to get answers to difficult situations.

b. a threat to my status as a professional.

c. valuable to have when I reach an impasse with a client.

d. a way for me to learn about myself and to get insights into how I work with clients.

e. _____

47. When it comes to working within institutions, I believe that

a. I must learn how to survive with dignity within a system.

b. I must learn how to subvert the system so that I can do what I deeply believe in.

c. the institution will stifle most of my enthusiasm and block any real change.

d. I can't blame the institution if I'm unable to succeed in my programs.

e. _____

48. If my philosophy were in conflict with that of the institution I worked for, I would

a. seriously consider whether I could ethically remain in that position.

b. attempt to change the policies of the institution.

c. agree to whatever was expected of me in that system.

d. quietly do what I wanted to do, even if I had to be devious about it.

e. _____

_____ _____ 49. In working with clients from different ethnic groups, I think it is most important to
     a. be aware of the sociopolitical forces that have affected these clients.
     b. understand how language can act as a barrier to effective cross-cultural helping.
     c. refer these clients to some professional who shares their ethnic and cultural background.
     d. help these clients modify their views so that they will be accepted and not have to suffer rejection.
     e. _____

_____ _____ 50. To be effective in helping clients from a different culture, I think that a human service practitioner must
     a. possess specific knowledge about the particular group he or she is helping.
     b. be able to accurately "read" nonverbal messages.
     c. have had direct contact with this group.
     d. treat these clients no differently from clients from his or her own cultural background.
     e. _____

Group Work

Bring completed inventories to class so that you can compare your views. Such a comparison may stimulate some debate—which might help get the class involved in the topics to be discussed. In choosing the issues you want to discuss in class, you might go back over the inventory and circle the numbers of those items that you felt most strongly about as you were responding. Ask others how they responded to these items in particular.

NOTES

1. Adapted from *Expanding Your Experience: Exercises and Activities,* by L. Hughes (1996, p. 12).
2. Adapted from *Clinical Ethics and Values: Issues and Insights in a Changing Healthcare Environment,* by D. B. Uustal (1993, p. 25).
3. Adapted from *Expanding Your Experience* (pp. 13–14).
4. From "Validation of a Clinical Measure of Self-Esteem," by W. R. Nugent and J. W. Thomas (1993, pp. 191–207).
5. From "The Belief in Personal Control Scale: A Revised, Short Form," by J. L. Berrenberg (1987, pp. 17–22). Adapted from Hughes, 1996.
6. Adapted from *Expanding Your Experience* (p. 32).
7. Adapted from "The Social Readjustment Rating Scale," by T. H. Holmes and R. H. Rahe (1967, 213–218).
8. Adapted from *Expanding Your Experience* (pp. 61–62).
9. From *Targets: How to Set Goals for Yourself and Reach Them!* by L. Tec (1980, pp. 8–9). Adapted by Hughes, 1996.
10. Adapted from "Development of a Values Conflict Resolution Assessment," by R. T. Kinnier (1987, p. 34).
11. Adapted from *Issues and Ethics in the Helping Professions,* by G. Corey, M. S. Corey, and P. Callanan (1993, pp. 15–25) and (1997, pp. 19–29).

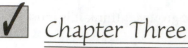 Chapter Three

Ethical Standards of Human Service Professionals

Codes of ethics are living documents that change over time. They can do no more than reflect our state of knowledge and general consensus on ethical issues at the time they are written.

— Barbara Herlihy and Gerald Corey, 1997

PROFESSIONAL CODES AND STANDARDS

Most professions have identified ethical guidelines for members of that profession. These guidelines, published as codes or **standards,** are distributed to the members of the profession, included in textbooks for students, and made available to the public.

The process of compiling, adopting, publishing, and revising the ethical guidelines is usually completed by a national organization in its role of promoting the development of the profession and its members.

Enforcement of the ethical guidelines, if there is any, involves action on the part of the organization that developed them. Many organizations have ethics committees or review boards that consider complaints about members from the public or other professionals. When a member of an organization is found to be in violation of that organization's ethical guidelines, the member may suffer consequences that include reprimand, suspension, or permanent loss of membership privileges. Some organizations report to appropriate state professional licensing boards for possible legal action.

NOHSE AND CSHSE[1]

The statement on ethical standards for human service professionals was adopted by the members of the National Organization for Human Service Education (NOHSE) and the Council for Standards in Human Service Education (CSHSE) in 1994/1995.

NOHSE is the professional organization for human service practitioners, students, and faculty. It acts as a leader and advocate for the profession. CSHSE is the professional organization for educational programs in human services. It has developed standards for educational programs and awards national program approval to those that meet its stan-

60

dards and complete a program review process. There is more information about these organizations in Appendixes B and C.

Human services is an emerging profession with a history that goes back to the 1960s. Some initial ethical statements were developed during the 1980s (Mehr, 1995, pp. 300–301; Woodside & McClam, 1994, pp. 252–253). These did not, however, gain widespread acceptance and use. In the early 1990s the membership asked NOHSE to develop a statement on ethical standards that could be accepted and used by all members of the profession. The development process was lengthy and involved many members of NOHSE and CSHSE[2] (National Organization for Human Service Education, 1996).

ETHICAL STANDARDS OF HUMAN SERVICE PROFESSIONALS

The statement on ethical standards for human service professionals is organized into seven parts: the Preamble (introduction) and separate clusters of standards that present the human service professional's responsibilities to clients, to the community and society, to colleagues, to the profession, to employers, and to self.

The order in which the clusters are presented has some significance. The professional's responsibilities to clients and community come first because these are the consumers or recipients of services. The next three clusters—colleagues, the profession, and employers—are those with whom the human service professional shares responsibility for providing services. The last cluster addresses the human service professional's responsibility to himself or herself.

In the rest of this chapter we will consider each section of the standards separately.

PREAMBLE

Peace we want because there is another war to fight against poverty, disease and ignorance. We have promises to keep to our people of work, food, clothing, and shelter, health and education.

—Indira Gandhi, 1966

The introduction sets the stage. It tells us something about what the profession of human services is, what human service professionals do, and the purposes of the ethical standards that follow.

Read the Preamble.

Preamble

Human services is a profession developing in response to and in anticipation of the direction of human needs and human problems in the late twentieth century. Characterized particularly by an appreciation of human beings in all of their diversity, human services offers assistance to its clients within the context of their community and environment. Human service professionals, regardless of whether they are students, faculty, or practitioners, promote and encourage the unique values and characteristics of human services. In so doing human service professionals uphold the integrity and ethics of the profession, partake in constructive criticism of the profession, promote client and community well-being, and enhance their own professional growth.

The ethical guidelines presented are a set of standards of conduct which the human service professional considers in ethical and professional decision making. It is hoped that these guidelines will be of assistance when the human service professional is challenged by difficult ethical dilemmas. Although ethical codes are not legal documents, they may be used to assist in the adjudication of issues related to ethical human service behavior.

Human service professionals function in many ways and carry out many roles. They enter into professional-client relationships with individuals, families, groups, and communities who are all referred to as "clients" in these standards. Among their roles are caregiver, case manager, broker, teacher/educator, behavior changer, consultant, outreach professional, mobilizer, advocate, community planner, community change organizer, evaluator and administrator.* The following standards are written with these multi-faceted roles in mind.

*Southern Regional Education Board (1967). *Roles and functions for mental health workers: A report of a symposium.* Atlanta, GA: Community Mental Health Worker Project.

Reflection

1. How does the Preamble define human services?

2. According to the Preamble, what are the purposes of the written ethical standards?

3. List the 13 roles of human service professionals that are mentioned in the Preamble. As you list them, consider what you know about each role.

4. Identify those roles that are unfamiliar to you.

Class Discussion

1. Compare your understanding of human services with the other students. Can you develop a definition together, in your own words?
2. Discuss the purposes of the written ethical standards. Can you add other purposes that you think are important?
3. Review the roles. Ask your instructor to explain those roles with which you are not familiar. Are some roles more common in your community than others? Does your educational level affect the roles you might be eligible for?

THE HUMAN SERVICE PROFESSIONAL'S RESPONSIBILITY TO CLIENTS

While an ethic of justice proceeds from the premise of equality—that everyone should be treated the same—an ethic of care rests on the premise of nonviolence—that no one should be hurt.

—Carol Gilligan, 1982

This first cluster includes nine statements. As the Preamble says, clients may be individuals, families, groups, and communities. Clients are those who seek our assistance, both voluntarily and involuntarily. As we help them, we also protect their rights and safeguard them from harm.

Read "The Human Service Professional's Responsibility to Clients." As you read, highlight—or underline—the terms that are unfamiliar to you.

The Human Service Professional's Responsibility to Clients

Statement 1. Human service professionals negotiate with clients the purpose, goals, and nature of the helping relationship prior to its onset, as well as inform clients of the limitations of the proposed relationship.

Statement 2. Human service professionals respect the integrity and welfare of the client at all times. Each client is treated with respect, acceptance, and dignity.

Statement 3. Human service professionals protect the client's right to privacy and confidentiality except when such confidentiality would cause harm to the client or others, when agency guidelines state otherwise, or under other stated conditions (e.g., local, state, or federal laws). Professionals inform clients of the limits of confidentiality prior to the onset of the helping relationship.

Statement 4. If it is suspected that danger or harm may occur to the client or to others as a result of a client's behavior, the human service professional acts in an appropriate and professional manner to protect the safety of those individuals. This may involve seeking consultation, supervision, and/or breaking the confidentiality of the relationship.

Statement 5. Human service professionals protect the integrity, safety, and security of client records. All written client information that is shared with other professionals, except in the course of professional supervision, must have the client's prior written consent.

> **Statement 6.** Human service professionals are aware that in their relationships with clients power and status are unequal. Therefore they recognize that dual or multiple relationships may increase the risk of harm to, or exploitation of, clients, and may impair their professional judgment. However, in some communities and situations it may not be feasible to avoid social or other nonprofessional contact with clients. Human service professionals support the trust implicit in the helping relationship by avoiding dual relationships that may impair professional judgment, increase the risk of harm to clients, or lead to exploitation.
>
> **Statement 7.** Sexual relationships with current clients are not considered to be in the best interest of the client and are prohibited. Sexual relationships with previous clients are considered dual relationships and are addressed in Statement 6 (above).
>
> **Statement 8.** The client's right to self-determination is protected by human service professionals. They recognize the client's right to receive or refuse services.
>
> **Statement 9.** Human service professionals recognize and build on client strengths.

Reflection

1. Find each unfamiliar term in the glossary, another human service textbook, or a standard English dictionary. List the term and the most appropriate definition below. Use a separate piece of paper if you need more space.

Term	Definition

2. Identify the statements with which you agree, those that seem unclear to you, and those with which you disagree.

	I agree	This is unclear	I disagree
Statement 1	_____	_____	_____
Statement 2	_____	_____	_____
Statement 3	_____	_____	_____
Statement 4	_____	_____	_____
Statement 5	_____	_____	_____
Statement 6	_____	_____	_____
Statement 7	_____	_____	_____
Statement 8	_____	_____	_____
Statement 9	_____	_____	_____

3. Consider *why* you agreed with those you marked as "I agree." Is this something you learned as a child? A result of your experiences as a consumer of human services? Something you have come to appreciate from your work or volunteer experiences? Or are there other reasons?

4. Consider *why* you disagreed with those you marked as "I disagree." Is this something you learned as a child? A result of your experiences as a consumer of human services? Something you have come to appreciate from your work or volunteer experiences? Or are there other reasons?

5. Now, think about those that you marked as unclear. Write below some questions you might ask in class that would help you understand these statements.

Class Discussion

1. Share your responses to reflection item #1. Make sure the terms are clear to all of you and that you agree on the basic definitions before you continue. Don't skip this sometimes tedious and difficult step, or you may talk at cross-purposes with one another during further discussion.
2. Consider: How can you differentiate between informed and uninformed opinions and argument in such issues as ethical guidelines?
3. Statement by statement, discuss your responses to reflection items #2, #3, #4, and #5. It may help to first tabulate all of your responses to item #2 and display the

tabulation where you can all see it as you talk. This discussion by itself will create an ethical challenge for you—most of you will be tempted to argue when there is disagreement and support one another when there is agreement. Some of you will tend to say little, rather than exposing your opinions to others who may disagree with you. Seek to treat one another "with respect, acceptance, and dignity" and to understand others' experiences and reasoning, rather than trying to find one correct response or change others' minds. This may well bring you to a new level of understanding of yourself, one another, and future clients.

4. Professionals expect their colleagues to adhere to established ethical guidelines, even when these guidelines are in conflict with personal standards. Do you think you will be able to do this? What implications do your answers have?

THE HUMAN SERVICE PROFESSIONAL'S RESPONSIBILITY TO THE COMMUNITY AND SOCIETY

In this section of the standards are 12 statements that direct our attention to the community and society in which we live and work. The standards here begin to focus on advocacy responsibilities, telling us we must seek to improve social systems that potentially or actually harm people.

Read "The Human Service Professional's Responsibility to the Community and Society." As you read, highlight—or underline—the terms that are unfamiliar to you.

Statement 17. Human service professionals provide services without discrimination or preference based on age, ethnicity, culture, race, disability, gender, religion, sexual orientation, or socioeconomic status.

Statement 18. Human service professionals are knowledgeable about the cultures and communities within which they practice. They are aware of multiculturalism in society and its impact on the community as well as individuals within the community. They respect individuals and groups, their cultures and beliefs.

Statement 19. Human service professionals are aware of their own cultural backgrounds, beliefs, and values, recognizing the potential for impact on their relationships with others.

Statement 20. Human service professionals are aware of sociopolitical issues that differentially affect clients from diverse backgrounds.

Statement 21. Human service professionals seek the training, experience, education, and supervision necessary to ensure their effectiveness in working with culturally diverse client populations.

Reflection

1. Find each unfamiliar term in the glossary, another human service textbook, or a standard English dictionary. List the term and the most appropriate definition below. Use a separate piece of paper if you need more space.

Term	Definition

2. As you review these statements individually, identify which you already follow, which are unclear, and which you do not yet follow.

	I already do this	This is unclear	I have never done this
Statement 10	_____	_____	_____
Statement 11	_____	_____	_____
Statement 12	_____	_____	_____
Statement 13	_____	_____	_____
Statement 14	_____	_____	_____
Statement 15	_____	_____	_____
Statement 16	_____	_____	_____
Statement 17	_____	_____	_____
Statement 18	_____	_____	_____
Statement 19	_____	_____	_____
Statement 20	_____	_____	_____
Statement 21	_____	_____	_____

3. Give two or three examples of your activities that represent one or more of these ethical standards. Note which standard(s) is (are) related to your activity.

4. Look at those standards you marked in the third column, "I have never done this." Is there a reason why you haven't done anything in relation to these standards? Do you agree that they are important? If not, why not?

5. Think about those that you marked as unclear. Write below some questions you might ask in class that would help you understand these statements.

Class Discussion

1. Share your responses to reflection item #1. Again, make sure the terms are clear to all of you and that you agree on the basic definitions before you continue.
2. Statement by statement, discuss your responses to reflection items #2, #3, #4, and #5. Tabulate the responses to #2 and display the tabulation where you can all see it

as you talk. Our ethics are not simply words we say, but actions we take. Sometimes our profession asks for a higher level of ethical responsibility than we think we can deliver. In your discussion consider whether this might be true for you. If it is, how might you handle the conflict between what is expected of you and what you are willing to deliver as a human service professional?

THE HUMAN SERVICE PROFESSIONAL'S RESPONSIBILITY TO COLLEAGUES

Four statements pertain to our relationship with our peers, the other professionals who also act to meet the needs of our clients. The standards tell us that we should cooperate with one another and take action to resolve issues so clients are protected.

Read "The Human Service Professional's Responsibility to Colleagues." As you read, highlight—or underline—the terms that are unfamiliar to you.

The Human Service Professional's Responsibility to Colleagues

Statement 22. Human service professionals avoid duplicating another professional's helping relationship with a client. They consult with other professionals who are assisting the client in a different type of relationship when it is in the best interest of the client to do so.

Statement 23. When a human service professional has a conflict with a colleague, he or she first seeks out the colleague in an attempt to manage the problem. If necessary, the professional then seeks the assistance of supervisors, consultants, or other professionals in efforts to manage the problem.

Statement 24. Human service professionals respond appropriately to unethical behavior of colleagues. Usually this means initially talking directly with the colleague and, if no resolution is forthcoming, reporting the colleague's behavior to supervisory or administrative staff and/or to the professional organization(s) to which the colleague belongs.

Statement 25. All consultations between human service professionals are kept confidential unless to do so would result in harm to clients or communities.

Reflection

1. Find each unfamiliar term in the glossary, another human service textbook, or a standard English dictionary. List the term and the most appropriate definition below. Use a separate piece of paper if you need more space.

Term	Definition

Term	Definition

2. In your own words explain what Statement 22 means.

3. What do you do now when you have a conflict with a coworker or another student? Consider Statement 23. What would you do differently if you used this procedure when you had a conflict? Do you think the results would differ?

4. Describe an incident when you became aware that another student or professional was acting unethically. What did you do? Why? Compare and contrast your behavior with the process described in Statement 24.

Class Discussion

1. Share your responses to reflection item #1. Make sure that the terms are clear to all of you and that you agree on the basic definitions before you continue.

2. Share with one another how you have dealt with conflict and/or unethical behavior. Is it difficult to be as straightforward as the standards say you should be? Why or why not?

THE HUMAN SERVICE PROFESSIONAL'S RESPONSIBILITY TO THE PROFESSION

In this section are six statements that relate to our commitment to protect the profession of human services from harm and to promote its well-being. Being a member of this profession carries with it an obligation to strengthen the profession, its association with other professions and the public, and its recognition.

Read "The Human Service Professional's Responsibility to the Profession." As you read, highlight—or underline—the terms that are unfamiliar to you.

The Human Service Professional's Responsibility to the Profession

Statement 26. Human service professionals know the limit and scope of their professional knowledge and offer services only within their knowledge and skill base.

Statement 27. Human service professionals seek appropriate consultation and supervision to assist in decision making when there are legal, ethical, or other dilemmas.

Statement 28. Human service professionals act with integrity, honesty, genuineness, and objectivity.

Statement 29. Human service professionals promote cooperation among related disciplines (e.g., psychology, counseling, social work, nursing, family and consumer sciences, medicine, education) to foster professional growth and interests within the various fields.

Statement 30. Human service professionals promote the continuing development of their profession. They encourage membership in professional associations, support research endeavors, foster educational advancement, advocate for appropriate legislative actions, and participate in other related professional activities.

Statement 31. Human service professionals continually seek out new and effective approaches to enhance their professional abilities.

Reflection

1. Find each unfamiliar term in the glossary, another human service textbook, or a standard English dictionary. List the term and the most appropriate definition below. Use a separate piece of paper if you need more space.

Term	Definition

Term	Definition

2. Students and entry-level professionals commonly have difficulty knowing their own limits and seeking supervision. Reflect on the following questions: Because you tend to worry about what others will think about you, do you try to hide your lack of knowledge or skill? Do you avoid using new knowledge and skill because you're afraid you'll make a mistake? Do you find it difficult to ask your instructor or supervisor for assistance?

3. What can you do to create a situation where you are free to learn, but also seek help when you need it?

4. Do you know students or professionals in other related disciplines? Have you worked with them? Why or why not?

Class Discussion

1. Share your responses to reflection item #1. Make sure the terms are clear to all of you and that you agree on the basic definitions before you continue.
2. Discuss the process of supervision. How can a supervisor help the worker use available assistance? How can a worker seek the assistance he or she needs?
3. Invite students or practitioners from another discipline into class. Discuss the interdisciplinary interaction that happens at your college or within your community. Are there examples of cooperation? Are there examples of competition and backbiting?

THE HUMAN SERVICE PROFESSIONAL'S RESPONSIBILITY TO EMPLOYERS

Because human service professionals usually work for an employer rather than in private practice, there are three standards that define our responsibilities to employers. Statements 33 and 34 insist that we must take action when we find deficiencies at our employing agency.

Read "The Human Service Professional's Responsibility to Employers." As you read, highlight—or underline—the terms that are unfamiliar to you.

The Human Service Professional's Responsibility to Employers

Statement 32. Human service professionals adhere to commitments made to their employers.

Statement 33. Human service professionals participate in efforts to establish and maintain employment conditions which are conducive to high-quality client services. They assist in evaluating the effectiveness of the agency through reliable and valid assessment measures.

Statement 34. When a conflict arises between fulfilling the responsibility to the employer and the responsibility to the client, human service professionals advise both of the conflict and work conjointly with all involved to manage the conflict.

Reflection

1. Find each unfamiliar term in the glossary, another human service textbook, or a standard English dictionary. List the term and the most appropriate definition below. Use a separate piece of paper if you need more space.

Term	Definition

Term	Definition

2. Have you ever kept a commitment you made to your employer although you would have preferred to break it? Have you ever broken a commitment you had made and claimed an acceptable—but untrue—excuse, like illness? Do you think you might have difficulty following Statement 32?

3. If you saw something at your agency that was detrimental to clients, what would you do? Think of an example, then consider Statement 33. Would your action evade or fulfill what the profession requires of you?

4. Consider an example of a time you saw a conflict between the professional's responsibility to his client and his responsibility to his employer. How was it handled? What do you think of that in relation to the requirements of Statement 34?

Class Discussion

1. Share your responses to reflection item #1. Make sure the terms are clear to all of you and that you agree on the basic definitions before you continue.
2. Share and discuss some of your examples. Are the responsibilities of a student to an agency providing a field practicum different from the responsibilities of an employee? Can human service professionals who are trying to decide how to handle an employment-related ethical issue find assistance in your community? Where?

THE HUMAN SERVICE PROFESSIONAL'S RESPONSIBILITY TO SELF

Parents can only give good advice or put them on the right paths, but the final forming of a person's character lies in their own hands. . . .

—Anne Frank, 1944

The last three statements pertain to our responsibilities to ourselves as people and as professionals. Certain values and characteristics are considered essential in human service professionals. Achieving those values and characteristics requires a high degree of self-awareness.

Read "The Human Service Professional's Responsibility to Self." As you read, highlight—or underline—the terms that are unfamiliar to you.

Reflection

1. Find each unfamiliar term in the glossary, another human service textbook, or a standard English dictionary. List the term and the most appropriate definition below. Use a separate piece of paper if you need more space.

Term	Definition

Term	Definition

2. Are you active in seeking your own personal and professional development? Describe some examples.

3. Is your educational program fostering your self-awareness and personal growth? If not, what can you do to make a difference in the program?

Class Discussion

1. Share your responses to reflection item #1. Make sure the terms are clear to all of you and that you agree on the basic definitions before you continue.
2. Discuss self-awareness, personal growth, and the professional characteristics identified in Statement 35.
3. Explore your responsibilities and those of your educational program in fostering your personal and professional development.

USING THE ETHICAL STANDARDS OF HUMAN SERVICE PROFESSIONALS

You now have a fairly clear understanding of basic concepts in ethical decision making, your own values, and the ethical guidelines of your profession. Using the ethical decision-making process requires not only understanding, but also practice and reflection in response to issues that have ethical aspects. The next chapter uses a case study to illustrate use of the ten-step ethical decision-making process.

NOTES

1. Teaching note: The remainder of this chapter focuses on assisting the student to understand the *Ethical Standards of Human Service Professionals*. If you are using the workbook in another professional field, the exercises can be adapted by having the students substitute the ethical code or standards of that field, many of which are also organized into clusters. See Appendix A.

2. When the NOHSE Board adopted the *Ethical Standards of Human Service Professionals*, it also established a review process, anticipating that as the standards are used, improvements will be recognized and suggested. As you use this workbook, consider what changes in the standards you would find helpful. A form is included at the back of this workbook for your use in making comments about these standards.

Chapter Four

Welfare Reform Impacts a Student: A Case Study

To be in good moral condition requires at least as much training as to be in good physical condition.

—Jawaharlal Nehru

Ethical guidelines and ethical decision making can seem quite difficult and vague when discussed abstractly. And as long as this uncertainty persists, when we actually face human service issues, it is easy to overlook the ethical aspects. As with any other knowledge or skill, concrete examples and practice help to develop one's ability to engage in ethical decision making with ease and certainty.

Through consciously noticing, describing, and discussing ethical issues and the ethical decision-making process one masters the concepts and the process. As you read the following **case study,** I recommend you prepare to discuss it in your seminar or class by taking notes. Note aspects that seem particularly important to you. Are there omissions? Do you think other values, ethical principles, or guidelines should be mentioned? Would you prefer another resolution to the dilemma? Why?

SHARED GOALS BUT DIFFERENT REGULATIONS: STUDENT AND INSTRUCTOR FACE A CONFLICT

Barbara and Joanne

Background. In 1995 adult students at a small Southwestern community college started presenting faculty with slips to sign showing they had attended class that day. The slips originated with the Department of Public Welfare, the agency responsible for administering welfare benefits in the state. To maintain their eligibility, welfare recipients were being required to spend a specified number of hours weekly in a job, volunteer placement, or academic program as part of a new WORK program. Students were generally apologetic about asking faculty to sign these forms every class day. Some faculty members felt their embarrassment and considered it demeaning for adult students to be presenting attendance slips to the teacher.

Although some faculty believed this signature process served to impede the students' achievement of a personal and cultural identity that promoted full participation in and success with the academic and subsequent work environments, it seemed nothing could be done to alter the procedure. The faculty believed that whatever damage was being done to students was limited and could be undone by faculty's simply handling the forms as pieces of paperwork necessitated by another bureaucracy. When it did come up in discussion with students, human service program faculty promoted the impersonal view of it as a way for the WORK caseworker to demonstrate accountability, not any sort of personal statement about students and their motivations, reliability, or personal lifestyles.

Joanne. In January 1997 Joanne, a very good student who was entering her last semester in the human service program, told the human service field placement instructor, Barbara, that she couldn't figure out how she was going to meet the requirements of her third semester field practicum. The WORK program had suddenly changed its rules in response to federal welfare reform and was now requiring her to complete 30 hours of volunteer placement or paid work each week in addition to her full-time academic load. As a single parent of two children, one a preschooler, she was trying to figure out how to balance the demands on her time.

Field placement Agency A, at which Joanne had completed her Fall 1996 field placement, had invited her to continue there—as a volunteer 20 hours weekly and as an employee 10 hours weekly. This would fulfill the WORK program requirements. The human service program, however, required that Joanne—like all other students— complete her field practicum of 6 hours weekly in a different agency and with a different population from either of her previous two field placements.

Joanne said, "My class times are not flexible. My schedule for taking my son to school and picking him up is not flexible. The Department of Public Welfare will not pay for child care except when I'm in class or doing my WORK program requirement. I don't have much extra money, so it's a financial problem as well as a time problem. I contracted to complete my next practicum at field placement Agency B, but now I don't have any other hours in my week for a field placement at Agency B in addition to volunteering and working at Agency A. And Agency B staff say they cannot use me for 30 hours weekly!"

She described how she had attempted to negotiate with the WORK caseworker. It seemed to both Barbara and Joanne that the caseworker was following a new set of rules in a changed program and would not—or could not—consider being flexible. Joanne was on the verge of tears, frustrated and overwhelmed.

Barbara told her that she wanted Joanne to have a valuable learning experience in the field practicum and to be in position for seeking her first full-time job in May or June. "I also want you to succeed in a human service career, not be tied to one specific program or agency."

Joanne answered, "I know. I understand why you want me to do my field placement at another agency. I want to do it at another agency, too. I would learn a lot at Agency B. And I want to get a job as soon as I can after I graduate. But I don't think I will want to stay at Agency A, even if they offered me a full-time job."

APPLYING THE DECISION-MAKING MODEL

Step 1: Describe the Issue

In many ethical issues faced by human service professionals, another bureaucracy's policies create or worsen the dilemma yet are out of the control of the professional and client. Changing the WORK program's regulations would have solved the issue faced by Barbara and Joanne but was not possible. No matter what decision they made about Joanne's field placement agency for the semester, Joanne's learning and her well-being would be affected, probably adversely.

Joanne and Barbara recognized that this issue belonged to each of them individually and together. Both had the right and the responsibility to share the decision-making process. Joanne accepted the responsibility of making a decision that benefited herself, her learning, and her family. Since Barbara held the academic authority for the decision, she would be the one who made the official decision and was held accountable for the decision by the program, the college, and the agencies involved.

Step 2: Consider Ethical Guidelines

Relevant societal values and guidelines were in conflict. They included (1) obeying laws and regulations, (2) getting people off welfare and into employment, (3) limiting current public spending, (4) promoting education, and (5) supporting good parenting. Because public regulations were also involved, legal requirements could be expected to supersede ethical preferences if there were a conflict between them.

Barbara's personal values and professional ethical guidelines were closely tied in this issue. They included autonomy, respect, education, and beneficence. Barbara reported, "I've been teaching for over 20 years. In that time I've encountered a wide variety of students and their personal and academic problems. I'm convinced that part of their learning and preparation for the 'real world' comes from coping successfully with conflicting demands and stressors. Basically I consider autonomy and beneficence to be the highest of ethical principles. I respect students and their ability to discover their own resources. I am not quick to offer solutions or directions—although I have always been willing to listen as they describe their problems, offering challenges or support that I think they need. And I *very* seldom solve their problems for them. At the same time, when I respond to students' decisions and choices, I am seeking the options that I believe are best for all concerned—at the very least, options that limit the harm. And I really do value education as both an end in itself and as a means to the end of improving people's well-being."

Another ethical guideline that influenced Barbara was that of academic freedom (the right to teach without restriction or interference). "I felt a responsibility to respond to Joanne's need, not simply to follow the written procedure that we had in place," Barbara said. Academic freedom means, among other things, that the faculty have the responsibility to adapt their educational approaches as needed. Faculty consider their own knowledge, experience, and skills; the students' knowledge, experience, and skills; available resources (including time and energy); the environment in which learning will take place; and other influences that will impact the processes of teaching and learning.

Again, Barbara: "This is one of the reasons I like teaching—I am allowed and expected to be responsive and creative, rather than following a formula or approach designed by a bureaucracy. I also believe that academic policies and procedures are designed for good reasons and should usually be followed. The reason the human service program at my college requires field placements at three different agencies with a variety of special populations is to ensure that each graduate has a human service generalist's knowledge, attitudes, and skills—this, in turn, makes each graduate's initial job search easier and promotes career development."

Professional guidelines in the *Ethical Standards of Human Service Professionals* underscored Barbara's personal guidelines:

- Treat the client (the student, in this case) with respect, acceptance, and dignity (Standard 2): Barbara could not demean Joanne and her problem by ignoring it.
- Protect the client's (the student's, in this case) right to self-determination (Standard 8): As Joanne thought through her options and the risks for her and her family, Barbara needed to make sure Joanne's thinking was not flawed, then support her choices if possible.
- Be practical (Standard 35): Barbara recognized they needed to be realistic in considering Joanne's options.

Step 3: Examine the Conflicts

Barbara reported experiencing one internal conflict. She wanted to evade the regulatory requirement and go on with the semester's experience already planned. "I am a person who does not like many rules and regulations, especially when I think they are unreasonable in terms of human well-being and even more so when I believe the rules actually impede the attainment of the goal they purport to support. In this case, by requiring an overcommitment in Joanne's hours, I really believed the regulations interfered with her personal goal and the societal goal of getting her off welfare and into employment. I considered getting help from Agency A to document volunteer hours without requiring Joanne to complete all of the hours. I realized, after a bit of reflection, that although I might feel emotionally justified in doing this, it would not be in any of our best interests—it would have placed Joanne, Agency A, the college, and myself at risk of legal consequences."

The only significant external conflict arose from the contradictory societal values and guidelines. Barbara added, "There was no conflict between my personal values and professional guidelines. I have been in a professional role for so many years now that I find my personal values have been influenced by professional guidelines. Those conflicts don't happen for me as often as they used to."

Step 4: Resolve the Conflicts

Joanne and Barbara discussed the practical, ethical, educational, and societal conflicts in this situation. They agreed that they had no control over the outside regulations in relation to her immediate situation and agreed to abide by the WORK requirements. They accepted their highest ethical principle as Joanne's autonomy, current and future. Again, Barbara: "This, by the way, isn't something we actually discussed, but, rather, it was implicit in our consideration of our options and consequences. The sooner we could get her into her career and free of the requirements of the WORK program, the better it would be for her and her family."

Step 5: Generate Action Alternatives

Barbara and Joanne identified four options.

1. Joanne could return to Agency A to complete the 30 hours required by the WORK program, receiving concurrent credit for her field practicum hours. That would save her 6 hours weekly plus transportation time.

2. Joanne could ask the WORK caseworker to accept 24 hours weekly at Agency A and allow her to complete 6 hours weekly at Agency B. This would total 30 hours weekly and would require extra transportation time three or four days weekly.
3. Joanne could withdraw from her field experience course, continuing her WORK program requirement and other coursework. This would lighten the load on her time and energy, would ensure that her subsequent field placement experience was a high-level learning experience, and would delay her graduation by as much as a year.
4. Joanne could begin a new search for another placement agency at which she could complete the 30 hours for the WORK program and the 6 hours for her field practicum concurrently. The semester had already started and this would delay her start-up in a placement for several days or weeks, during which WORK would continue to require her 30 hours weekly at Agency A. When and if she did gain the new placement agency, she would lose her current 10 hours weekly of paid employment at Agency A.

Step 6: Examine and Evaluate the Action Alternatives

Of the four options, Barbara and Joanne seriously considered only the first two. The third alternative they eliminated for ethical reasons: Withdrawing from the course for the semester would create too great a probable harm to Joanne by interrupting her education, delaying her graduation, and delaying her attainment of economic self-sufficiency. "Although Joanne said she would accept this option if I thought it was best, I decided it would not meet the principles of universality, publicity, and justice," Barbara said.

The fourth alternative Barbara and Joanne eliminated for pragmatic reasons. Had Joanne been informed by the WORK program a couple of months earlier (say, in early November) of the upcoming requirement of a 30-hour commitment, Barbara said this option would have been her preferred option. "It would have given her a field placement experience in a new human service agency, where she could gain additional knowledge and skills as a generalist human service professional. It would have met the requirements of the WORK program. And, with sufficient time to plan her academic, volunteer, and personal schedules, she could have developed a plan that balanced the demands on her time and energy. But the WORK program had notified her of the change during the break between semesters and there wasn't time for her to seek a new placement while meeting concurrent academic, volunteer, and personal demands."

Both the first and second options met the principles of universality, publicity, and justice. Both were consistent with Joanne's and Barbara's values and the ethical guidelines. Both would satisfy the requirements of the WORK program. And both were achievable.

The second option would require that Joanne master the new skills and knowledge required at Agency B and a role with which she was not familiar. Barbara explained, "She was already showing signs of exhaustion from the emotional turmoil and stress of the added WORK program demands, so it seemed reasonable to me that additional responsibilities at her field placement site would increase her level of stress. In addition, the extra time she would spend in traveling between sites would be taken from her time with her two children—an impact she and I were both reluctant to have happen, since her time with them was already limited." The probable consequences of the second option would include a decrease in Joanne's and her family's well-being throughout the semester. Possible consequences included Joanne's developing a broader knowledge base, new helping skills, and increased employment and career options.

The first option would not require Joanne to become familiar with a new agency and special population, so she would have to master less new knowledge and fewer new skills. She also would spend less time traveling between placement sites so would have more time with her children. Barbara discussed this option: "I believed the probable consequences of this option included at least a stabilization in Joanne's and her family's well-being, but also a more limited knowledge and skill base with reduced employment and career options."

On balance, Barbara thought that the first option would result in doing the least harm. She also said she thought that Joanne could more easily compensate in the future for any limitation to her knowledge and skill base through continuing education than she could compensate for the semester's decrease in her and her family's well-being.

"When I recommended to Joanne that we choose the first option, continuing her placement in Agency A and granting her credit for her placement hours concurrently with the WORK program requirements, she seemed surprised. I did suggest to her that she should seek out opportunities to take on new roles and participate in new learning experiences at Agency A—I didn't believe she had exhausted all the possibilities for new knowledge and skills there."

Step 7: Select and Evaluate the Preferred Action

Joanne initially preferred the second option, saying she valued the learning opportunities at Agency B, although she still couldn't figure out where she'd find the time to arrange it. She challenged Barbara about taking the easier option. Barbara shared her thinking about the short-term and long-term consequences of the options they were considering. "I pointed out that I was particularly concerned that if she were under undue stress, her mastery of new knowledge and skills would be impaired anyway, and our reasons for sending her to Agency B would be defeated."

Joanne asked some questions, then expressed relief about being allowed to select the first option, despite the program's policy for selection of field placement sites.

Step 8: Plan the Action

Joanne made all the necessary arrangements with Agency A and the WORK program, and explained the decision to her fellow students. In her placement she actively sought out new learning experiences and coped with several changes that occurred during the semester.

Step 9: Evaluate the Outcome

Joanne did master new knowledge, skills, and attitudes through this second semester's placement in Agency A. During her placement, administrative and clinical changes occurred in the agency and Joanne contributed positively to the change process in the agency from her perspective as a student. Her contributions were valued by Agency A; she was hired for additional hours during the semester. By her graduation date she had been hired full-time by Agency A; two months later, she had earned a promotion. It won't be possible to judge any further impact on her career opportunities and choices for a few years.

Barbara summarized, "In retrospect, I think the decision worked out better than I expected. Benefits were attained for Joanne, her family, the agency, and society."

Step 10: Examine the Implications

There are implications here for the human service program and for the college. The program needs to reconsider the rationale for guidelines regarding selection of field placement agencies by students. A broader issue is that of the college and its adult students who are on welfare.

If the 1996 federal welfare reform rules as implemented by the states are going to require students to take on essentially three full-time commitments—academics, parenting, and a community volunteer and/or work assignment—then welfare reform will not bode well for the academic success of these students.

Many of them are precisely the people who the politicians and reformers say should be moved off welfare and into productive employment. Employment prospects today are poor for people with limited education. As currently defined at state and federal levels, welfare reform and related regulations appear to be creating a "no win" dilemma for students, colleges, and society. This is not simply an ethical issue: It is also a political and a legal issue.

Professional guidelines are relevant to this broader issue. The *Ethical Standards of Human Service Professionals* include the following responsibilities:

- Advocate for change in regulations and statutes when laws conflict with client rights (Statement 10).
- Keep informed about current social issues (Statement 11).
- Act as advocates in addressing unmet client and community needs (Statement 13).

Faculty and students in many human service programs across the United States are advocating for change in some aspects of the welfare reform statutes and regulations. Barbara reported that one outcome of her experience with Joanne has been her assumption of an activist role in the local community. She has brought guest congressional speakers into classes, testified at legislative hearings, facilitated a public hearing about welfare reform and its impact on college and university students, and is participating in meetings that involve staff members from the educational and welfare communities in collaborating for the benefit of students.

REFLECTION

1. What features of Barbara's and Joanne's issue seem particularly important to you?

2. Were there other aspects that should have been considered?

3. Do you think other values, ethical principles, or guidelines should be mentioned?

4. Would you prefer another resolution to the dilemma? Why?

5. What questions do you have about the 10-step ethical decision-making model now?

CLASS DISCUSSION

Explore your responses to the reflection questions.

SUMMARY AND PREVIEW

Barbara and Joanne, faced with an ethical dilemma created by conflict between the regulations of the local welfare office and the policy of the human service program, used the ethical decision-making process together to resolve the issue.

Now, it's your turn! In chapter 5 we address issues that commonly occur in academic settings.

Chapter Five

Ethical Issues for Students in the Academic Environment

*Borrowed thoughts, like borrowed money, only show the poverty of
the borrower.*

—Marguerite Gardiner

Human service students encounter ethical issues in college. These issues involve getting into college, succeeding in their coursework and field practicums, sustaining relationships with faculty and other students, and preparing for the world of employment. The rewards of success and the risks of failure are so great as to create an environment in which philosophical questions of right and wrong can be set aside in favor of practical outcomes.

Age-old questions recur for students. "Do the ends justify the means?" "Should I betray a friend if he or she does something wrong?" "How can I disagree with a faculty member who has more power than I?" "Does it really matter what I do while I'm in college? Real life happens after I earn the degree."

EXAMS: THREE EXPERIENCES

Clarita and the Tired Professor

I received an exam back; we went over it in class. The professor was up late and made a couple of mistakes in my favor. I had received an A. If graded correctly, I would have earned a B. I needed the A to keep my class standing.

Whose Issue Is This?

Is this the professor's issue?	Yes ____	No ____
Is this Clarita's issue?	Yes ____	No ____
Is this the college's issue?	Yes ____	No ____

Action

If you were Clarita, would you speak up and point out the errors? Or would you say nothing and accept the professor's mistakes?

How would you feel about doing this?

If you chose to speak up, would you ask for extra credit for honesty? Should taking the right action be rewarded more often in the classroom than it is or should it be reward enough just to do the right thing?

Frank and Henry

I was taking a test and saw Henry, who was sitting next to me, cheating. Henry was a friend of mine. He realized I noticed his cheating. Now Henry knew that I was the only one who knew that he cheated. If I did nothing, then I would be considered part of the cheating. If I told the faculty, Henry would fail and I would probably lose a friend.

What Is Frank's Dilemma?

Frank has well-developed personal values—like loyalty, keeping secrets, and allowing Henry to make his own choices. In his developing commitment to academic standards and the human service profession, he has accepted some ethical obligations that conflict with these values—like veracity, universality, and utility.

What ethical principles or values are most important in this situation?

Action

What do you think Frank should do?

Marcia and Diane

I was in my first semester as a faculty member in a community college human service program. Prior to this I had worked for many years as a human service professional, helping clients cope with often unresponsive systems. One of my students, Diane, was a single parent with a three-year-old daughter. Diane attended class regularly, participated actively in class discussions, and seemed very committed to a career in human services. She occasionally mentioned the "hardships" she faced daily.

During an in-class exam, I saw her glancing at another student's paper. I had never challenged a student about cheating nor had I ever talked with other faculty members about whether it was a problem at this college and how they handled it. I thought Diane should not earn a undeserved grade, but I was also worried about jeopardizing Diane's chance for success in the program.

What Is Marcia's Dilemma?

What ethical principles underlie the general rule that students should not copy each other's work?

What ethical principles underlie the responsibility of the human service professional to act as an advocate for clients who are working against great odds to succeed?

Marcia was both a human service professional and an educator. Describe your understanding of her dilemma as she faced Diane.

Action

What do you think Marcia should do? Explain why.

Class Discussion

1. Share your action decisions in response to these first three anecdotes. Do you think Marcia and Frank faced the same ethical dilemma? Or did their dilemmas differ because of their roles in relation to the student who was cheating?
2. Clarita faced a slightly different issue. Share your thinking about Clarita's dilemma.
3. Discuss whether cheating can be justified.
4. Identify academic policies that you believe faculty could or should implement that would reduce the frequency of cheating in your college. How would you devise these policies so they wouldn't reflect a lessening or watering down of academic standards?

ACADEMIC PAPERS: THREE EXPERIENCES

If you steal from one author, it's plagiarism; if you steal from many, it's research.

—Wilson Mizner

George

While I was enrolled in a community college program in human services, I frequently used the computer lab to prepare my assignments. One day I discovered a research paper saved on the hard drive of the computer I was using. According to the date on it, it was submitted the previous semester for Biology 101 with Dr. Playa.

I was enrolled at the time in Biology 101 with Dr. Hendricks. I was a student who did good work, earning grades of A and B. But that semester I was behind because my wife had been seriously ill and unable to work. I had taken an additional part-time job and, in my few available hours after work and school, had been taking care of my wife and two children, ages 4 and 6. I had not yet started work on my own Biology 101 research paper—which was due in two weeks.

I copied the paper to my own disc. I could change it a bit in terms of my own style and submit it as my own. It was a large biology department and it was unlikely that Dr. Hendricks and Dr. Playa would ever find out.

Definition

Define the term *plagiarism*.

Whose Issue Is This?

Is this George's issue?	Yes _____	No _____
Is this the original writer's issue?	Yes _____	No _____
Is this Dr. Hendricks's issue?	Yes _____	No _____
Is this Dr. Playa's issue?	Yes _____	No _____
Is this the computer lab's issue?	Yes _____	No _____

Your Preference

What would you want to do if you were George? Why?

Ethical Guidelines

What values and ethical principles are involved?

List the other issues that seem to be involved.

Action Alternatives

Briefly describe three possible things George could do.

Evaluating the Alternatives

Would each of these three actions meet the test of universality? (Would you approve it if other students did it? Would the faculty approve it?)

Would each of these three actions meet the test of publicity? (If you were George, would you be willing to explain your action to other students and to faculty? Would they accept your explanation?)

Would each of these three actions meet the test of justice? (Would you suggest the same actions to other students in similar situations? What if they were A students? What if they were D students?)

Describe the most likely consequences of each of these three possible actions.

Action

What do you think George should do?

Implications

What did you learn about yourself, your values, and your ethical decision making from this exercise?

Pamela and Alan

Alan is a male Native American student in his second year of a human service program at a community college. He is in his late 50s and wants to work at a local school for Native American youth. Alan is in recovery from chemical dependency and has a lot to give to Native American youth. In class, however, his work is marginal.

It has become apparent to several of his instructors, including me, that his papers—which are quite well written—are completed for him by someone else. This conclusion is supported by a substantial difference between his other work and these papers: His in-class work is not well written and his journal has many misspellings, instances of poor grammar, and incomplete ideas.

The Issue

The profession of human services claims a strong commitment to multiculturalism (*Ethical Standards of Human Service Professionals*: Statements 16, 17, 18, 19, 20, 21). Alan's Native American background probably means he has had limited experience in the writing traditions of the European American culture. He may well not value writing in the process of learning as highly as the dominant culture—and the faculty—do. Additionally, he has been impacted by his history of chemical dependency.

What do you think Pamela wanted to do?

Was she required legally to take or to avoid any particular action?

Should the fact that Alan is in recovery influence Pamela's action? Why or why not?

Action

What do you think Pamela should do? What values, ethical principles, or guidelines are most important in guiding your choice of action for her?

Yvette

As a student in human services, I developed close relationships with many of the other students. We frequently helped each other with course assignments as well as with personal problems. The faculty in our program emphasized the importance of developing collegial relationships among students to help us prepare for interdependency, teamwork, and networking, which would be essential parts of our careers in human services. They did, however, require that we complete some assignments on our own.

In a course requiring a research paper (to be completed independently) I became aware that some students were borrowing and copying completed research papers from students who had previously taken the course.

What Are the Issues?

What is Yvette's issue?

What is the faculty's issue?

What are the other students' issues?

Are these issues ethical, legal, academic, or personal? Or are they not actually issues—for anyone except faculty—in the real world of academic competition and unreasonable expectations?

Ethical Guidelines

What values and ethical principles are involved?

Action

What would you do if you were Yvette? Would you be following the ethical guidelines that you think are pertinent?

Class Discussion

1. Ask questions about any parts of these three anecdotes and exercises that were unclear to you.
2. Share your decisions about what George, Pamela, and Yvette should do. Notice how much similarity or difference there is among your decisions. What do you think this indicates?
3. Do you think you will be willing to give your completed research papers—or other work—to current students after you have finished a course? Why or why not?
4. Share what you learned about your own ethical decision making.
5. Should faculty prepare students to deal with these kinds of issues? How?
6. Discuss the relationship between plagiarism and copyright. Agencies—often with very limited funds—may use illegal copies of videotapes, computer software, and published printed materials in providing client services. Since purchasing legal copies for such use may cost much more than the agency budget can bear, the agencies justify the use of such illegal copies by saying, "Better this than nothing." What do you think?

FALSIFYING DOCUMENTATION FOR PERSONAL GAIN: TWO EXPERIENCES

Jeanine

Students at my college are falsifying their applications to obtain federal aid to attend school with disregard for ramifications for others. Lying to the federal government about the application really bothers me because if the students have the guts to lie to the federal government, then most likely they are lying elsewhere.

The Issue

Is this Jeanine's issue?	Yes ____	No ____
Is this the federal government's issue?	Yes ____	No ____
Is this the college's issue?	Yes ____	No ____

Do you think this is a legal issue, an ethical issue, or both? Explain your thinking.

Do you agree with Jeanine that if "students have the guts to lie to the federal government, then most likely they are lying elsewhere"?

Why do you think students falsify their financial aid applications? Give at least three possible explanations.

What are the relevant situational features? Are there extenuating circumstances?

Assume that Jeanine is correct that this behavior reflects a character defect—that the person who lies to get financial aid is likely to lie elsewhere. If the student is majoring in human services and graduates, how may clients be harmed?

Do you think educational institutions and faculty should do more to identify students who have such character defects and prevent their entry into helping fields? Explain your answer. How might human service students and potential students be harmed by such action on the part of their educational institutions?

Currently in most academic institutions, the provider of financial assistance is responsible for discovering any fraud, and the human service faculty and future employers are responsible for recognizing and intervening in response to unprofessional behavior in helping. Do you think that this is the best approach? What alternative would you recommend?

Bob

In our human service program faculty have told students to falsify documents to get state licenses by answering "no" to questions about mental illness or chemical dependency because it will take longer to get a license or they may not get a license at all.

The Issue

Is this Bob's issue?	Yes ____	No ____
Is this the state government's issue?	Yes ____	No ____
Is this the profession's issue?	Yes ____	No ____
Is this the human service program's issue?	Yes ____	No ____

Do you think this is a legal issue, an ethical issue, or both? Explain your thinking.

Do you believe that civil disobedience is ethical? If you don't agree with a law or the regulations that enforce it, should you: (1) Obey the law anyway? (2) Disobey the law, but protect yourself by not telling anyone? (3) Disobey the law and tell others? (4) Obey the law and become politically active in an effort to change the law and regulations? or (5) Do something else? Explain your thoughts.

Perhaps you, like many others, believe that it is okay to disobey a law if you're not likely to harm someone else, but not okay to disobey a law if someone else might be hurt. How do you decide whether someone else is at risk or not? Do you think you—or anyone else—can be objective in this type of decision? Are your own interests and desires likely to interfere with clear consideration of potential risk?

Perhaps you believe it is not okay to engage in civil disobedience at all. No matter what your personal opinions are, you follow the law and regulations to the best of your ability. Do you think such obedience might put you or others at risk for harm?

Class Discussion

1. Discuss your beliefs about obeying and disobeying current laws and regulations. Share your own experiences in relation to your personal behavior or in relation to your activities in helping others as a volunteer, a student, or a professional.
2. Do you think your membership in a group of colleagues—at your workplace or in a professional organization—would help you deal with the dilemmas that occur when there is a conflict between what action is legally required and what action is ethically acceptable?
3. Not only in experiences like this as a student, but also as a human service professional, documentation serves important purposes. The rule is often stated as, "If it isn't documented, it didn't happen." Usually the reverse is also considered a rule: "If it is documented, it was done." Discuss documentation.
4. How might you be tempted to document in a way that would put you and your actions in a better light than if you actually wrote the truth? What might keep you from doing so?

INSIDE THE CLASSROOM: THREE EXPERIENCES

The code of morality is to do unto others as you would have them do unto you. If you make that the central theme of your morality code, it will serve you well as a moral individual.

—Barbara Jordan, 1986

Manuel: Conflict

We had a guest speaker from another department on campus in our helping relationship class. (Our professor was not in the classroom during her presentation.) The guest speaker's topic was diversity. She showed us a film on the differences between people. Several black students felt it was racist and became very angry. I didn't feel it was racist at all—it could have been any difference. The students became very angry and verbally attacked the speaker. She locked the door and said they couldn't leave. One student unlocked the door and stormed out, almost breaking the door.

The Issue

It sounds like the situation in this classroom was out of control, with the speaker and some students responding emotionally to one another.

What ethical issues do you see on the part of the professor, the speaker, and the students?

Can you decide whether Manual's perception or the black students' perception was correct? Why or why not?

What are your values in relation to expressing or resolving conflicts between students in a classroom?

Action

How would you have handled your reaction during the class if you had been Manuel? What would you have done afterward? (Would you have gone to the professor and spoken to him about this incident? Would you have gone to the speaker in her office and talked about your reactions? Would you have kept your feelings to yourself and tried to forget what happened?)

What ways have you found to help you clarify and express your feelings, so you can be active in discussions of sensitive issues when there is disagreement and conflict among the participants?

Rebecca: Dominance

Each semester a clique of garrulous individuals respond to queries readily and insistently. I believe they are inconsiderate of others who want to participate in response to questions and issues in the class. I think these individuals are usually either paraphrasing or mimicking what has already been said without further substance or insight.

The Issue
Is this an ethical, personal, or situational issue?

Action Alternatives
Whose responsibility is it to assure that all class members have an equal opportunity to participate?

What should the "clique" do?

What should Rebecca do?

Elizabeth and Anna: Sexism

We are both human service students. We talked in private and discovered that we were both feeling intimidated by three male students in our classes: Tom, Juan, and LeRoy.

Between and during classes, Tom, Juan, and LeRoy frequently make remarks about women in general and female students in particular. These remarks seem to be directed at us and the other female students in the program. Recently these male students started responding sarcastically when either of us contributed to the class discussion.

At the beginning of the semester, all the female students in the classroom seemed shocked by the comments made by these men. Now, after eight weeks or so, a couple of women in the class—the most assertive ones—have become friends with the men; they laugh at their comments and seem to encourage their behavior. Most of the other women try to ignore the men and participate in class activities, at least some of the time. The faculty don't seem to take the men's behavior and comments seriously.

We are still attending classes, but we no longer participate in class discussions. We don't know what we can do. Although both of us want to become human service professionals, we are considering withdrawing from classes because we feel so uncomfortable.

The Issue

Is this Elizabeth's and Anna's issue?	Yes ___	No ___
Is this Tom's, Juan's, and LeRoy's issue?	Yes ___	No ___
Is this the faculty's issue?	Yes ___	No ___
Is this the human service program's issue?	Yes ___	No ___
Is this the college's issue?	Yes ___	No ___

Is this an ethical issue? A legal issue? An educational issue? A combination of these? Explain your thinking.

What would you want to do in this situation? Why?

Ethical Guidelines

Are any of the participants legally prohibited from doing something? Are any of them legally required to do something? What are they legally entitled to do?

The teachers are legally required to step in and talk to her but

Separate from any legal considerations, what are the ethical duties for the participants? Identify the ethical values and principles involved. The teachers should be taking care of they student

What guidance does the *Ethical Standards of Human Service Professionals* give the participants? It gives them the of what to do

Action Alternatives

Identify three things Elizabeth and Anna could do.

They should stand up for themselves

Change classes - online

Talking to teachers/higher ups

Evaluating the Alternatives

Would Elizabeth's and Anna's values, as shown by their initial approach to the issue, allow them to take these actions?

No, they don't like confrontation

Would each of these actions pass the rule of universality? (Would you recommend the actions to other students? Would you approve them if others did them? Would the faculty approve them?)

Change online classes + telling the boys to f— off. It would be fine for them to do online classes. They wouldn't like to ...

Would each of these actions pass the rule of publicity? (Would you be willing to explain the action to colleagues or the public? Would they accept your explanation?)

Online classes yes, but telling boys to ...

Would each of these actions pass the rule of justice? (Would you suggest the same action to other people in similar situations—for example, professionals in a work group or clients in a therapy group?)

Eliminate any option that didn't pass the three rules. Describe the probable consequences of each of the remaining alternatives.

Action
What should Elizabeth and Anna do? Why?

Class Discussion

1. Ask questions about any parts of the exercises that were unclear to you.
2. Share your thoughts about these classroom issues. Do you think you need to approach the issues differently, depending on whether you think they are legal, ethical, or personal?
3. Consider: If the action that seemed best to address the issue was inconsistent with the students' values and beliefs—Manuel's, Rebecca's, or Elizabeth's and Anna's— does this action introduce new ethical issues? What would you do?

Chapter Six

Personal Issues and Relationships

> *But what's more important? Building a bridge or taking care of a baby?*
>
> —June Jordan, 1975

Most of us experience conflicts among our obligations and responsibilities to family, friends, work, school, and others. Sometimes we consciously review those conflicts as they occur and decide which should take priority. More often, though, we respond to what seems most urgent or is closest to us. Personal values, societal values, and professional guidelines influence the decisions we make.

FEELINGS ABOUT CLIENTS

Kayla

I am a foster parent. These foster children have been taken from homes where they have often been neglected or not cared for. It's a dilemma for me to see those parents at visits and not want to help them as well—or, at times, feel angry toward them.

Definition

Define the term *dilemma*.

The Issue

As a foster parent Kayla is working as a human service practitioner in her family setting. A foster parent's obligation is to the children; usually the foster parents are required to refrain from judging or assisting the parents. Yet, as Kayla tells us, foster parents do have contact with the parents.

Is this an ethical issue for Kayla?	Yes _____	No _____
Is this an emotional issue for Kayla?	Yes _____	No _____
Is this a legal issue for Kayla?	Yes _____	No _____

Which values are involved here for Kayla?

Action

What would you do if you were Kayla?

Implications

As an entry-level human service professional, how do you think you will deal with your feelings about parents who have failed in their obligations to their children?

Class Discussion

1. Share your thoughts about how dealing with our feelings about clients and their families is an ethical issue.
2. Explore strategies for dealing with feelings about clients and their families.

CHANGING RELATIONSHIPS

Maria

I'm concerned about a dual relationship between a counselor and myself. I have been a client of this counselor and now—because of my human service education—I'm becoming a colleague.

Definitions

Define these terms:

dual relationship

multiple relationship

Dual or multiple relationships are common—particularly in small and rural communities where people's roles often overlap. The ethical concern about dual or multiple relationships between practitioners and their clients or former clients centers particularly around the potential for harm to clients because of unequal power and status. Review Statements 6 and 7 in the *Ethical Standards of Human Service Professionals*.

Maria's issue involves both Maria and her former counselor. What is the risk for the former counselor if this issue is not addressed effectively?

What is the risk for Maria if this issue is not addressed effectively?

Action Alternatives

How do you think Maria and the former counselor could deal with this concern? Describe at least two alternatives.

Class Discussion

1. Discuss the potential impact of multiple relationships with clients, former clients, and former helpers. How likely are such relationships to occur in your community?
2. What do you think you can do to prevent harm from occurring?

RELATIONSHIPS BETWEEN STUDENTS

Davis and Marilyn

Marilyn, a fellow student, has started talking with me about her relationship with a significant other that ended, eventually, as a result of domestic violence. In the time Marilyn spends with me she has given me enough information to suggest that she would fall into another relationship very easily. At the same time, she has said she is strong enough and smart enough to know how to "make it" alone, especially since her need to be a good student is also for the sake of her 3-year-old son.

I sincerely like Marilyn. I am single. I perceive Marilyn as a vulnerable person who needs support. Should I pursue a personal relationship with Marilyn? Should I let her work through her issues instead of coming in at a vulnerable point in her life?

The Issue

Davis and Marilyn are both students in a human service program. Is the issue an ethical one or a personal one? Explain your answer.

Is anyone else likely to be affected besides Marilyn, her son, and Davis?

Action Alternatives

What might Davis do? Describe at least three possible options.

Evaluating the Alternatives

Would each of these actions meet the test of universality? (Would you recommend them to others? Would you approve them if someone else did them?)

Would each of these actions meet the test of publicity? (Would you be willing to explain your action to other students and to faculty? Would they accept your explanation?)

Would each of these actions meet the test of justice? (Would you suggest the same actions to other students in similar situations?)

Eliminate any action that would not meet these three tests. Describe the most likely consequences of each of the remaining actions.

Class Discussion

Discuss to what extent your personal life will be impacted by your decision to seek a career in human services. Does *everything* become a potential professional ethical issue?

PARENT-CHILD RELATIONSHIPS

Vanessa's Son

We had been having difficulty with our 15-year-old son, Darrell. He was disobedient, in trouble in school, and had been arrested for gang-related activities a couple of times. We had been unable to control his behavior. Counseling did not help him, as he walked out of it. We did not know what was the right or the wrong action to take. We decided to file a "Children in Need of Services" petition with the juvenile court. Would it help him or would it hurt him? Then, we had to call the police when Darrell returned home after four days. He was arrested and taken to a facility.

Definition

Legal terms vary among the states. What do you think Vanessa means by a "Children in Need of Services" petition?

The Issue

Does this seem to be predominantly a personal (or family) issue, an ethical issue, or a legal issue?

How would you differentiate your obligations to your child from your obligations to a client? Are they the same? Why or why not?

How might Vanessa's experience influence her ability to help as a human service professional?

Class Discussion

1. Where can you get assistance in your community to figure out the right action to take as a parent?
2. Discuss the extent to which you think your personal experiences influence your ability to assist clients. If you have an unresolved issue (for example, a son like Darrell), will that make you less effective with clients who have a similar issue? In this situation, according to the ethical standards, what should you do?

FAMILY-SCHOOL CONFLICTS

Munro's Family Obligations

I have had a dilemma with regard to my own needs as a student versus the clear needs of some family members. I am in my second year in a human service program. One of my aunts—who lives a short distance from me—is a 92-year-old widow and needed housing maintenance assistance this year so she could remain in her home. My father—a 60-year-old man recovering from a recent stroke—also needed help with his activities of daily living, shopping, and local transportation. I had to decide whether to help them, knowing that my study time would be compromised and my grades might drop. Other family members live in the community and have more "free" time than I do, but they wouldn't make a commitment to help either my aunt or my father.

The Issue
Describe Munro's dilemma in terms of his personal values. What are his values and how are they in conflict?

Do you think anyone else he mentioned might be experiencing an ethical dilemma?

What do you think Munro feels?

What is at risk in this situation?

What are the relevant situational features?

Action

Do you think Munro should decide not to volunteer his help, hoping that the others will come forward if he doesn't? Or do you think he should set aside his needs and reach out to his aunt and father, hoping that he can maintain the quality of his academic work?

Evaluating the Action

Review your action preference. What does it tell you about your own values and their ranking?

Class Discussion

1. Share your experiences in choosing among your obligations to family, yourself, work, academic demands, friends, and others. Do others rank their priorities the same or differently from you? What does this ranking tell you about yourself and others?
2. How do faculty respond when you tell them you must miss class or be late with a paper because of a commitment to a family member? Does this reflect a difference in values, a misunderstanding, or something else? How can this be resolved?

PARENT-PARENT RELATIONSHIPS

Alice, Henry, and Iris

My 16-year-old son, Henry, came home from school and was upset because Iris, a friend of his, had been sexually assaulted by a boy at another friend's party. Henry was concerned about her well-being but hadn't talked with her about the experience—Iris was not the one who told him of the assault. Henry told me that the other friend's parents had allowed a party in their home without adult supervision.

I really wanted to hold those parents accountable for their failure to provide proper supervision. We live in a small community and the issue of confidentiality was important because the perpetrator was in school with Henry. I knew I had the following choices: (1) do nothing, (2) call Iris's parents so they could help her, (3) call the perpetrator's parents, (4) call the parents in whose home this took place.

The Issue

What types of issues are involved in this situation?

Who is involved?

Ethical Guidelines

In what ways is this an ethical problem for Alice? What do you expect would be the values or principles that would rank highest for Alice, as a human service professional?

Action

Should Henry have simply minded his own business, rather then get involved? Why or why not?

What do you think Alice should do? Why?

Class Discussion

1. Discuss the risks of action and inaction for Iris, Henry, and Alice. What are the potential consequences for each?
2. Is there agreement or disagreement in your group as to what Alice should do? What do you think about that?

Chapter Seven

The Field Practicum: Creating and Maintaining a Learning Environment

There is such a wide difference of opinion in the world that it is virtually impossible to settle on one single standard of behavior. But we can tell what that standard has been in the past and what it is today. We can, for instance, generally agree that murder, lying, cheating and stealing are wrong and that consideration, truthfulness and honesty are right!

—Jim Lichtman, 1996

The field experience—or practicum—provides an opportunity for students to apply attitudes, skills, and knowledge they have gained in the classroom to actual work in human service agencies. In their field practicum courses, students are responsible to staff whose perspectives may or may not differ significantly from those of their faculty. And students must, in relatively short periods of time, develop working relationships that promote their learning as well as contribute to an acceptable course grade.

Grading procedures vary from program to program, but invariably, agency supervisors and faculty are both involved. This means students must meet the expectations of both, regardless of whether their points of view differ or not. Sometimes the conflicts engendered involve ethical issues.

GETTING THE PLACEMENT: TWO EXPERIENCES

Alec, a Student

In seeking a placement for the next quarter's field practicum, I recently was offered a practicum I was more than qualified for. During the interview all went well until the agency placement coordinator said she wanted people to work an entire year. In our previous discussions she had said nothing about this. By not telling her I would only work one quarter, I would be a shoo-in for the position. If I volunteered that I would graduate in December and would not continue the placement, I realized I might not only lose the position, but also would have to scramble for another practicum so I could graduate in time.

The Issue

We don't know from what Alec tells us, but the agency placement coordinator probably considered that she was looking after the best interests of the agency, its staff, and its clients. Possibly it was a placement where clients were vulnerable and frequent changes in staff and volunteers would make them more vulnerable. Possibly the staff had told the coordinator that they were willing to help in educating students, but only if the students stayed long enough after the orientation period that they developed knowledge and skills and could actually lighten the staff work load. And Alec, registering for the last quarter before graduation, probably ranked his own academic needs as equally as important as or more important than agency, staff, or client needs or preferences.

Is the coordinator ethically correct to insist on a one-year commitment although the student placement is made college quarter by quarter? Explain your thinking.

Is Alec ethically correct to rank his own academic needs so highly? Explain your thinking.

Ethical Guidelines

What personal values or ethical principles are involved?

What professional ethical standards are involved? Consult the *Ethical Standards of Human Service Professionals*. List any standards that you think are relevant.

Action

What do you think Alec should do? Why?

Stacey, a Faculty Member

As a coordinator of a large human service internship program, I interview, accept, or reject students for a full-time internship semester. Part of the process requires the student to develop a résumé, following established guidelines, to take to the agency interview. Occasionally when reviewing a student's résumé and questioning the student about accomplishments, I find the student has misrepresented himself or herself.

Should I reject the student's eligibility for a placement that semester? Should I simply discuss the consequences of misrepresentation and have the student redo the résumé correctly? Should I continue to work with the student in the internship? Should I establish particular conditions for continuing the internship placement?

The Issue

A student thinks he or she can increase the likelihood of gaining a desired field placement by being dishonest. Although honesty is widely praised as a value in our society, we witness daily events that testify to a widespread preference for dishonesty when it enhances our self-esteem, gets others to like us, protects others' feelings, or brings some gain for ourselves or our group. Although our society claims honesty is a high value, it may be that other considerations frequently outrank honesty—to the point that it can be acceptable to be dishonest as long as we don't get caught or we don't really hurt someone else.

Ethical Guidelines

Comment on the values of honesty and pragmatism. What experiences have you had in which you had to decide between being honest and doing what might bring the most favorable results?

Action

In her last paragraph Stacey asks four questions about what she should do when she faces a student who used misrepresentation in the résumé. What do you think Stacey should do?

Do you think faculty, agency supervisors, and students might answer her questions differently from each other? Why or why not?

Class Discussion

1. Review Statement 14 of the *Ethical Standards of Human Service Professionals*. Discuss the influences of personal values, societal values, and professional guidelines on your decisions about how to represent yourself to others.
2. Does your group consider that other, nonethical issues—like self-esteem or the personal reactions of others—are more influential than values on your decisions about being honest in your self-representations?
3. Do you think human service faculty should actively foster honesty in students? How do you think they should do that?

HELPING EACH OTHER: TWO EXPERIENCES

Renee, an Agency Supervisor

I take class attendance and collect papers if the instructor won't be in that day. Students sometimes ask me to lie for them to the instructor about things such as practicum and class attendance and turning in papers that are due.

Samantha, a Student

One time when I was getting overwhelmed by academic and personal demands, I missed some of my field practicum hours. It looked like I might be unable to make up the hours I'd missed. My agency supervisor, wanting to help me, told me to go ahead and document practicum hours that I hadn't put in—she would certify that I had put in those hours. "It's no big deal, Samantha," she said.

Ethical Guidelines

List the personal values that seem to be involved in these two anecdotes—from the student's and also the supervisors' viewpoints.

What societal values do you think are involved?

Resolving the Conflicts

What do you think are the primary influences on supervisors' decisions in these situations? (Their ethical positions? Personal relationships with the students? Habits and attitudes? Something else?)

Class Discussion

1. Did Renee's and Samantha's anecdotes bring to your mind additional nonethical factors that can influence decision making?
2. Review the list of ethical principles in chapter 1. Do any of them apply to this issue of considering nonethical factors as influential? How?

STUDENT COMPETENCY AND RISK: FOUR EXPERIENCES

Frank, a Faculty Member

Our program's human service students are in their field placements without malpractice and liability coverage—such coverage is not available for human service students and faculty at this time. The students also have little knowledge of current standards and procedures for practice. We do give them guidelines in their field practicum manual, but situations arise in their placements that are not covered by these guidelines or that require rapid decisions on their part. The other faculty members in my department aren't willing to address this as a problem.

Definitions

Define these terms:

liability

malpractice

liability insurance

professional malpractice insurance

professional practice standards

The Issue

Did you know that many who work in human service professions (counseling, nursing, psychology, social work) as students or practitioners have professional liability insurance? Why do you suppose they carry such coverage?

Do you have liability insurance coverage? Why or why not?

How is the situation Frank describes an ethical issue? How is it a legal issue?

Earl and Pamela

I was required to complete a volunteer placement for the introduction to human service course. I did mine at a homeless shelter. About halfway through the semester, Pamela, my staff supervisor, told me to put a DSM-IV diagnosis on one client's record and sign it. I didn't even know what DSM-IV was. Pamela told me to just copy what the last person wrote and sign it. She implied that if I didn't do it, then I'd be dismissed from the placement—and, therefore, wouldn't complete the course requirements.

The Issue

Is this an ethical issue?   Yes ____   No ____
Is this a legal issue?   Yes ____   No ____

Whose issue is it?

Agency's ____

Pamela's ____

Earl's ____

Client's ____

Action

What should Earl do?

Should Earl consult with anyone else?

Ron

I was completing my field placement at a residential program for adolescents. Often the teenagers acted out physically when they got upset and the staff had to restrain them. I had not been trained in physical restraint procedures and had been told by my instructor that I should not assist in any procedures involving physical control. One evening when the facility was short-staffed because a couple of staff members were ill, two residents began acting out at the same time. The staff demanded that I assist them in restraining one teenager.

The Issue

If Ron didn't help, staff members or residents might be injured. If he did, he might be injured.

Ethical Guidelines

Let's look at the legal aspects first:

Who might be liable for any harm resulting from Ron's action? (More than one may be marked.)

Agency ____

Staff ____

Ron ____

Instructor ____

Would anyone risk liability if Ron refuses to assist? Yes ____ No ____

Now, to ethics:

What values and professional guidelines are involved?

Action Alternatives

What different things could Ron do?

Evaluating the Alternatives

Would each of these possible actions meet the test of universality? (Would you recommend them to other students? Would you approve them if other entry-level professionals did them?)

Would each of these actions meet the test of publicity? (Would you be willing to explain the action to other students and to faculty? Would they accept your explanation?)

Would each of these actions meet the test of justice? (Would you suggest the same actions to other students in other field placements?)

Eliminate any action that would not meet these three tests. What would result from the remaining alternatives? Are these consequences certain, probable, possible, or unlikely?

Remaining alternatives	Consequences	Likelihood

Action

What do you think Ron should do? Why?

Do you think your instructor will agree with you? Why or why not?

Ali and Arnold

As a practicum student I arrived at my site to find my supervisor (a social worker) gone for the day. I went to another social worker, Arnold, for suggestions of things to do. Arnold gave me psychosocial histories to do on new clients—I had never completed a psychosocial history by myself, although we had studied them in class. I later discovered that Arnold was in the pool room with clients while I was reading the clients' records in preparation. I loved the challenge, but two dilemmas arose: (1) Am I competent enough to do the histories? (2) Am I enabling Arnold to "dump" his duties on me?

The Issue

Ali identifies two dilemmas. What do you think: Was he competent enough to do the histories? Was he enabling Arnold to "dump" his duties on him?

Do you think Arnold acted unprofessionally? Why or why not?

What was involved? What was at risk for Ali? What was at risk for Arnold? What was at risk for the clients?

What might Ali gain from this? What might Arnold gain from this? What might the clients gain?

Ethical Guidelines

What values and professional guidelines are involved?

Do these values and guidelines conflict with each other? If they do, how should they be ranked or evaluated to minimize the conflict and provide guidance to Ali?

Action Alternatives

Should Ali have completed the intake histories?

What else might Ali have done?

Class Discussion

1. Clarify the legal concepts introduced in these four anecdotes.
2. Discuss liability and professional malpractice insurance. What kind of protection does it provide the insured?
3. Discuss the risks of harm to client, staff, and agency involved in physical restraint and control.
4. Discuss the risks of harm to client, staff, and agency involved in allowing students to complete client assessments at which they are unskilled.
5. How do agencies and academic programs usually limit risks of harm?

FURTHER EXPLORATION

Contact insurance agencies, human service agencies, or professional organizations for information about liability insurance for students. Invite a guest speaker to class to address this issue.

FACILITATING THE BEST LEARNING EXPERIENCE: FOUR EXPERIENCES

Curtis, a Student

One ethical dilemma I found troubling in my role as a student intern was that an objective in my learning contract was not met. This objective stated that I would be given case management responsibilities for no more than three clients with direct supervision of the assistant director. When this was called to the attention of my placement supervisor, he stated that this objective could not be met due to legal regulations involved with the writing of treatment plans required by the case manager. I was given case management responsibilities for many different clients, just not my own clients. I felt this was just because I was a student.

Definition

Define the term *contract*.

The Issue

Curtis defines this as an ethical issue. Do you agree with him or would you define it differently?

Curtis says that he had a learning contract that included his learning objectives. Explain your understanding of a learning contract. Who would be involved in creating a learning contract?

Curtis tells us the supervisor said there were "legal requirements." What might those have been? How might Curtis have determined the real reason(s) he was denied a caseload?

Action Alternatives

List as many possible things Curtis could have done as you can think of.

Evaluating the Alternatives

Would each of these actions meet the test of universality?

Would each of these actions meet the test of publicity?

Would each of these actions meet the test of justice?

Eliminate any action that would not meet these three tests. Predict the possible consequences of all the remaining possible actions. Are these consequences certain, probable, possible, or unlikely?

Remaining alternatives	Consequences	Likelihood

Action

What do you think Curtis should have done? Why?

Terry, a Student

This may come across pretty vague, but my dilemma is the negativity of some staff that is verbalized in my presence. These complaints may be about other people, power struggles, or the manner in which things are accomplished or operated. My choices are (1) to ignore it—let it roll off my shoulders, (2) to report to my agency supervisor how the negativity affects me, or (3) to walk away or give no response.

The Issue

Describe Terry's issue.

Whose dilemma is it?

What are the relevant situational features?

Ethical Guidelines
What values and ethical principles are involved?

Are any professional guidelines relevant?

Sheila, an Agency Supervisor

Some students do not maintain boundaries at a professional level and do not benefit from supervision about these issues—for example: students with an immature sense of personal values and professional identity, students who see helping as a form of self-enhancement, and students who see themselves as independent agents.

It is difficult to explain what is "known and accepted" in supervisory feedback to these types of students. They tend, also, to blame the agency supervisor and demonstrate poor problem-solving skills in relation to their own performance and learning needs. Sometimes the time and energy I must devote to them is more than I have available.

The Issue
In Sheila's anecdote, there are educational, personal, ethical, and, possibly, legal issues involved. Let's focus on the ethical aspects.

Describe Sheila's ethical dilemma.

Who is involved?

What are the relevant situational mfeatures?

Ethical Guidelines

What values and ethical principles seem pertinent?

Review the *Ethical Standards of Human Service Professionals*. **What professional guidelines are relevant?**

Conflicts

Describe the internal conflicts Sheila may be experiencing.

Describe the external conflicts she may be experiencing.

Resolving the Conflicts

Should Sheila consult anyone? Who?

List as many possible ways Sheila could handle these situations as you can think of.

John, a Faculty Member

I have difficulty figuring out whether to intervene for students experiencing a "difficult" internship. If I intervene prematurely, the student may miss an important growth and decision-making opportunity. If I hesitate, the student may be placed in a potentially harmful situation.

The Issue

Describe the issue John faces.

Describe possible relevant situational features.

Conflicts

Describe the internal conflicts John may be experiencing.

Describe the external conflicts he may be experiencing.

Class Discussion

1. What do you think is required of each participant in the field practicum (student, instructor, agency supervisor)?
2. How much help should instructors and supervisors give to students who have problems? Whose responsibility is it to initiate discussion and action?
3. How can we determine, in the most ethical way, if difficulties are caused by students, are caused by other participants, and/or are the result of an interaction among the participants? How do we decide what the difficulty is? How do we get objective information or balance the subjective information?
4. How should overt conflicts be handled? How should covert conflicts be handled?
5. Discuss how you would design and implement a student's learning contract to prevent or deal with these types of issues. Is that the way learning contracts are handled in your program? If not, why not? Are there other issues with the learning contracts in your program?

HIDDEN AGENDAS AND LEARNING

Monica, Barry, and the Seminar

Barry, one of the students in our on-campus seminar (which accompanies the field practicum), claims he is being treated unfairly. In private conversations with other students Barry says he was, apparently, a threat to his first supervisor (who was young and new in her job) and that he was unjustly discriminated against and forced to quit that placement because of internal office politics. He says he was older than she and expressed his ethical standards in relation to things they were doing at the agency. He has been given another placement and says he is demanding the training he is there for and has been given some—grudgingly. He says one of our field instructors is a good listener, but this faculty member did nothing to encourage Barry to stand up for his rights. He says his new field instructor made him take the initiative he needed to.

Barry never talks about this in the seminar when the faculty are present. I am quite uncomfortable with his attitude and I think other students are, too. No one is saying much now in the seminar. The faculty know something is bothering us and have asked us what it is, but none of us have said anything. We don't want Barry to attack us.

The Issue

Monica, the other students, and the faculty are all aware there is something wrong, but the faculty members don't know what it is and, therefore, are not addressing it effectively.

Whose issue is this?

Monica's	____
Barry's	____
Faculty members'	____
No one's	____

Is this an ethical or another type of issue—or are there several types of issues involved? Explain your thinking.

Action Alternatives
List at least three things Monica could do.

Evaluating the Alternatives
Would each of these actions meet the test of universality?

Would each of these actions meet the test of publicity?

Would each of these actions meet the test of justice?

Eliminate any action that would not meet these three tests. What would result from the remaining alternatives? Are these consequences certain, probable, possible, or unlikely?

Remaining alternatives	Consequences	Likelihood

Action

What do you think Monica should do? Why?

Do you think most students would do what you have recommended? Why or why not?

Class Discussion

1. Share your thinking about what Monica could or should do and how most students would handle this type of situation.
2. Is this a situation where personal comfort may take precedence over the most ethical approach? What do you think about that?
3. How should other students respond to a student in a seminar or a field practicum when they think the student is creating the difficulty?

NOT QUITE A STAFF MEMBER: TWO EXPERIENCES

Gardner

Gardner was doing his field placement at an adult day care. He reported to the faculty and other students in their seminar that when the supervisor wasn't at adult day care, some of the workers sat at a table, eating, playing cards, socializing, and ignoring the clients. Gardner wasn't sure what he should do because he was only a student.

Action

Do you think Gardner should have ignored what he saw? Should he have told his supervisor? Should he have confronted the workers?

Ethical Guidelines

What ethical or other reasons underlie your recommendation to Gardner?

Virginia Ann

I was doing my internship in a substance abuse treatment program. In this internship the agency supervisor would give me my course grade for the internship. In a group therapy session, Rachel—one of the clients—admitted to abusing her 2-year-old daughter while on a weekend pass. I knew that professionals in this situation are legally required to report child abuse in our state. Later, at a staff meeting, I raised the question of reporting the abuse to the police or child protective services. The doctor, counselor, and supervisor did not want it reported: They said it might scare Rachel so that she would leave the program before she finished treatment. She would, as a result, lose the opportunity to relate better with her child in the long run.

The Issue

Describe Virginia Ann's dilemma.

Ethical Guidelines

What values, professional guidelines, and legal requirements are relevant?

Conflicts

What internal conflicts are involved?

What external conflicts are involved?

Resolving the Conflicts

Would you seek assistance in deciding what you should do if you were Virginia Ann? What assistance?

Action Alternatives

List four things Virginia Ann could do.

Evaluating the Alternatives

Would each of these actions meet the test of universality?

Would each of these actions meet the test of publicity?

Would each of these actions meet the test of justice?

Eliminate any action that would not meet these three tests. What would result from the remaining alternatives? Are these consequences certain, probable, possible, or unlikely?

Remaining alternatives	Consequences	Likelihood

Action

What do you think is the best approach from an ethical point of view? Why?

What do you think you would actually do if you were Virginia Ann? Why?

Class Discussion

1. Share your thinking about what Gardner and Virginia Ann could or should do and how most students would handle these situations.
2. Are these situations where personal comfort may take precedence over the most ethical approach?
3. How should students respond to staff in a field practicum when staff don't seem to be fulfilling their responsibilities?

FURTHER EXPLORATION

Learn about the Americans with Disabilities Act and rights of access to educational opportunities. Discuss in class how legal changes have altered faculty decision making about students and student progress. Relate that to your planned career in human services.

Chapter Eight

Confidentiality

I usually get my stuff from people who promised somebody else that they would keep it a secret.

—Walter Winchell

Confidentiality is central to the success of all helping professions. Without some assurance of confidentiality, most clients would be reluctant to tell practitioners much about themselves or their issues. Practitioners would then be unable to help clients.

In human services the confidentiality that is most often practiced is **relative confidentiality,** rather than **absolute confidentiality.** Relative confidentiality allows practitioners to privately discuss clients with other professionals in their agencies in the interest of improving services to those clients. It also means that in some circumstances we can be required by law to reveal information that was revealed to us by clients.

CONSENT AND CONFIDENTIALITY

Emery's Former Client

I have an old client who confided to me about sexual abuse. She asked for my help. I had a field practicum last year under the supervision of the Adult Protective Services (APS) worker who is assigned to her case. She does not know the APS worker. She asked me to talk with the worker and explain her situation as she is afraid and the worker has not returned her call.

I do not have her written consent to use her name when talking with the worker. If the worker asks her name, what can I do ethically? Name her? Or just tell the worker the story and that I will call the client and have her call the worker right away?

Definitions
Define these terms:

confidentiality

absolute confidentiality

relative confidentiality

privacy

written consent

The Issue
Why is maintaining confidentiality important?

In his last paragraph Emery asks three questions. How would you answer them if you were him?

How do you think Emery's "old client" would answer them?

What are the risks being faced by Emery and his former client?

Action
What would you do if you were Emery?

What values of yours were important in deciding what you would do?

Prevention

What could Emery have done differently to prevent this situation from developing? Describe at least two things he could have done.

Class Discussion

1. Compare and contrast the concepts of privacy and confidentiality.
2. Discuss your responses.
3. Preventing situations that involve ethical issues is often easier than dealing with them once they've happened. Discuss how you might prevent situations like this.

RESPONDING TO COWORKERS' BREACHES OF CONFIDENTIALITY

Martha and Her Coworkers

I was a certified nursing assistant working at an adult care facility. I overheard a day shift nursing assistant talking to one of my shift coworkers at a local food market. They were discussing how badly Mrs. N, a patient at our facility, had acted up during the shower that day. They called Mrs. N by name. I happened to be a friend of Mrs. N's granddaughter.

The Issue

Put yourself in Martha's place. What would you probably do?

Describe the personal and ethical aspects of Martha's issue.

What is at risk for Mrs. N? For the coworkers? For Martha?

What professional guidelines are involved? Consult the *Ethical Standards of Human Service Professionals*. Identify the statements that are most relevant to Martha's situation.

Action Alternatives

What, following the professional guidelines, should Martha do? List at least three options for her.

Evaluating the Alternatives

What is likely to happen as a result of each of these optional actions?

Action

Based on the probable consequences, which option would be preferable?

Class Discussion

1. Should the fact that Martha was a friend of Mrs. N's granddaughter have influenced her decision? Would it have influenced your decision?
2. Taking ethically correct actions can make human service professionals unpopular with their coworkers, especially when negative consequences result for the coworkers. Discuss what you might do in your workplace to maintain a high level of ethics as well as maintain positive working relationships with others.

CONFLICT: NEEDS OF CLIENTS VERSUS NEEDS OF OTHERS

Max, Sylvia, and David

As part of my field practicum I was providing brief premarital counseling for couples. I saw each couple individually, then together. While interviewing Sylvia and David individually, it was clear to me that they loved each other very much. Sylvia, however, told me she had tested positive for HIV and didn't want to tell David. She refused to tell him for fear of losing him.

The Issue

Is this an ethical issue?	Yes ____	No ____
Is this a clinical issue?	Yes ____	No ____
Is this a legal issue?	Yes ____	No ____

Is anyone else involved besides Max, Sylvia, and David? Explain your answer.

Whose issue is it?

What is involved or at risk?

Ethical Guidelines

What values and ethical principles are involved?

What professional guidelines are involved? Consult the *Ethical Standards of Human Service Professionals.*

Action Alternatives

List at least four things Max could do.

Evaluating the Alternatives

Cross out (but leave readable!) any alternative that would impose Max's values on Sylvia. Also, cross out any alternative for which there seem to be no resources or support.

Cross out any alternatives that don't pass the ethical tests of universality, publicity, and justice.

For each of the alternatives remaining, predict the probable consequences.

Remaining alternatives	Probable consequences

Review the remaining alternatives and consequences. Rank them with 1 being best. Which best protects Sylvia's rights and welfare? Which best protects David's rights and welfare? Which best protects society's rights and interests? Which causes the least harm possible?

According to your rankings, prioritize the acceptable alternatives.

Action

If you were Max, what would you do if Sylvia did not accept your alternatives? Would you terminate your counseling relationship with the couple? If so, how would you explain it to David?

Would you continue to work with them? How would you address the secret if you did?

Andy, Loretta, and Merrill

Disclosures about one resident's case to another resident is unethical and a breach of confidentiality. When one resident is in danger because another resident happens to be a perpetrator, however, what should the human service worker do?

In the crisis residential center where I work, a 16-year-old girl, Loretta, has a crush on a convicted teenage sex offender, Merrill, who is also a resident. The treatment plan calls for the residential techs to keep them apart without telling them why or disclosing Merrill's background. Loretta thinks we're just being unreasonable adults.

Wenona

In residential programs (alcohol/mental health, crisis, acute care), often clients are admitted without the knowledge of their family or significant others. The family or significant others may be very concerned about the welfare of the client and may call hospitals, clinics, law enforcement agencies, and residential programs in the community in their efforts to locate the person. Based on confidentiality, this information cannot be provided. But as a human service worker I hear and understand the fears and concerns of the callers.

Ethical Guidelines

List at least three values or ethical principles that you think are involved in the ethical dilemmas described by Andy and Wenona.

List the statements from the *Ethical Standards of Human Service Professionals* that you think are relevant to these two dilemmas.

Conflicts

Is there conflict among t he values and professional guidelines in terms of what the professional should do? Explain your thinking.

Action

What would you do if you were Andy? How did you make that decision? Describe the steps you took in moving from (1) your selection of the pertinent ethical guidelines, through (2) the alternatives you considered, through (3) your evaluation of those options, to (4) your decision.

Would your preferred action meet the three tests of universality, publicity, and justice?

Predict the consequences of the action.

What would you do if you were Wenona? Again, trace the steps in your thinking.

Would this action meet the three tests of universality, publicity, and justice?

Predict the consequences of the action.

Class Discussion

1. Evaluate the three preceding scenarios and your preferred actions in relation to Statement 3 of the *Ethical Standards of Human Service Professionals*. How do you define "cause harm" to others? Do you think other professionals would agree with your definition and support your preferred actions?

2. Review together how you ranked (prioritized) the values, principles, and professional guidelines that were involved in these situations. Clarify any similarities and differences among yourselves in terms of values and rankings. Discuss what you can learn from this.

EVERYONE KNOWS EVERYTHING

New England

In my school placement everyone is talking about everyone. All the staff (secretaries, teacher aides, faculty, housekeeping) know everything about all the students. They talk about students, their families, and their problems on the playground, at the copier, in the lunchroom, in their offices, and in the hallways.

Southwest

Gossip and rumors about other staff as well as clients are exchanged in the lunchroom, bathroom, and hallways. If you don't want to hear, where can you go?

Northwest

Working with a variety of agencies in my practicum and networking, I came to deal with a counselor from a homeless agency who constantly broke her client's confidentiality with her friends and family members.

The Issue

The breaches of confidentiality described by these students from across the U.S. reflect a—sad, but true—commonly reported practice in human services. The students describe well-established patterns of gossiping in which staff, friends, and family members are involved. Because of this practice, information about clients becomes widely available in the community, risking not only the clients' well-being, but also that of the agency and the staff. Examples: A father might suffer a harmed reputation at his job because his boss hears from a secretary at the school that the father is accused of child abuse. Staff at other human service agencies might stop referring consumers to the homeless agency because they've heard that confidentiality is broken at the homeless agency.

Students at agencies for practicum or field experiences and their faculty are in difficult positions in relation to such practices. In relation to agencies, students and their faculty are outsiders with minimal influence on the agency functioning. Students are more likely than employees (to whom such information sharing seems commonplace) to notice such practices, yet students are usually not in positions where they are encouraged—or even allowed—to criticize the staff.

In relation to their course enrollment, students are challenged by their faculty and other resources to approach their work with clients professionally—including maintaining appropriate confidentiality. In the face of the actual practice they see role-modeled at their agencies—and in which they are often expected to participate—students may learn to accept such unethical behavior as characteristic of "the real world."

Ethical Guidelines

What statements from the *Ethical Standards of Human Service Professionals* are relevant?

In developing as a human service professional, do you think the influence of actual role models—reflecting societal values—is stronger than the influence of resources and faculty—reflecting professional guidelines?

Internal Conflicts

What internal conflicts would most students experience?

What do you think most students in one of these situations would want to do to maintain their comfort?

What do you think most students in one of these situations would think they should do?

External Conflicts

What external conflicts would most students experience?

What do you think most students in one of these situations would want to do to continue being accepted by the staff and welcome at the agency?

What do you think most students in one of these situations would want to do out of their commitment to clients?

Action

What do you think most students would do in one of these situations?

What should they do?

Class Discussion

1. Share your experiences with gossiping in human service agencies. What additional points do you think are important to mention?
2. Were you able to resolve the internal and external conflicts and find action alternatives? Discuss and evaluate those alternatives.

Chapter Nine

Client Rights and Needs, Agency Policy, and Law, Part 1

Judge your character by (a) how well you treat those who can't do you any good and (b) how you treat those who can't fight back.

—Anonymous

Individual providers of human services are limited in the knowledge, skills, and resources they can muster to assist clients. They, therefore, join together, pooling their knowledge, skills, and efforts for the benefit of **consumers** and developing human service agencies and voluntary organizations to provide services. The judicious use of bureaucracy makes these organizations more effective and efficient in service provision than the individual can be.

Most human services are provided under the auspices of such bureaucracies—both public and private organizations. The existence of these bureaucracies, which are supported by donations and by tax money, reflects a societal commitment to assist people who have difficulty meeting their needs by themselves. Each **entry-level professional** shares his or her commitment to helping others with the society, the employer, and the other professional and nonprofessional workers in the agency.

Human service organizations are built on some sense of mission and purpose. This is expressed through an organizational structure and culture that includes such aspects as shared norms, standards, values, and assumptions (Clifton & Dahms, 1993, pp. 39–42). The life of the organization—sometimes overt, sometimes covert—involves issues as diverse as making administrative and clinical decisions, developing funding sources, meeting legal and regulatory requirements, and understanding the needs of clients.

The structure and culture are expressed overtly in explicit **policies** and **procedures,** which are developed to ensure that the organization meets the requirements of statutory law and regulations as well as expresses its mission consistently. Employees and volunteers are expected to read, understand, and follow established policies and procedures. By doing so, workers support and protect the agency and its clients.

The written rules reflect only part of an organization's culture, however. The new professional must come to understand and decide how to reconcile sometimes conflicting written and unwritten rules. He or she must also figure out whether and how particular rules reflect or do not reflect personal and professional ethical guidelines. To do this, he or she must apply an understanding not only of ethical decision making, but also of organizational dynamics and the balancing of ethical, legal, clinical, and pragmatic considerations in the particular agency.

CLIENT RIGHTS AND NEEDS

Joe

Two retarded clients, a man and a woman, in a group home locked themselves in a bathroom. I did not know what they were doing in the bathroom.

Definitions
Define these terms:

policy

procedure

The Issue
What other information does Joe need to have before he decides whether he has a clinical or an ethical issue?

How might the agency's policies and procedures be important?

Do the clients have a right to privacy together in the home? In the bathroom?

Does Joe have a responsibility to leave them alone? To intervene?

Class Discussion

Discuss your responses. What personal values influenced your thinking? What societal values influenced you? What else influenced you?

CLIENT RIGHTS AND AGENCY PROCEDURES

Rosalinda

I observed the director of my agency satellite that catered to walk-in clients ignore a client for over 20 minutes; the director was on a personal phone call. What irked me the most was the fact that she had told all the volunteers not to answer clients' questions—she would greet all of them. I was also angry because I knew the phone call was personal. The client, a young woman with two small children, was very upset.

The Issue

What type of issue is this (ethical, legal, personal, clinical)?

Who is involved? How are they related? How does that complicate the issue?

Whose dilemma is this?

Rosalinda's	Yes _____	No _____
Client's	Yes _____	No _____
Director's	Yes _____	No _____
Agency's	Yes _____	No _____

What is at risk for each of the participants?

Ethical Guidelines

Review the *Ethical Standards of Human Service Professionals*. What values and professional guidelines are involved?

Action Alternatives

Considering Rosalinda's role and authority, what is she most likely to do?

What do you think Rosalinda would want to do? What would she do if she felt safe from retaliation?

What do you think Rosalinda should do? Considering her role and authority, feelings, and the potential harm to the client, what do you think would be the most ethical thing she could do and still protect herself from retaliation?

Class Discussion

1. What do you consider the most important values or ethical principles in this anecdote?
2. The differences among our decisions when we are (a) primarily protecting ourselves, (b) giving vent to our emotional reactions, and (c) choosing what we believe is the most ethical approach (protecting all participants from harm) are important to note. Compare and contrast your responses to the questions under "Action Alternatives." Did you follow your highest-ranking values in deciding what Rosalinda should do?

TRUST, CONFIDENTIALITY, AND AGENCY POLICY

Connie and Maria

My first human service field placement was in a domestic violence shelter. I was pretty self-directed and responsible in this placement. My agency supervisor had to be out of the shelter frequently for agency business—she had told me in supervision that I was doing fine. I spent a lot of time with the clients at the shelter, listening to their stories and helping them set their own goals and plan what they were going to do next. I had developed a particularly close relationship with Maria, a victim who had been in the shelter for several weeks, when Maria told me that she was going to spend an upcoming holiday with the perpetrator. I didn't want to betray Maria's trust in me, but I knew that such a visit was against the shelter's rules.

Ethical Guidelines

What are Connie's personal values that are pertinent to this situation?

What societal values may be pertinent?

What professional guidelines are pertinent? Consult the *Ethical Standards of Human Service Professionals.*

Rank these values and guidelines by numbering the one you consider most important with a 1, the second most important with a 2, and so forth.

Evaluate your ranking. What guided your decisions? Why did you decide what you did?

Class Discussion

Compare and contrast your rankings of values and guidelines. What can you learn from this in terms of your values and ethical decision making?

PERSONAL VIEWS AND CLIENT NEEDS

Camilla

My field practicum is as an entry-level child care worker. I wonder if I would be able to objectively discuss the subject of homosexuality with an adolescent who needs help and advice in identifying and accepting his or her sexual identity, particularly since my views are conservative toward the matter of homosexuality. I know my options will be: (1) refuse to talk with the adolescent about the subject, (2) refer the adolescent to another worker, (3) pretend to be liberal in my view, (4) persuade the adolescent that homosexuality is a choice, (5) tell the adolescent that homosexuality is wrong. I don't feel safe talking with anyone in my program about this issue and my feelings.

The Issue

What do you think Camilla means by "my views are conservative toward the matter of homosexuality"?

Is it ethically acceptable that she plan a career working with adolescents if her values and beliefs will be different from their values and beliefs? Explain your thoughts.

How would you approach a conflict you didn't feel safe talking about with faculty, students, or colleagues?

Ethical Guidelines

What do you think is Camilla's highest value in relation to this situation?

What do you think is the most important societal value in relation to this situation?

What standards in the *Ethical Standards of Human Service Professionals* are pertinent?

Camilla lists five possible actions. Do they all follow relevant ethical guidelines? Explain your answer.

What other options can you think of?

Class Discussion

Review Statements 25 and 36 in the *Ethical Standards of Human Service Professionals.* One aspect of situations like Camilla's is trust: Will peers, colleagues, faculty, or supervisors help us with our conflicts without judging us or telling other people? We all have issues sometimes where our values differ significantly from those of others around us and from our professional guidelines, and we fear others' responses if they knew. What do *you* do when you realize you have such an issue?

INFORMED DECISIONS: TWO EXPERIENCES

Andre

In the nursing home where I am a human service worker, the staff sometimes encourage residents to accept interventions and treatments that the residents do not want. I think the staff may have the best health-related interests of the patient in mind when they encourage the medication, therapy, or diet, but my concern is that the residents really have the rights to refuse and to give informed consent.

Definitions

Define these terms:

autonomy

beneficence

informed consent

nonmaleficence

paternalism

right to refuse treatment

The Issue

When a human being is dependent on a person or an agency for shelter, food, clothing, and care, it becomes very difficult for that person to refuse an intervention that the provider wants him or her to accept. Even when no threat is intended by the provider, the power difference in their relationship often carries an underlying message of "If you don't agree, then I might reject you, depriving you of shelter, food, clothing, or care." In reality, this happens more often than we like to admit: Practitioners are, after all, human beings, and when clients refuse their recommended intervention, they may feel hurt or angry. As a result, the provider may spend a bit less time and effort with this client, at least while the provider copes with his or her feelings. This is a deprivation of care by the practitioner and is recognized as such by the client.

Andre is describing a common dilemma in residential human service agencies. If the client has agreed to the staff's recommendation, is this informed consent or did the client say yes because he or she didn't want the practitioner to be upset?

On what ethical principle is informed consent (a legal concept) based?

On the basis of what ethical principle do practitioners encourage a client to accept an intervention in his best interests, although he may be reluctant?

Oscar

In a senior center for disabled adults, one of the clients refused to eat her lunch. She was very underweight and her family expected her to eat the hot meal served at the center. It was written in the contract that a nourishing meal is served to every client daily. I believe in client autonomy and each person's right to refuse treatment.

The Issue

Informed consent is a legal concept that requires three criteria be met: competence, knowledge, and voluntariness (Saltzman & Proch, 1990, pp. 343–346). **Competence** (or **capacity** means the person consenting must be capable of making the decision.

Knowledge (or **comprehension of information**) means the person must understand the procedure, its benefits, risks, alternatives, and potential consequences. Voluntariness means the person must be making a decision freely (he or she must not be coerced—or feel coerced—into the action).

The **right to refuse treatment,** also a legal concept, is derived from the concept of informed consent: Refusal should be informed.

Do we need additional information about this client's competence? What does the anecdote imply about her competence?

What additional information do we need about this client's knowledge?

Do we need additional information about this client's voluntariness?

If our decision were to be based on legal, rather than ethical, grounds, could the client be fed against her will? Explain your answer.

Ethical Guidelines

Is the highest ethical principle here autonomy? Is it beneficence? Is it nonmaleficence? Defend your answer.

Class Discussion

1. Review Statement 8 in the *Ethical Standards of Human Service Professionals*. Compare and contrast the ethical concepts of autonomy and beneficence with the legal concept of informed consent.
2. Discuss the information that must be collected before deciding what type of issue (ethical, legal, clinical) we face.
3. Students enter field placements without having detailed information about clients, the staff, and how decisions are made in that agency. What should a student do when he or she sees a staff member doing something to a client that seems unethical or illegal?
4. If you do decide staff are doing something illegal or unethical to a client, what are your options?

CLIENT NEEDS AND TRUTH

Chandra

At a nursing home the activities staff are working with an elderly man who is upset about being in the nursing home, particularly since he thinks the cost is being borne by the taxpayers. He is in the beginning stages of Alzheimer's disease, but he is still capable of understanding most information. The staff assure him that the money is coming out of his own savings through the guardian who is managing his money, although it actually is coming out of long-term care money (tax-supported). He feels better, so he participates more.

Ethical Guidelines

What values and ethical principles are involved here?

What professional guidelines are relevant?

Evaluating the Alternatives

What action alternatives and potential consequences are involved here?

What do you think: Is it okay to lie in the best interests of a patient?

Class Discussion

Discuss whether it is okay to lie in the best interests of a client. Would you have to decide among relevant ethical principles and potential consequences?

RESPONDING TO A COWORKER'S BREACH OF CLIENT RIGHTS

Louis, Melody, and a Group of Boys

I work in a residential program for hearing-impaired children. It was on the schedule of activities that a certain group of boys would go to the therapeutic cottage to bake cookies for snacks, and Melody was assigned to assist and supervise them. The boys all did a good job of baking and cleaning up. They all used sign language to ask, "Cookie, please." But Melody refused to give them cookies. She told them that they did not deserve it and she took the whole batch of cookies to her own home instead.

The Issue

What is the decision Louis has to make? Is it an ethical or another type of decision?

Who is involved? How are they related?

What is involved? What is at risk?

What are the relevant situational features?

Ethical Guidelines

What personal and societal values are involved?

What professional guidelines are involved?

Conflicts

Is there an internal conflict? If so, describe it.

Is there an external conflict? If so, describe it.

How would you resolve the conflicts?

Action Alternatives

List at least three things Louis could do.

Evaluating the Alternatives

Would the alternatives you listed pass the tests of universality, publicity, and justice? Eliminate any that wouldn't. (Cross them out in your list.)

What would be the probable consequences of the remaining actions?

Rank the remaining alternatives by numbering them.

Class Discussion

Most of you probably said that Louis should do something besides ignore Melody's action. Discuss whether—in the real world—you would or would not actually "do something." Why or why not?

CLIENT NEEDS VERSUS AGENCY POLICY

Esteban

I work with children and adolescents in their home and community while they and their parents are under supervision from Child Protective Services, so these clients have not had very responsive parenting and often have many unmet needs, emotionally, physically, socially, intellectually, etc. Agency policies prohibit my talking with them about sex. My ongoing dilemma is what to do when one of them asks me to discuss something about sex with him or her. If I avoid the conversation, I protect myself and the agency, yet prevent the client from access to a knowledgeable source of information (myself). If I respond, the client's needs are met, yet I put myself, my job, and my agency at risk.

The Issue

Esteban is describing an ethical dilemma in which he believes his best action is contrary to his agency's policy, a topic we will consider in more depth in the next chapter.

Describe his issue. Who is involved? What is their relationship? Whose dilemma is it? What is at risk? What are the relevant situational features?

Ethical Guidelines

If you were Esteban, what values and ethical principles of your own would be involved?

What societal values may be involved?

What professional guidelines are relevant?

Conflicts

Is there an internal conflict?

Is there an external conflict?

If you were Esteban, could you resolve the conflicts?

Class Discussion

1. If you knew one of your clients needed open communication about sex and no other responsible adult was providing it, do you think you would: (a) avoid the subject, (b) bring it up, or (c) discuss it only when he or she brought the subject up?
2. If you broke agency policy in what you believed were the client's best interests, would you inform the client you were breaking agency policy?
3. Review Statement 34 of the *Ethical Standards of Human Service Professionals*. Would you bring the policy at Esteban's agency up for review?

Chapter Ten

Client Rights and Needs, Agency Policy, and Law, Part 2

It is not desirable to cultivate a respect for the law, so much as for the right.
—Henry David Thoreau

The anecdotes included in this chapter have more legal components than those in chapter 9. At the entry level of human services, most professionals make every effort to follow relevant law, regulations, and agency policies and procedures. They understand the major repercussions that would occur if they were caught doing something that skirted the law, rules, or agency policies. And, generally, following the law is the most ethical thing they can do.

The ethically preferred and the legally mandated actions are usually in agreement with each other, making the decision fairly easy. When there is conflict, however, the professional faces a dilemma. Entry-level workers see that some experienced professionals don't always follow the rules. They take risks to do what they consider ethical and seem to have developed support networks that protect them in their actions. Other times, entry-level workers encounter experienced professionals who never break the rules: Regardless of the situation, they enforce the letter of the law.

For the entry-level practitioner, finding a compromise between what seems ethically appropriate and what is legally mandated can be a source of professional burnout. Feeling forced to make decisions and to take actions that cause internal conflict leads to feelings of helplessness and a belief that one is ineffective. Fear of others' opinions often accompanies this internal conflict: "If I tell my colleague or boss that I think what the rules say I'm supposed to do is wrong, what will he or she say? Might I be fired?"

In meeting human service professionals and in discussing ethical dilemmas they have faced, I have encountered their sense of isolation particularly when they describe dilemmas that involved conflict between the rules (law, regulations, agency policies) and their own values or the guidelines of the profession. Often I have been the first person they have told of the dilemma; some have even glanced around repeatedly as we talked to make sure no one else was listening.

I hope that the process of thinking and talking about the following anecdotes not only gives you some experience in making decisions where the rules and your values conflict, but also helps you begin to build a recognition that all of us in this field have faced such conflicts and that it really is okay to talk with other human service professionals about how to cope with them. Do not, however, approach this unrealistically: There *are* administrators and colleagues who would be judgmental about even considering breaking the rules, so be selective about those you seek out for consultation.

THE CLIENT'S DECISION: BREAK THE RULES

Isaac and Eloise

I am in a field placement with the elderly, making home visits and helping with home care and shopping. Eloise is on Medicaid. She is keeping the insurance checks instead of paying the medical providers. She's very poor and really needs the extra money. I know she trusts me.

The Issue

Describe Isaac's issue from both the ethical and the legal perspectives.

Action

What would you do if you were Isaac? Would you tell your supervisor or the Medicaid worker? Would you let them catch up on their own—if they do? Explain your reasoning.

Class Discussion

Discuss the possible consequences of the actions Isaac could take.

THE CLIENT: CAUGHT IN THE SYSTEM

Phoebe and Melissa

The problem of bail and the indigent creates many ethical problems and hard decisions for defendants who are poor. Melissa, a 22-year-old woman, was arrested for selling crack cocaine to an informant for the police. Conviction carries a mandatory sentence of 5 years and up to 30 years in prison. Melissa had spent the last 10 days in jail. She had a 2-year-old daughter who was being cared for by Melissa's mother, who had taken time off work to do this. Bail was set at $50,000; Melissa did not have the $5,000 (10 percent) necessary to post bail.

She would have had to spend the next few months in jail, awaiting trial, or admit guilt and accept the State's plea bargain offer: a suspended sentence with 8 years of probation. Her constitutional right to a trial was, in effect, never available. She had no choice but accept the plea bargain agreement and admit guilt (although at trial she would have had a good shot at an acquittal because the State's snitch was not guaranteed to show up to testify). So, for the next 8 years, she must live in the same environment and "keep the peace," or face violation of probation and incarceration.

The Issues

Phoebe has explained the legal situation Melissa faced. She doesn't tell us whether human service professionals were involved in helping Melissa. Melissa probably had a lawyer or a paralegal as her advocate and may also have had one or more community service practitioners who were supporting her in chemical dependency treatment and in protecting the welfare of her child.

Describe the ethical dilemma that these professionals probably faced.

Whose dilemma is this?

What is involved? What is at risk?

Describe the relevant situational features (legal system, human service systems, family, community).

Ethical Guidelines

What are your personal values that are important in relation to the situation Phoebe described?

What societal values do you think are important?

Which statements in the *Ethical Standards of Human Service Professionals* do you think are pertinent?

Conflicts

Describe the internal conflicts you would experience if you were working with Melissa.

Describe the external conflicts that seem important.

Could you minimize these conflicts and make a decision about how best to advise or assist Melissa? On what basis would you make that decision?

Resolving the Conflicts

If you could not decide the best approach to helping Melissa, what would you do or who would you consult?

Class Discussion

1. Do you believe that in deciding the best action to take as a practitioner when faced with situations like Melissa's, you should hold societal values to be more important than the professional guidelines? Why or why not?
2. What do you know about the ethics of the legal profession? In what ways are they similar to or different from those of the human service profession?

FURTHER EXPLORATION

Obtain copies of codes of ethics of the legal profession and law enforcement professionals to read and discuss in class.

CLIENT NEEDS VERSUS THE REGULATIONS

Ben and Charles

Charles, an adult offender under my supervision, is behind in his payments. He has not made a payment in over a year. He is mentally retarded and is on disability, lives alone, and, despite numerous reminders, has not turned in the required paperwork to verify his disability and his inability to pay. His mother is willing to help him by making the payments for him.

I believe that he does not understand the potential consequences of his failure to pay or to complete the paperwork. My agency, the probation department, requires that I take action. According to the rules, I am not allowed to advocate for Charles, complete the paperwork for him, nor request the assistance of an outside advocate—my efforts must stay within the criminal justice system. I can: (1) request a court hearing, which could mean jail time, (2) request a bench warrant, which would mean jail time, (3) recommend "no action," which would reinforce Charles's "noncompliance is okay" attitude, (4) request the paperwork again and wait, or (5) accept the payment from his mother and reinforce his "noncompliance is okay" attitude.

The Issue

Describe the ethical dilemma Ben is facing. Who is involved? What are their relationships with each other? Whose dilemma is it? What is involved or at risk? What are the relevant situational features?

If no agency policies were involved, what do you think would be the best action for Ben to take?

Ethical Guidelines

Why do you think the probation department has the policies and procedures that seem to be keeping Ben from doing what seems best for Charles?

What personal values and principles are important in this situation?

What societal values do you think are important in this situation?

Which statements in the *Ethical Standards of Human Service Professionals* do you think apply?

Conflicts

Describe the internal conflicts you think Ben is experiencing.

Describe the external conflicts that Ben is experiencing.

Could Ben minimize these conflicts and make a decision? How?

Resolving the Conflicts

What should Ben do or who should he consult for assistance in his decision?

Class Discussion

1. In what way are these ethical issues unique to the criminal justice system? Do you think you would be better prepared to cope with the ethical issues in law enforcement than in other human service fields?
2. Would being part of an informal network of human service professionals help you cope with issues like this? How?
3. What do the *Ethical Standards of Human Service Professionals* say we should do when we disagree with our agency's policies? Do you think it is okay to simply fail to follow policies and procedures you consider to be unethical? Why or why not? What would be at risk?

A STUDENT FEARS FOR HER SAFETY

Meira and Felix

When I was a practicum student at a juvenile training facility (a prison for adolescents), Felix, a convicted multiple arsonist, told me about criminal behavior he had engaged in at the prison. The prison staff didn't know about it. If I reported it to the staff, it would probably stop his upcoming parole for at least six months. I knew, however, that he would eventually be paroled to my small hometown—where he could easily find my home.

The Issue

Is this a legal issue?	Yes ____	No ____
Is this an ethical issue?	Yes ____	No ____
Is this a personal issue?	Yes ____	No ____

Ethical Guidelines

If you were Meira, what facts, beliefs, and values would you consider in deciding what you were going to do? How would you weigh your personal and family safety against Felix's responsibility for his own behavior?

Resolving the Dilemma

Would you seek consultation from anyone? If you would, what do you think the consultant would advise?

Action Alternatives

List four things Meira could do.

Evaluating the Alternatives

Would each of these actions meet the tests of universality, publicity, and justice? Eliminate any action that would not meet these three tests.

What would result from the remaining alternatives? Are these consequences certain? Are they probable? Are they possible? Are they unlikely?

Action

What would you do if you were Meira?

Class Discussion

1. Compare and contrast your thoughts and decisions.
2. Human service students and professionals do not commonly experience threats to their safety within the course of their profession, but it does happen. As a group, consider the types of danger you may face and how you might handle those dangers ethically.

DEINSTITUTIONALIZATION: TWO EXPERIENCES

Hassan

I had a position as a psychiatric technician in a state mental hospital and witnessed the results of the ongoing downsizing of state mental institutions. Long-term institutionalized consumers are moving into their own apartments in the community. They are not properly prepared, educated, and supported in doing this. It is important to understand that the communities are also not prepared or educated to accept this.

Lois and Douglas

As a case aide, I have the responsibility of medicating a client, Douglas, twice daily, four days weekly, at his apartment with a high dosage of psychotropic medication. Douglas is very delusional, even when he is taking his medication. Children in the surrounding apartments tease him about his appearance and behavior. His apartment is filthy—feces are smeared on the walls, garbage is stacked up, and maggots develop in food left on the kitchen counter. I have helped him clean up many times and have made suggestions to him how to do it himself. Each time I return after a few days off, I find a similar situation. We have discussed Douglas in staff meetings. Because of current laws he cannot be institutionalized in the state mental hospital and there is no medication that would be more effective in managing his symptoms.

The Issue

Issues with deinstitutionalization are encountered by human service professionals across the U.S. They include client rights, societal rights, and the politics of limited resources. One way of supporting Douglas in a relatively sanitary and safe environment would be to provide him with twice-daily visits, seven days a week, from entry-level professionals in an effort to assure that his self-care and preventive health needs are met. To be effective, not only is intervention needed with Douglas, but also the neighbors and their children need education and support.

In terms of resource use, what are the ethical issues such an approach creates?

What other interventions can you suggest?

Ethical Guidelines
Describe the societal values that are involved.

Describe the personal values that would be involved if you were Hassan or Lois.

What do the *Ethical Standards of Human Service Professionals* say that is pertinent?

Class Discussion

Review Statements 10, 11, 12, and 13 in the *Ethical Standards of Human Service Professionals*. Discuss what the human service profession is doing and should be doing in advocacy for people with disabling mental illnesses. Be as specific and realistic in your ideas as you can be!

BALANCING CLIENT RIGHTS, CLIENT NEEDS, AND LEGAL APPROACHES

Dolores, Her Supervisor, and Ms. Doe

While I was completing my field placement at Adult Protective Services (APS), Ms. Doe, a woman in her 90s, was reported to us. She lived alone in a cockroach-infested, filthy apartment. She was underweight but refused services. Against her will, APS took her to the local hospital emergency room for physical and mental status assessments. Neither assessment revealed any particular pathology, but my supervisor, wanting to protect her, insisted the physician admit Ms. Doe to the hospital. The physician, who had worked with APS on many other cases, agreed to admit her for a more extensive work-up and, because of Ms. Doe's condition, was able to justify the admission for Medicare. The physician implied to us that although this was legal, it was not ethical—the real reason for her admission was not medical, but rather was to confine her against her wishes until APS made arrangements for her to live in a new setting.

My supervisor wanted Ms. Doe to be in an assisted living facility or nursing home. Ms. Doe did not want to move out of her home or lose her possessions. While she was hospitalized, my supervisor went to court and got an order that gave a niece—the only local relative—guardianship. The niece was willing to do whatever APS suggested. Ms. Doe's sister, also in her 90s, lived about 200 miles away and supported Ms. Doe's right to live independently and make her own decisions, but the sister wasn't willing to take Ms. Doe in or come to live with her.

The Issue

In our society, we value the individual's right to autonomy. Legislation and judicial decisions over the past 40 years have been effective at limiting the State's authority to intervene in response to people with issues related to mental illness, chemical dependency, family violence, and—as is illustrated in this anecdote—aging. In general, the State is allowed to intervene only if it is likely that direct and immediate harm (danger to self or to others) could occur or if it is clear that the individual is incapable of making informed decisions (gravely disabled).

Ethicists and practitioners are beginning to question whether this narrow legal definition of when the State has a right to interfere with a person's autonomy is humane or civilized. Is it best for the person's well-being to allow him or her autonomous decision making when the results may be harmful? Or do the needs and rights of society supersede the occasional need of the individual: Is it best, especially in a multicultural society, to continue to limit State intervention because it protects all citizens against interference in decisions that might not be approved by those in authority?

Ethical Guidelines

What personal values, societal values, and statements from the *Ethical Standards of Human Service Professionals* do you think are most relevant?

Conflicts

Describe the internal and external conflicts for Dolores.

Describe the internal and external conflicts for the APS worker.

Action Alternatives

What would you want to do about Ms. Doe if you were the student?

What other things could the APS worker do?

Evaluating the Alternatives

Which actions do not meet the tests of universality, publicity, and justice?

What are the possible consequences of the remaining alternatives? Are these consequences certain? Are they probable? Are they possible? Are they unlikely?

Action

What would you do if you were the APS worker?

Would you do anything if you were Dolores and the situation were progressing as she described it?

Class Discussion

1. In your community, does APS use a narrow or a broad definition of when intervention is permitted?
2. Share your thoughts about our current ethical and legal climates and how they relate to Ms. Doe and her professional helpers.
3. If you were to follow through on the approach you consider most ethical, would you be deciding to take social action? What action would you take?

FURTHER EXPLORATION

1. Invite local legislators, judges, or representatives of Adult Protective Services into class to discuss these issues.
2. Find out how social policy decisions are made in your state.
3. Discuss how you might start taking a role in influencing policy decisions locally or in your state.

Chapter Eleven

Dual Relationships and Self-Disclosure

One thoughtful person suggested that while a certain amount of A.A. contact with patients was inevitable,[1] most of the traps could be avoided by two measures. One was that there be no scheduled appointments with former patients, although awkward and artificial measures to avoid casual contact were impractical. The other was to avoid situations in which he would be alone with former patients, particularly those of the opposite sex.

—LeClair Bissell and James E. Royce, 1987

Dual, or **multiple, relationships** in the course of counseling have been placed under an ethical microscope in the past 10 to 15 years. Pick up many of the recent resources in psychology, psychiatry, and counseling and you will find sections concerned with harm or potential harm from sexual relationships with clients and former clients, from the exchange of services between client and practitioner, from the conflict for faculty and students when the same person is teacher, evaluator, and personal counselor, and from other relationships that may impair the professional's judgment and capacity to help the client.

Dual and multiple relationships also occur in the relationships between entry-level human service professionals and their clients. They are not always avoidable, nor are they always potentially harmful to clients. The intent of this chapter is to assist the reader to, first of all, recognize dual relationships and, then, to apply ethical thinking before proceeding.

CASUAL CONTACT

Eloise

How should I respond when I meet a client on the street with whom I have been or am currently working? If I greet the client, I may be violating confidentiality. If I don't, he or

---

[1]Many addiction counselors continue to participate in Alcoholics Anonymous groups as part of their own recovery. They may encounter their former patients in those groups.

> *she may feel ignored. This is more complex if they or I am with other people. Example:*
> *If I work in a mental health setting and say "hi," the person might feel exposed.*

The Issue

In some communities, a large population makes it unlikely that a human service profes-sional will encounter a consumer apart from the helping context. In many communities, however, it is likely that we will meet clients, not only on the street but also in social groups, religious organizations, and service clubs.

What is involved in Eloise's anecdote? What is at risk?

Whose issue is this? Eloise's   Yes ____   No ____

Client's   Yes ____   No ____

Ethical Guidelines

What values, ethical principles, and professional guidelines are relevant?

Do you think this type of situation reflects a dual or a multiple relationship? Explain your thoughts.

Action Alternatives

List at least three possible alternatives for Eloise.

Who should make the decision as to the most preferable action? Explain your thinking.

Class Discussion

Share your ideas about ways to prevent this from becoming an issue for entry-level professionals.

ACQUAINTANCES AND HELPERS: FOUR EXPERIENCES

Ramona

As a student intern in an agency that serves the general population, I was faced with counseling the child of another student at my college. I wasn't sure I could be effective if we knew each other and I didn't want it to be uncomfortable for her and her child, due to some very sensitive and personal problems they faced as a family.

Jessica

Three people I graduated from high school with were admitted to the mental hospital where I did my internship. It was very awkward. I had not seen them in such a long time and now I had access to their medical records, and, at times, I would chart their progress and sit in on their therapy sessions. I approached these individuals separately and explained that my internship was a training period for an occupation I was very serious about pursuing. I assured them of confidentiality. In the company of other patients, I maintained a professional demeanor and with my old friends I was slightly more approachable during working hours. After hours I would pay friendly visits to them.

Della

As a practicum student at a mental health center, I work one on one with clients. A woman came in who I knew from when we were both in prison and in treatment. If I decided not to work with her, she would have had to wait weeks to see one of the full-time staff members. She and my supervisor both were comfortable with my working with her. After some strong soul searching I came to the decision to go ahead and work with her.

The Issue

Ramona, Jessica, and Della wrote about similar situations. Jessica and Della told us how they took action to handle the dilemmas early in their helping relationships.

Ethical Guidelines

What professional guidelines are relevant?

Are there any relevant legal considerations?

Are there other relevant clinical issues?

Action Alternatives

If, in your internship, you encountered a friend or acquaintance who was also a client, what would you want to do?

What should you do? Explain your thinking.

Valerie

I was working with a family as a case aide. Their adult daughter and I became acquainted socially. We wanted to develop our relationship further. In the context of family services, she could be considered a client, but she lived on her own, separate from the family. In that context, she was probably not considered a client. I was taught in my human service program that while social relationships with clients are dual relationships, there is more latitude for this than with other dual relationships, like sexual relationships.

The Issue

Do you agree that this might be a dual relationship? Explain your thinking.

Resolving the Dilemma

Should Valerie talk with anyone about her decision? Who? Why?

Action

What do you think Valerie should do? Why?

Class Discussion

1. In working with a friend or acquaintance, what would you do to make sure your professional judgment was clear and that you were not risking harm to or exploitation of the client?
2. You ask a friend or acquaintance who is your client if she is uncomfortable. Would you believe her response? Why or why not?
3. Do you think the ethical issues in working with members of your own family are the same as those involved in working with friends or acquaintances? Why or why not?
4. How would you decide whether to develop a social relationship with someone who had previously been a client?

EXCHANGE OF SERVICES

Yolanda and Emma

While I was working as a teacher's aide in an adult education classroom, I met Emma, a student. Emma needed extra help to understand the lessons, so I translated the lessons and tutored her on my own time. Because Emma had no money to pay me, we agreed that she would work for me, cleaning my house in exchange for the tutoring. In Emma's and my culture this is not an ethical dilemma nor is it a problem to find employment this way.

The Issue

Is this Yolanda's ethical issue?   Yes ____   No ____

Is this Emma's ethical issue?   Yes ____   No ____

How might this arrangement be beneficial to Emma?

How might it harm her?

Ethical Guidelines

Do values and ethical principles really differ with culture?

In making your own ethical decisions, are you most likely to apply the values with which you were raised? Explain your thinking.

What guidance does the *Ethical Standards of Human Service Professionals* give Yolanda?

Evaluating the Action

Was Yolanda's action consistent with Emma's and
        her own values?   Yes _____   No _____
Did her action meet the test of universality?   Yes _____   No _____
Did her action meet the test of publicity?   Yes _____   No _____
Did her action meet the test of justice?   Yes _____   No _____

Predict the consequences of Yolanda's action. Are they certain? Are they probable? Are they possible? Are they unlikely?

Do you approve Yolanda's decision? Explain your thinking.

Class Discussion

1. Share your thoughts about the influence of culture on values and ethical principles.
2. Do you believe that professional ethical standards override personal ethical preferences? Why or why not?

A PROFESSIONAL'S CONCERN ABOUT HIS CLIENTS' SAFETY

Nikolai

I work with clients in an evening program where they often don't have transportation home. I find it difficult to leave clients late at night in dangerous neighborhoods, inclement weather, or alone with an infant.

The Issue

What type of issue is this?

Clinical?	Yes ____	No ____
Legal?	Yes ____	No ____
Ethical?	Yes ____	No ____

What are the relevant situational features?

Ethical Guidelines

What values and principles are pertinent?

Are any statements in the *Ethical Standards of Human Service Professionals* relevant to Nikolai's issue?

Action Alternatives

If you were Nikolai, would you want to offer these clients a ride? Identify the possible consequences of providing transportation to clients in your personal vehicle.

What other options does Nikolai have?

Evaluating the Alternatives

Cross out any alternatives listed above that you consider inconsistent with your values and principles and with professional guidelines.

Eliminate any alternatives listed above for which you think there would be no resources or support.

Eliminate any alternatives that don't pass the tests of universality, publicity, and justice.

Predict the possible consequences of the remaining alternatives.

Rank the remaining alternatives in order of preference.

Selecting the Action

Select the action you consider best. Is it the one you ranked highest? If not, evaluate why you selected it over the one you had ranked highest.

Class Discussion

1. What do you think is the best course of action for Nikolai? Why?
2. Review Statement 13 in the *Ethical Standards of Human Service Professionals*. Is there a need for social action in your community or at local agencies to better protect clients from dangers imposed by getting transportation to obtain services? Discuss what you know and what is being done.

MONEY CHANGING HANDS: THREE EXPERIENCES

Luis

My field practicum was in a large residential setting for elderly and demented clients. I had developed a relationship with Mr. Rodriguez—we spoke together in Spanish, I translated for him to other staff, and I helped him participate in activities. One morning in his room, he gave me $400 in cash, saying it was a gift for me to keep.

The Issue

What are the ethical issues involved in a human service professional's accepting money, freely offered, from a client?

Are there also legal or clinical issues? Explain your thinking.

Action Alternatives

If you were Luis, would you have been tempted to keep the money?

What should he have done?

Clay and Joe

I work in a residential setting with children who have developmental disabilities. Joe was badly in need of a pair of sneakers. Money for clothing is allocated for each child on a weekly basis. I had been asking for money to get his shoes for almost three weeks and failed to get the money from my supervisor. I bought the shoes with money from my pocket. Later I was reimbursed for the money I spent.

The Issue

Why do you think Clay decided to buy the shoes out of his own money?

Describe the ethical issue Clay faced.

Are there also other issues?

Ethical Guidelines

What values are involved?

What professional guidelines are involved?

Christian and the Volunteer

A volunteer at our agency was helping a child in a big sister–little sister relationship. The volunteer took it on herself to hire a psychologist to help the child. The child's parent (with whom the child lived) gave permission. It was forbidden by the agency, but by the time I found out, the sessions were already in progress.

The Issue

Why do you think the volunteer "took it on herself to hire a psychologist"?

Were there ethical aspects to the volunteer's decision? Explain your answer.

Describe the ethical issue Christian faced.

Ethical Guidelines

What values and ethical principles are involved?

What professional guidelines are relevant?

What laws and regulations are involved?

Conflicts

If you were the volunteer, what internal conflicts do you think you would have faced?

If you were Christian, what internal conflicts do you think you would have faced?

Describe the conflicts among the volunteer, the agency, and Christian.

How could they minimize these conflicts?

Resolving the Conflicts
What do you think the participants should do to resolve this?

Action Alternatives
What can Christian do? List as many options as you can think of.

Evaluating the Alternatives
Which alternatives do you think the child and her parent would find acceptable? Explain your answer. What further information would help you answer this question better?

Cross out any alternatives that are inconsistent with relevant ethical principles and/or the child's and parent's preferences.

Cross out those alternatives for which there are no resources or support.

Cross out any alternatives that don't pass the tests of universality, publicity, and justice.

Predict the possible consequences of the remaining alternatives.

Rank the remaining acceptable alternatives in order of priority.

Action
What should Christian do?

Is this the alternative you ranked as 1? If not, why not?

Class Discussion

1. Discuss how the situations described by Luis, Clay, and Christian are ethically similar and/or ethically different.
2. Do these situations represent dual relationships?
3. How can human service professionals best evaluate whether a dual or multiple relationship with a client "may increase the risk of harm to, or exploitation of, clients, and may impair their professional judgment" (Statement 6, *Ethical Standards of Human Service Professionals*)?

RESPONDING TO A COLLEAGUE'S DUAL RELATIONSHIP

Louise and Isabella

I knew another student, Isabella, had become personally involved with a male client in the chemical dependency program where we were both doing our field practicums.

The Issue
Describe Louise's issue in ethical terms.

Ethical Guidelines
What professional guidelines are relevant?

Action Alternatives
What are Louise's options for action?

Evaluating the Alternatives
Describe the potential consequences of each alternative.

Action
What do you think Louise should do?

Class Discussion

1. Review Statement 24 in the *Ethical Standards of Human Service Professionals*. Do you all agree about the steps Louise should take?
2. If you were Louise, would you be most likely to do what you should do—or something else? Why?

PERSONAL DISCLOSURE

Elaine and Helena

The ethical issue that comes to mind is that of when to make a personal disclosure to a client, especially when the disclosure is of something that would be considered negative about myself. In my field placement I worked with women who lived in abusive relationships. One woman, Helena, had low self-esteem and felt that she would fail at any attempt to reach goals. She felt life was not worth living. I used to be in an abusive relationship and still sometimes, even though I am a student in a human service program, feel doomed to fail. If I disclosed this, would the commonality help Helena? Or would it limit my ability to help her? Would I just be unloading on her—meeting my own needs?

The Issue

Describe the ethical and clinical issues that Elaine is facing.

Ethical Guidelines

What professional guidelines are relevant to Elaine's situation?

Resolving the Conflict

Do you think Elaine can resolve the issue on her own? Explain your answer.

With whom might Elaine consult about this?

Class Discussion

1. Self-help groups rely on self-disclosure; it is accepted that participants can be meeting their own as well as others' needs at the same time through this self-disclosure. Is there a difference between the relationships in a self-help environment and a professional helping relationship? Should there be a difference?
2. How can helper self-disclosure benefit the client? How might it harm the client?

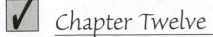

Chapter Twelve

Relationships with Colleagues and Supervisors in the Work Setting

The nice thing about teamwork is that you always have others on your side.
—Margaret Carty

Entry-level professionals work closely with colleagues in settings that encourage getting work done efficiently. The nature of the working relationships they develop with their colleagues influences how difficult their own work loads are and whether others support and assist them. And that, in turn, influences their job satisfaction, the level of service they give to consumers, and how long they stay in the job. Success in working as a team can mean the development of interrelationships that encourage openness, challenge, and mutual support. It can also mean minimizing conflict, thus reducing the time and effort spent in identifying and resolving disagreements.

The process of **socialization**—seldom acknowledged openly—to the specific work environment and work group is intense. Most new professionals join the team by quickly accepting the norms, values, and beliefs that characterize their employment setting and organizational culture.

This chapter presents anecdotes from entry-level professionals describing issues they have faced in working with colleagues. Most reflect situations in which the professional writing the anecdote had not accepted the norms and values of the work group—and, as a result, was not accepted by coworkers.

CONFLICTS WITH COWORKERS' PERFORMANCE STANDARDS

Wendy

My greatest dilemma occurred in a residential community-based group home with entry-level colleagues who displayed very little professionalism in relation to the clients or other staff. This was difficult because I strive to have above-average job performance; this often made coworkers uncomfortable with their performance and with me. I felt the problem occurred because most of the entry-level personnel had had no formal education in human services and were not committed to excellence in service.

The Issue

What is Wendy's responsibility to her clients?

What is Wendy's responsibility to her colleagues—coworkers?

What is Wendy's responsibility to herself?

Action Alternatives

Should Wendy change her standards for her own job performance so her coworkers will accept her more fully?

In what ways might changing her standards contribute to better services to the clients?

In what ways might changing her standards contribute to poorer client services?

Class Discussion

1. Discuss how you should relate to workers who have less human service education than you have.
2. Identify ways in which you might maintain high standards for your own behavior while avoiding or minimizing conflict with your coworkers.

PEER PRECEPTORSHIP

Ralph and Omar

I work as a residential technician in a crisis center. We deal with a lot of troubled teens. I was assigned to train a new residential tech, Omar. As time went on, I discovered that Omar's boundaries with our residents were low: He often pushed them, apparently as a playful gesture. My talking to him about this did not seem to help.

The Issue

Was this Ralph's issue?	Yes _____	No _____
Was this Omar's issue?	Yes _____	No _____
Was this the supervisor's issue?	Yes _____	No _____

Ralph says he was assigned to be Omar's trainer. What do you think were Ralph's responsibilities in his relationship with Omar?

What do you think were Omar's responsibilities in his relationship with Ralph?

Have you ever been in a work role where peer preceptorship was used in the orientation and training of new employees?

If you have seen peer preceptorship used, what benefits did you see from it?

What problems occurred with it?

Evaluating the Alternatives

Consider the following possible actions: (1) Ralph could report Omar to his supervisor, (2) Ralph could continue to talk with Omar about boundaries, (3) Ralph could let it go, hoping that the supervisor would notice Omar's behavior eventually.

Describe the most likely consequences of each of these three actions. How would each affect Ralph's relationship with Omar? How would it affect the residents' well-being? How would it affect Ralph's job and his relationship with the supervisor?

Action

If you were Ralph, which of these three actions would you most likely take?

Consider your preference. Are you being guided by your personal needs, your personal values, or professional guidelines?

Class Discussion

Discuss the benefits of and risks in using peer preceptorship for new employees.

WHISTLE BLOWING: TWO EXPERIENCES

I am speaking now of the highest duty we owe our friends, the noblest, the most sacred—that of keeping their own nobleness, goodness, pure and incorrupt. . . . If we let our friend become cold and selfish and exacting without a remonstrance, we are no true lover, no true friend.

—Harriet Beecher Stowe, 1865

Hazel

I work part-time in a nursing home doing personal care. One evening I witnessed a female resident fall. The nursing assistant put the resident back in her chair and went about her business. I called the nurse on call, who came over to see the resident. The nursing assistant was suspended for two weeks and now won't speak to me.

The Issue

Many of us, facing a situation like this in which we observe a colleague fail to take action that might help a client, initially react with the childhood rule, "Don't be a tattletale!" We might:

- Pretend we didn't witness the event.
- Tell ourselves: "It's none of my business."
- Assume the consequences are minimal: "She falls all the time—she's probably not hurt."
- Pass the responsibility on to someone else: "If they didn't expect us to do so much with so few staff, that wouldn't have happened! What can we do, taking care of 15 patients at a time?"
- Identify with the colleague: "I wouldn't want anyone else to interfere with my decision."
- Worry about the consequences for ourselves: "If I report the nursing assistant, she and the rest of the nursing assistants will get mad at me. I don't like to have others mad at me."

Describe how you think you would have felt initially if you had been Hazel.

What is the clinical issue here?

What is the legal issue?

What are the personal issues for Hazel and the nursing assistant?

Ethical Guidelines

What values and ethical principles did Hazel apply?

Review Statement 24 in the *Ethical Standards of Human Service Professionals.* Do you think you will find it difficult to do something about a colleague's unprofessional behavior?

Jeffrey

At the nursing home where I work as an activities aide, I know a member of the social services staff "borrowed" money from a resident to pay a personal bill. We are not allowed to borrow money or to accept gifts from residents. I told my boss, who reported it to the administrator. The staff started treating me like a "tattletale." The coworker was fired, but only after she made a huge scene.

The Issue

In Jeffrey's story, bodily harm to the resident is not an issue. Some human service professionals would describe their ethical obligations differently when the principle of the protection of life is not involved. Some professionals would justify their borrowing from the resident's account because they plan to pay the money back after their next paycheck and they know the resident won't be using the money for anything in the meantime.

What do you think?

What are the issues here?

Ethical Guidelines

What ethical values and principles did Jeffrey apply?

Review Statements 5 and 6 in the *Ethical Standards of Human Service Professionals.* Do either or both of these statements seem pertinent to Jeffrey's situation? Why or why not?

Class Discussion

1. Discuss how you might respond to unprofessional behavior in your colleagues. What options would you have?
2. What support is available in your community, at agencies, or in your college to help you face such decisions?

A COWORKER'S REQUEST

Rose and Harriet

We don't have a time clock at work and the supervisor is auditing our hours. My co-worker and friend, Harriet, asked me to verify that she was at the agency for 40 hours this week. We work different schedules. I was at work with her for 15 hours this week; I really don't know if she was there the other 25 hours.

The Issue

Harriet is Rose's friend. What do you think she would want to do?

Ethical Guidelines

What personal ethical principles might be involved?

Action Alternatives

List as many possible things Rose could do as you can think of.

Evaluating the Alternatives

What do you think might happen to Rose's relationship with Harriet if she does not verify the full 40 hours for her?

What may happen to Rose if she does verify the full 40 hours?

What are the possible consequences of the options you listed?

Action

What should Rose do?

Class Discussion

1. Discuss among yourselves and with your faculty how and why such monitoring of staff hours occurs. Does it mean the administration does not trust its employees? What other reasons are there?
2. Share the possible consequences you identified.
3. How would you weigh the risks of verifying or not verifying?

REPORTING WORKPLACE HARASSMENT

Evelyn

I work in a governmental human service agency. I heard a coordinator—who worked with both volunteers and paid staff—start conversations with volunteers about issues in the news. Each time it would come out as a racial discussion and he would use derogatory remarks that bothered me. I knew it was against the law for him to do this and I felt it was not right, but I could not bring myself to confront him or report him to my supervisor. After many incidents of the coordinator making more slurs and racial remarks, I went to my supervisor, who in turn reported the incidents to people higher than her. One morning the coordinator confronted me as a result of his being reported, so I told him I believed his behavior was wrong.

The Issue

Is this Evelyn's issue? Why or why not?

Do you believe Evelyn should have done anything differently in this situation? Explain your thinking.

Review Statement 25 in the *Ethical Standards of Human Service Professionals*. Should the administrators have kept Evelyn's identity confidential in talking with the coordinator? Why or why not?

How do the relationships among the participants in this situation influence the ethical dilemma for Evelyn?

Ethical Guidelines

What values and ethical principles are involved?

Does the *Ethical Standards of Human Service Professionals* have any other standards that are relevant?

Conflicts

Describe the internal conflicts you would experience if you were Evelyn.

Could you minimize them?

Action Alternatives

If you faced this situation at your workplace, what are the possible courses of action you could take? List as many as you can.

What would you be most comfortable doing? Why?

Class Discussion

1. Explore your understanding of the legal mandates pertaining to harassment related to race.
2. How assertively do you think we should act as advocates for other staff or volunteers?

REPORTING COWORKERS' UNPROFESSIONAL BEHAVIOR: TWO EXPERIENCES

Expedients are for the hour; principles for the ages.

—Henry Ward Beecher

John and Roderick

When I graduated from my human service program, I obtained a position working in an adolescent treatment facility. I noticed that most of the staff who have been employed at the facility for very long didn't "make waves." They completed their assigned responsibilities, reported to the incoming shift, and went home.

> One employee, Roderick, had been employed at the facility for a couple of years. Roderick generally developed constructive relationships with the adolescents, frequently came in on his days off to cover when other staff members were ill, and was close to the supervisor. Working with Roderick on weekends, I observed him coming to work intoxicated.
>
> When I asked other employees about this, they agreed that Roderick frequently came to work intoxicated, but no one wanted to talk about it to supervisors. I found out that the person whose position I took—Martha—had reported Roderick's drinking to the supervisor. Martha had been accused by the supervisor of gossiping and had been fired shortly afterwards.
>
> Having a family to support, I knew there were very few available jobs in the community—if I lost my job, I would be unemployed for a long time.

The Issue

Describe your thoughts and reactions to John's anecdote.

In what ways is this an ethical issue?

In what ways is it a legal issue?

In what ways is it a clinical issue?

Compare and contrast the issue from John's, Roderick's, the supervisor's, the clients', and the agency's perspectives.

Ethical Guidelines

What are your personal values in relation to this situation? Do you think there are any societal values that are similar to or different from your personal values?

What guidance does the *Ethical Standards of Human Service Professionals* provide?

What is more important: John's ethical responsibility to clients and the profession or John's responsibilities to his family and dependents? Do you think most entry-level human service professionals would agree with you and base their action on this?

Action Alternatives

List as many possible things John could do as you can think of.

Evaluating the Alternatives

Draw a line through those alternatives that you consider ethically unacceptable.

Do the remaining alternatives pass the tests of universality, publicity, and justice? Draw a line through any that don't.

Describe the possible consequences of the remaining actions in your list.

Rank the remaining actions, numbering the one you think is the best with a 1.

Review your ranking. Why did you put them in this order? What ethical principles did you use? What consequences seemed most important?

Which did you follow most closely: your personal standards, societal standards, or professional guidelines?

How do you think others in your class will respond to your decisions?

Ramona, Her Colleagues, and Kathy

While working in a program for offenders, I noticed that my supervisor, Kathy, frequently wore clothing that was quite revealing. Some other counselors also engaged in sexually inappropriate behavior on the job with each other and, occasionally, with offenders. A male counselor in the program, Bob, was accused by a female counselor, Lita, of sexual harassment. Kathy put Bob on a work improvement program as a result of this accusation.

As I saw it, Bob was one of the few staff members who did not engage in inappropriate behaviors with other staff and clients. I wanted the facility to maintain the highest standard of care and a good reputation in the community. I was pretty sure that if I brought up the patterns of behavior I had observed to Kathy or to Kathy's superior, I would be put on a work improvement program or be fired—and the behavior patterns would not change.

The Issue
How is Ramona's dilemma similar ethically to John's?

How is it different?

Ethical Guidelines

What are your personal values in relation to Ramona's situation? Do you think there are any societal values that are similar to or different from your personal values?

What guidance does the *Ethical Standards of Human Service Professionals* provide?

What is more important: Ramona's ethical responsibility to the program and the clients or her need to prevent harm to herself? Do you think most entry-level human service professionals would agree with you and base their action on this?

Action Alternatives

List as many possible things Ramona could do as you can think of.

Evaluating the Alternatives

Draw a line through those alternatives that you consider ethically unacceptable.

Do the remaining alternatives pass the tests of universality, publicity, and justice? Draw a line through any that don't.

Describe the possible consequences of those actions you consider ethically acceptable.

Rank your possible actions, numbering the one you think is the best with a 1.

Review your ranking. Why did you put them in this order?

How do you think others in your class will respond to your decisions?

Class Discussion

1. Consider how you think you will cope when faced with a situation in which doing the ethically correct thing means you might lose your job.
2. Do your local community standards seem to support doing the most expedient thing or the most ethical thing?
3. Are there regulatory agencies that might help if you were faced with John's and Ramona's dilemmas? Are there professional groups that would provide guidance and support in your decision making?

Chapter Thirteen

Professionals, Agencies, and Other Entities

We believe that students need to know and understand the effects of values on policy, planning, and service delivery.

—Tricia McClam and Marianne Woodside, 1993

Human service agencies—board members, administrators, and staff members—often face difficult ethical decisions. Most maintain a high degree of ethical and legal practice. This makes it easier for us as employees to recognize and manage the ethical and legal dilemmas that we face on a daily basis when working with clients and colleagues.

Occasionally, however, agencies do not follow expected standards of ethical or legal practice. Professionals who work for these agencies must make decisions about how to respond to practices that may promote the agency or its administration at the expense of client well-being, that may send the wrong message about the agency to the community, or that may be illegal. In these situations, the agency may not be caught in its illegal or unethical activity unless the professional decides to become a **whistle blower.**

Statements 33 and 34 in the *Ethical Standards of Human Service Professionals* address our responsibility to our employer: The professional works to maintain employment conditions that promote high-quality client services, and when there is a conflict between responsibilities to employers and clients, speaks up about the conflict and works to resolve it. How, though, are you to recognize these agency issues? What about the situations—often political—that arise in which community members are seeking information about the agency and you're not sure whether they will use the information to help or harm the agency? What are the internal and external dilemmas involved? How can you make a decision that protects you, your clients, the agency, and the community?

It is particularly difficult for students in their field practicums and for entry-level professionals to cope with these situations: They don't have a broad base of information and experience from which to judge the practices of an agency. They typically have very little power within the agency from which to work for change. They frequently recognize that most actions they could take would jeopardize their placement or employment status and, therefore, the well-being of themselves and their own dependents.

FUND RAISING

Lydia

I work in a women's and children's domestic violence shelter that has suffered many funding cutbacks, so it is putting more efforts into fund raising. Of course, many episodes of family violence occur while the perpetrator—and sometimes the victim—is under the influence of alcohol or drugs. Is it ethical for the shelter to raise money through a wine-tasting party? How about a "fun run" with the support of a local beer wholesaler?

The Issue

There are conflicting ethical viewpoints here.

Describe the thinking of someone who would consider such fund-raising activities to be ethical.

Describe the thinking of someone who would consider such activities unethical.

What do you think?

Ethical Guidelines

What values and professional guidelines do you think are most important?

What other factors are involved?

Class Discussion

The board is particularly responsible for making sure its human service agency fulfills its mission. To ensure that the mission is not jeopardized, how do you think a board should proceed in considering money-raising ideas? If you were a board member, how would you want your agency to approach the decision?

THE PUBLIC'S QUESTIONS ABOUT THE AGENCY

Flora

I worked on a crisis line as part of my field practicum. The staff told me that some people in the community—not in crisis—would call from time to time and start asking about the sexual preferences of staff members and volunteers: "Is she a lesbian? Is he gay?" They sometimes would ask if you were homosexual. If I answered either "yes" or "no," I risked harming other volunteers, staff, or myself—compounding the stereotyping or being perceived as a liar. If I refused to answer, telling the caller it is none of their business and is irrelevant, then the agency risked losing some community support.

The Issue

Small agencies in small communities are particularly sensitive to public scrutiny. Flora says that anonymous members of the community call with very intrusive questions about the sexual preferences of staff members. Consider not only the questions Flora describes (it's pretty easy to defend an answer of "This is none of your business!"), but also less intrusive inquiries. Statement 32 of the *Ethical Standards of Human Service Professionals* says that we adhere to commitments made to employers. One of the (often implicit) commitments we make to employers is to be loyal. Another is to help them maintain their standing in the community.

How do you think Flora wants to answer the questions she reports?

How do you think she should answer these questions?

What have you been asked by others about your employer or field placement agency?

What have you said about your employer or field placement agency in public?

What do you think of that ethically?

Conflict

Have you experienced a conflict between your loyalty to the agency and your personal or professional ethical principles? Explain it.

Class Discussion

What do you think are the best ways to show loyalty to your human service employer?

THE OPTION TO BECOME A WHISTLE BLOWER: THREE EXPERIENCES

Inez

I was working as a teacher in a child day-care center and witnessed violations of the licensing requirements. Examples: The director and his assistants hid children during an inspection to get the ratio of students and teachers down. To save money, they regularly changed the posted menu of meals to much less nutritious meals. When I voiced my concerns, my supervisor—the director—threatened to dismiss me. I reported the violations after some children were locked in a closet. I was fired by the director, who guessed I had made the report. He told me that he would see to it that I would never be able to work in another day-care center.

The Issue

Inez is describing a failure to maintain standards that meet licensing guidelines for child day-care centers and deliberate efforts to deceive site inspectors. She had to decide between her own willingness to risk her employment status and her concern about the safety and well-being of the children.

In this situation it is easy to say that she would have had the grounds to file legal action against the employer for unfair dismissal, but, in reality, very few employees at entry level who are illegally fired from their positions even attempt to contest the dismissal, much less succeed. It is in the nature of entry-level employment that the employer has the upper hand because of power and knowledge of legal requirements in personnel matters.

The network among human service providers also lends credibility to her boss's claim that he could "see to it that I would never be able to work in another day-care center."

Ethical Guidelines

What personal and societal values do you think were involved for Inez?

What professional guidelines are relevant?

Conflicts

Review the principles involved. Do you think Inez experienced internal conflict about this dilemma? Explain your answer.

Review the anecdote. Do you think Inez experienced external conflict? Explain your answer.

Resolving the Conflicts

Inez doesn't tell us whether she sought assistance. What assistance do you think might have been available for her to help her resolve the conflict and her dilemma?

Action Alternatives

Can you identify any alternatives for Inez that might have been at least as good as the one she selected, or possibly better? Describe them.

Elizabeth

In the residential school where I teach, the developmentally disabled students have programs and tasks to complete. It is important that you understand that based on my experience with many similar residential programs, this school provides very good services to its students and is an excellent placement for them.

Individualized Educational Programs (IEPs), established by our behavior specialists, direct our work with the students. Some of the tasks and programs set for the students in these IEPs are very unrealistic—for example, we are expected to be teaching one student to brush his teeth independently, yet he is incontinent, oblivious to any of his body's needs, and unable to control his arms or legs. Throughout the day we (residential workers/teachers) are required to record data on student behaviors.

Our behavior specialists are doing research, publishing their findings, and gaining national recognition for the effectiveness of their approaches. The real results of our interventions and teaching do not correspond to the results these behavior specialists/researchers want. Documentation that supports their research efforts favorably has become more important than accurate documentation about the students. If I follow the IEPs and record accurate data, it will make me look less competent than those staff members who are recording favorable results. If I am less accurate in recording data, the programs will look like they are working. If I, an entry-level professional, try to change the programs to more realistic ones and record the data correctly, I will be labeled as someone who rocks the boat, making my relationships with the other staff difficult and possibly endangering my job.

The Issue

Elizabeth is facing a situation in which she knows of unethical research methodology and the publishing of inaccurate results. At best, such research practices may confuse the efforts and findings of other researchers. At worst, such practices can lead to unrealistic habilitation expectations for clients, unfair funding criteria, and unreachable program guidelines. This could result in disadvantage and possible harm to developmentally disabled students served by this or other agencies. Yet, despite the irregularities in research methodology, Elizabeth—who has worked in many such programs—tells us that this school is among the best when judged by the services it provides to clients.

Describe the ethical dilemma that Elizabeth is facing.

Is the ethical dilemma Elizabeth's? Or is it someone else's responsibility? Defend your answer.

Ethical Guidelines

What personal values and principles, societal values, and professional guidelines are involved?

Might any legal requirements be pertinent?

Conflicts

Describe the internal conflicts that Elizabeth might be experiencing.

What are the external conflicts she is experiencing?

Resolving the Conflicts

Where might Elizabeth get assistance in deciding what to do?

Action Alternatives

List all the options you can think of for Elizabeth.

Evaluating the Alternatives

Cross out the alternatives that you consider to be poor ethical choices. Why do you think they are poor choices?

Predict the consequences of the alternatives that you consider to be good ethical choices.

Rank these alternatives in order from most to least preferred.

Evaluating the Preferred Action

Describe why you think the one you ranked highest is best.

Bruce

I work in an agency that is not providing the services agreed to in exchange for grant money. Its brochures advertise the services as available and the agency documentation shows the services as provided, so the grantor believes the services are in place. The staff doesn't have the necessary resources, so those directly responsible for the care of the individuals who should be receiving the services are under a lot of stress. The consumers were promised something and are not getting it.

The Issue

Describe Bruce's issue. What kind of issue is it? Who is involved? Whose responsibility is it? What is at risk? Are there relevant situational features?

Ethical Guidelines

What values, ethical principles, and professional guidelines are pertinent?

Is there conflict among these guidelines? If so, how would you minimize the conflict?

Action Alternatives

List, evaluate, and rank Bruce's alternatives.

Class Discussion

1. Share your thoughts and feelings about Inez's, Elizabeth's, and Bruce's positions and dilemmas.
2. How are Inez's, Elizabeth's, and Bruce's ethical issues similar? How are they different?
3. What do you think you would do if you faced issues like these?

FURTHER EXPLORATION

Investigate what institutional review committees are. What are their roles in protecting client rights and the quality of human research? Do any local human service agencies have institutional review committees? If so, ask a member to come to your class and talk about how to handle concerns with research ethics.

Applying Ethical Thinking in Your Own Experience

Education moves you from the realm of cocksure ignorance to the sphere of thoughtful uncertainty.

—Anonymous

In the previous chapters of this workbook, I have asked you to respond to ethical issues that have been reported by other human service professionals. In this chapter I am asking you to consider the ethical issues that are part of your own experience.

Consider for a few moments: What ethical issues and dilemmas have you faced? How have you resolved those issues—or have you resolved them? How do you rank ethical principles? What ethical issues and dilemmas are common in your community? How do you think they should be addressed? What are you thinking about yourself and your chosen career in human services?

And so, we begin the next step of a process that will continue throughout your career: the deliberate application of ethical decision making to your own professional experiences. First, I want to remind you of a couple of definitions:

- *Ethical issue*—A matter that involves morality, rules, or standards by which one judges right and wrong. It may seem easy to resolve (the correct action is obvious to you) or difficult (the correct action is not clear).
- *Ethical dilemma*—An ethical issue that is especially complex because every option for action will result in some degree of harm or wrongdoing. Our ethical duties are in conflict and we can see no totally right action. Even taking no action is wrong.

YOUR ETHICAL ISSUES AND DILEMMAS

One of Your Own Ethical Issues

The issue. Describe as completely as possible one common ethical issue that you face in your own experience.

Ethical guidelines. What values, principles, and other guidelines are relevant?

Action alternatives. What options are there?

Selecting and evaluating an action. How do you usually resolve this issue?

Implications. What do you think—ethically—of that resolution?

One of Your Own Ethical Dilemmas

The issue. Describe one ethical dilemma that you find to be particularly troubling in your role as a student or professional in human services. Include as much detail (as many facts) as you can.

Ethical guidelines. What values, principles, and other guidelines are relevant?

Conflicts. Describe the conflicts. What makes it a dilemma?

Resolving the conflicts. What assistance have you sought with this decision? Did you get that assistance?

Action alternatives. What options are there?

Selecting and evaluating an action. Has this issue been resolved?

Implications. If it hasn't been resolved, why not? If it has been resolved, what do you think—ethically—of that resolution?

Class Discussion

1. Report the issues and dilemmas you've identified. There will probably be some that are shared among you.
2. On an issue-by-issue basis, explore the ethical guidelines, action alternatives, and selection and evaluation of action.
3. For each issue: Is there substantial agreement among you or do you disagree? Is that okay or does it represent an ethical problem?

RANKING OF ETHICAL PRINCIPLES[1]

Following is a list of the ethical principles that were presented in chapter 1. Now that you have completed the exercises in the workbook, your understanding of these ethical principles and their significance in your own decision making in human services has developed. This exercise is in two parts: In the first part you rank them according to your own beliefs. In the second, you compare your rankings with those of others in your class and attempt to develop a ranking by consensus among you.

Individual Work

In Column 1 place a number (between 1 and 15) that indicates your ranking of the principle in relation to all the other listed principles. Rank the principle you hold highest with a 1, the next with a 2, and so on.

	Column 1	Column 2
autonomy	_____	_____
beneficence	_____	_____
confidentiality	_____	_____
fidelity	_____	_____
finality	_____	_____
gratitude	_____	_____
justice	_____	_____
nonmaleficence	_____	_____
ordering	_____	_____
publicity	_____	_____
reparation	_____	_____
respect for persons	_____	_____
universality	_____	_____
utility	_____	_____
veracity	_____	_____

Small Group Work

Discuss the reasons for your rankings, using values, professional guidelines, and examples. Try to reach agreement on a ranking by group consensus. (Consensus is a group decision-making process in which a decision is made only when all members of the group have agreed to support the decision—as opposed, for example, to a decision by majority vote, in which a significant number of participants may disagree but are overruled by the majority.) In Column 2, enter numbers that reflect decisions by consensus.

Because of the differences among people and groups of people, the results of this will vary: You may find you agree on ranking very few or none of the principles; you may find you can agree on ranking those that are ranked highest, but not the rest; you may find you reach consensus on all of them.

After you have discussed ranking all the principles and entered numbers beside those on which you reached agreement:

1. Discuss the similarities and differences among yourselves. What are the sources of these similarities and differences? How do they influence your relationships?
2. How might your own beliefs affect your success in human services?

"DEAR CAREER..."[2]

Human services is not only a career, it's a commitment. Sometimes that commitment is a cause for celebration, other times it's frustrating. Wise professionals keep in touch with their thoughts and feelings about their career, using them to guide their development and directions.

We encourage our clients to write to a person or to inanimate objects to help them clarify their feelings and examine their thoughts and values. Some people keep a journal and address questions and concerns they have by writing to a problem in their lives as if it were able to understand. It's a healthy way to explore issues and reactions.

Write a letter to your career. It's not a letter you will mail, but rather it can serve as a springboard for personal growth or a mirror for personal reflection. Go ahead, tell your career what you think about it! Include: what you like, what you'd really like to be able to do, what you're unhappy with and want to change, what the stressors are, what goals you have, what conflicts in values you experience, what you'd like to learn or do, what brings you the most satisfaction. Don't edit your thinking. Let your thoughts and feelings find expression.

Write your "Dear Career" letter in the space provided on the next page.

Class Discussion

Ask volunteers to read their letters aloud. Respond, using the following questions or others that seem pertinent.

1. What can you do to increase your satisfaction with your career?
2. What can you do to decrease the stress of your job?
3. What does your ideal role or career look like?
4. Is human services a job, a career, a profession, or a mission for you?

Dear Career,

ETHICAL DILEMMAS IN YOUR OWN ACADEMIC AND SERVICE COMMUNITIES

In chapter 1 I mentioned an ethical dilemma faced by human service professionals in Arizona: their conflicting duties when working with clients who are undocumented aliens. Before you complete this workbook, I want you to consider the ethical issues and dilemmas that are common in your own professional communities, both academic and service.

Preparation

Decide how you will gather information about ethical issues and dilemmas that are common in your own community. You can do this individually or in your class group: Invite guest speakers to class, visit agencies, use your own knowledge if you already have some experience in human services in your community, or suggest another approach.

Gathering Information

Complete the activities you planned for gathering information about your community's ethical issues. Revise your activities as needed to gather more or different information.

Class Discussion

1. Share the information you've gained. Describe the issues.
2. Apply the ethical decision-making model in discussing each issue: What guidelines and standards are relevant? What are the conflicts? How might you resolve the conflicts—is assistance available? Generate, examine, and evaluate possible actions.
3. Identify at least three possible ethical action alternatives that you could use when faced with each issue.

NOTES

1. To review how some others have ranked ethical principles, see Lichtman (1996, pp. 246–248), Loewenberg and Dolgoff (1996, p. 63), and Reamer (1990, pp. 60–65).
2. Adapted from *Clinical Ethics and Values: Issues and Insights in a Changing Healthcare Environment* by D. B. Uustal (1993, pp. 46–47).

Appendix A

Ethical Codes and Standards of Other Helping Professions

- Ethical Standards of Alcoholism and Drug Abuse Counselors, National Association of Alcoholism and Drug Abuse Counselors (NAADAC, 1995)
- Code of Ethics and Standards of Practice, American Counseling Association (ACA, 1995)
- Ethical Principles of Psychologists and Code of Conduct, American Psychological Association (APA, 1992)
- Code of Ethics, National Association of Social Workers (NASW, 1996)

ETHICAL STANDARDS OF ALCOHOLISM AND DRUG ABUSE COUNSELORS (NATIONAL ASSOCIATION OF ALCOHOLISM AND DRUG ABUSE COUNSELORS)

Principle 1: Non-Discrimination

The NAADAC member shall not discriminate against clients or professionals based on race, religion, age, gender, disability, national ancestry, sexual orientation or economic condition.

a. The NAADAC member shall avoid bringing personal or professional issues into the counseling relationship. Through an awareness of the impact of stereotyping and discrimination, the member guards the individual rights and personal dignity of clients.

b. The NAADAC member shall be knowledgeable about disabling conditions, demonstrate empathy and personal emotional comfort in interactions with clients with disabilities, and make available physical, sensory and cognitive accommodations that allow clients with disabilities to receive services.

Principle 2: Responsibility

The NAADAC member shall espouse objectivity and integrity, and maintain the highest standards in the services the member offers.

a. The NAADAC member shall maintain respect for institutional policies and management functions of the agencies and institutions within which the services are being performed, but will take initiative toward improving such policies when it will better serve the interest of the client.

b. The NAADAC member, as educator, has a primary obligation to help others acquire knowledge and skills in dealing with the disease of alcoholism and drug abuse.

c. The NAADAC member who supervises others accepts the obligation to facilitate further professional development of these individuals by providing accurate and current information, timely evaluations and constructive consultation.

d. The NAADAC member who is aware of unethical conduct or of unprofessional modes of practice shall report such inappropriate behavior to the appropriate authority.

Principle 3: Competence

The NAADAC member shall recognize that the profession is founded on national standards of competency which promote the best interests of society, of the client, of the member and of the profession as a whole. The NAADAC member shall recognize the need for ongoing education as a component of professional competency.

a. The NAADAC member shall recognize boundaries and limitations of the member's competencies and not offer services or use techniques outside of these professional competencies.

b. The NAADAC member shall recognize the effect of impairment on professional performance and shall be willing to seek appropriate treatment for oneself or for a colleague. The member shall support peer assistance programs in this respect.

Principle 4: Legal and Moral Standards

The NAADAC member shall uphold the legal and accepted moral codes which pertain to professional conduct.

a. The NAADAC member shall be fully cognizant of all federal laws and laws of the member's respective state governing the practice of alcoholism and drug abuse counseling.

b. The NAADAC member shall not claim either directly or by implication, professional qualifications/affiliations that the member does not possess.

c. The NAADAC member shall ensure that products or services associated with or provided by the member by means of teaching, demonstration, publications or other types of media meet the ethical standards of this code.

Principle 5: Public Statements

The NAADAC member shall honestly respect the limits of present knowledge in public statements concerning alcoholism and drug abuse.

a. The NAADAC member, in making statements to clients, other professionals, and the general public shall state as fact only those matters which have been empirically validated as fact. All other opinions, speculations, and conjecture concerning the nature of alcoholism and drug abuse, its natural history, its treatment or any other matters which touch on the subject of alcoholism and drug abuse shall be represented as less than scientifically validated.

b. The NAADAC member shall acknowledge and accurately report the substantiation and support for statements made concerning the nature of alcoholism and drug abuse, its natural history, and its treatment. Such acknowledgment should extend to the source of the information and reliability of the method by which it was derived.

Principle 6: Publication Credit

The NAADAC member shall assign credit to all who have contributed to the published material and for the work upon which the publication is based.

a. The NAADAC member shall recognize joint authorship and major contributions of a professional nature made by one or more persons to a common project. The author who has made the principal contribution to a publication must be identified as first author.

b. The NAADAC member shall acknowledge in footnotes or in an introductory statement minor contributions of a professional nature, extensive clerical or similar assistance and other minor contributions.

c. The NAADAC member shall in no way violate the copyright of anyone by reproducing material in any form whatsoever, except in those ways which are allowed under the copyright laws. This involves direct violation of copyright as well as the passive assent to the violation of copyright by others.

Principle 7: Client Welfare

The NAADAC member shall promote the protection of the public health, safety and welfare and the best interest of the client as a primary guide in determining the conduct of all NAADAC members.

a. The NAADAC member shall disclose the member's code of ethics, professional loyalties and responsibilities to all clients.

b. The NAADAC member shall terminate a counseling or consulting relationship when it is reasonably clear to the member that the client is not benefiting from the relationship.

c. The NAADAC member shall hold the welfare of the client paramount when making any decisions or recommendations concerning referral, treatment procedures or termination of treatment.

d. The NAADAC member shall not use or encourage a client's participation in any demonstration, research or other non-treatment activities when such participation would have potential harmful consequences for the client or when the client is not fully informed. (See Principle 9)

e. The NAADAC member shall take care to provide services in an environment which will ensure the privacy and safety of the client at all times and ensure the appropriateness of service delivery.

Principle 8: Confidentiality

The NAADAC member working in the best interest of the client shall embrace, as a primary obligation, the duty of protecting client's rights under confidentiality and shall not disclose confidential information acquired in teaching, practice or investigation without appropriately executed consent.

a. The NAADAC member must provide the client his/her rights regarding confidentiality, in writing, as part of informing the client in any areas likely to affect the client's confidentiality. This includes the recording of the clinical interview, the use of material for insurance purposes, the use of material for training or observation by another party.
b. The NAADAC member shall make appropriate provisions for the maintenance of confidentiality and the ultimate disposition of confidential records. The member shall ensure that data obtained, including any form of electronic communication, are secured by the available security methodology. Data shall be limited to information that is necessary and appropriate to the services being provided and be accessible only to appropriate personnel.
c. The NAADAC member shall adhere to all federal and state laws regarding confidentiality and the member's responsibility to report clinical information in specific circumstances to the appropriate authorities.
d. The NAADAC member shall discuss the information obtained in clinical, consulting, or observational relationships only in the appropriate settings for professional purposes that are in the client's best interest. Written and oral reports must present only data germane and pursuant to the purpose of evaluation, diagnosis, progress, and compliance. Every effort shall be made to avoid undue invasion of privacy.
e. The NAADAC member shall use clinical and other material in teaching and/or writing only when there is no identifying information used about the parties involved.

Principle 9: Client Relationships

It is the responsibility of the NAADAC member to safeguard the integrity of the counseling relationship and to ensure that the client has reasonable access to effective treatment.

The NAADAC member shall provide the client and/or guardian with accurate and complete information regarding the extent of the potential professional relationship.

a. The NAADAC member shall inform the client and obtain the client's agreement in areas likely to affect the client's participation including the recording of an interview, the use of interview material for training purposes, and/or observation of an interview by another person.
b. The NAADAC member shall not engage in professional relationships or commitments that conflict with family members, friends, close associates, or others whose welfare might be jeopardized by such a dual relationship.
c. The NAADAC member shall not exploit relationships with current or former clients for personal gain, including social or business relationships.
d. The NAADAC member shall not under any circumstances engage in sexual behavior with current or former clients.
e. The NAADAC member shall not accept as clients anyone with whom they have engaged in sexual behavior.

Principal 10: Interprofessional Relationships

The NAADAC member shall treat colleagues with respect, courtesy, fairness, and good faith and shall afford the same to other professionals.

  a. The NAADAC member shall refrain from offering professional services to a client in counseling with another professional except with the knowledge of the other professional or after the termination of the client's relationship with the other professional.
  b. The NAADAC member shall cooperate with duly constituted professional ethics committees and promptly supply necessary information unless constrained by the demands of confidentiality.
  c. The NAADAC member shall not in any way exploit relationships with supervisees, employees, students, research participants or volunteers.

Principle 11: Remuneration

The NAADAC member shall establish financial arrangements in professional practice and in accord with the professional standards that safeguard the best interests of the client first, and then of the counselor, the agency, and the profession.

  a. The NAADAC member shall inform the client of all financial policies. In circumstances where an agency dictates explicit provisions with its staff for private consultations, clients shall be made fully aware of these policies.
  b. The NAADAC member shall consider the ability of a client to meet the financial cost in establishing rates for professional services.
  c. The NAADAC member shall not engage in fee splitting. The member shall not send or receive any commission or rebate or any other form of remuneration for referral of clients for professional services.
  d. The NAADAC member, in the practice of counseling, shall not at any time use one's relationship with clients for personal gain or for the profit of an agency or any commercial enterprise of any kind.
  e. The NAADAC member shall not accept a private fee for professional work with a person who is entitled to such services through an institution or agency unless the client is informed of such services and still requests private services.

Principle 12: Societal Obligations

The NAADAC member shall to the best of his/her abilities actively engage the legislative processes, educational institutions, and the general public to change public policy and legislation to make possible opportunities and choice of service for all human beings of any ethnic or social background whose lives are impaired by alcoholism and drug abuse.

Revised: 5/20/95

CODE OF ETHICS (AMERICAN COUNSELING ASSOCIATION)

Preamble

The American Counseling Association is an educational, scientific, and professional organization whose members are dedicated to the enhancement of human development throughout the life-span. Association members recognize diversity in our society and embrace a cross-cultural approach in support of the worth, dignity, potential, and uniqueness of each individual.

The specification of a code of ethics enables the association to clarify to current and future members, and to those served by members, the nature of the ethical responsibilities held in common by its members. As the code of ethics of the association, this document establishes principles that define the ethical behavior of association members. All members of the American Counseling Association are required to adhere to the Code of Ethics and the Standards of Practice. The Code of Ethics will serve as the basis for processing ethical complaints initiated against members of the association.

Section A: The Counseling Relationship

A.1. Client Welfare

a. *Primary Responsibility.*
   The primary responsibility of counselors is to respect the dignity and to promote the welfare of clients.

b. *Positive Growth and Development.*
   Counselors encourage client growth and development in ways that foster the clients' interest and welfare; counselors avoid fostering dependent counseling relationships.

c. *Counseling Plans.*
   Counselors and their clients work jointly in devising integrated, individual counseling plans that offer reasonable promise of success and are consistent with abilities and circumstances of clients. Counselors and clients regularly review counseling plans to ensure their continued viability and effectiveness, respecting clients' freedom of choice. (See A.3.b.)

d. *Family Involvement.*
   Counselors recognize that families are usually important in clients' lives and strive to enlist family understanding and involvement as a positive resource, when appropriate.

e. *Career and Employment Needs.*
   Counselors work with their clients in considering employment in jobs and circumstances that are consistent with the clients' overall abilities, vocational limitations, physical restrictions, general temperament, interest and aptitude patterns, social skills, education, general qualifications, and other relevant characteristics and needs. Counselors neither place nor participate in placing clients in positions that will result in damaging the interest and the welfare of clients, employers, or the public.

A.2. Respecting Diversity

a. *Nondiscrimination.*
   Counselors do not condone or engage in discrimination based on age, color, culture, disability, ethnic group, gender, race, religion, sexual orientation, marital status, or socioeconomic status. (See C.5.a., C.5.b., and D.1.i.)

b. *Respecting Differences.*
   Counselors will actively attempt to understand the diverse cultural backgrounds of the clients with whom they work. This includes, but is not limited to, learning how the counselor's own cultural/ethnic/racial identity impacts her or his values and beliefs about the counseling process. (See E.8. and F.2.i.)

A.3. Client Rights

a. *Disclosure to Clients.*

When counseling is initiated, and throughout the counseling process as necessary, counselors inform clients of the purposes, goals, techniques, procedures, limitations, potential risks and benefits of services to be performed, and other pertinent information. Counselors take steps to ensure that clients understand the implications of diagnosis, the intended use of tests and reports, fees, and billing arrangements. Clients have the right to expect confidentiality and to be provided with an explanation of its limitations, including supervision and/or treatment team professionals; to obtain clear information about their case records; to participate in the ongoing counseling plans; and to refuse any recommended services and be advised of the consequences of such refusal. (See E.5.a. and G.2.)

b. *Freedom of Choice.*

Counselors offer clients the freedom to choose whether to enter into a counseling relationship and to determine which professional(s) will provide counseling. Restrictions that limit choices of clients are fully explained. (See A.1.c.)

c. *Inability to Give Consent.*

When counseling minors or persons unable to give voluntary informed consent, counselors act in these clients' best interests. (See B.3.)

A.4. Clients Served by Others

If a client is receiving services from another mental health professional, counselors, with client consent, inform the professional persons already involved and develop clear agreements to avoid confusion and conflict for the client. (See C.6.c.)

A.5. Personal Needs and Values

a. *Personal Needs.*

In the counseling relationship, counselors are aware of the intimacy and responsibilities inherent in the counseling relationship, maintain respect for clients, and avoid actions that seek to meet their personal needs at the expense of clients.

b. *Personal Values.*

Counselors are aware of their own values, attitudes, beliefs, and behaviors and how these apply in a diverse society, and avoid imposing their values on clients. (See C.5.a.)

A.6. Dual Relationships

a. *Avoid When Possible.*

Counselors are aware of their influential positions with respect to clients, and they avoid exploiting the trust and dependency of clients. Counselors make every effort to avoid dual relationships with clients that could impair professional judgment or increase the risk of harm to clients. (Examples of such relationships include, but are not limited to, familial, social, financial, business, or close personal relationships with clients.) When a dual relationship cannot be avoided, counselors take appropriate professional precautions such as informed consent, consultation, supervision, and documentation to ensure that judgment is not impaired and no exploitation occurs. (See F.1.b.)

b. *Superior/Subordinate Relationships.*

Counselors do not accept as clients superiors or subordinates with whom they have administrative, supervisory, or evaluative relationships.

A.7. Sexual Intimacies with Clients

a. *Current Clients.*

Counselors do not have any type of sexual intimacies with clients and do not counsel persons with whom they have had a sexual relationship.

b. *Former Clients.*

Counselors do not engage in sexual intimacies with former clients within a minimum of two years after terminating the counseling relationship. Counselors who engage in such relationships after two years following termination have the responsibility to thoroughly examine and document that such relations did not have an exploitative nature, based on factors such as duration of counseling, amount of time since counseling, termination circumstances, client's personal history and mental status, adverse impact on the client, and actions by the counselor suggesting a plan to initiate a sexual relationship with the client after termination.

A.8. Multiple Clients

When counselors agree to provide counseling services to two or more persons who have a relationship (such as husband and wife, or parents and children), counselors clarify at the outset which person or persons are clients and the nature of the relationships they will have with each involved person. If it becomes apparent that counselors may be called upon to perform potentially conflicting roles, they clarify, adjust, or withdraw from roles appropriately. (See B.2. and B.4.d.)

A.9. Group Work

a. *Screening.*

Counselors screen prospective group counseling/therapy participants. To the extent possible, counselors select members whose needs and goals are compatible with goals of the group, who will not impede the group process, and whose well-being will not be jeopardized by the group experience.

b. *Protecting Clients.*

In a group setting, counselors take reasonable precautions to protect clients from physical or psychological trauma.

A.10. Fees and Bartering

(See D.3.a. and D.3.b.)

a. *Advance Understanding.*

Counselors clearly explain to clients, prior to entering the counseling relationship, all financial arrangements related to professional services including the use of collection agencies or legal measures for nonpayment. (A.11.c.)

b. *Establishing Fees.*

In establishing fees for professional counseling services, counselors consider the financial status of clients and locality. In the event that the established fee structure is inappropriate for a client, assistance is provided in attempting to find comparable services of acceptable cost. (See A.10.d., D.3.a., and D.3.b.)

c. *Bartering Discouraged.*

Counselors ordinarily refrain from accepting goods or services from clients in return for counseling services because such arrangements create inherent potential for conflicts, exploitation, and distortion of the professional relationship. Counselors may participate in bartering only if the relationship is not exploitive, if the client requests it, if a clear written contract is established, and if such arrangements are an accepted practice among professionals in the community. (See A.6.a.)

d. *Pro Bono Service.*

Counselors contribute to society by devoting a portion of their professional activity to services for which there is little or no financial return (pro bono).

A.11. Termination and Referral

a. *Abandonment Prohibited.*

Counselors do not abandon or neglect clients in counseling. Counselors assist in making appropriate arrangements for the continuation of treatment, when necessary, during interruptions such as vacations, and following termination.

b. *Inability to Assist Clients.*

If counselors determine an inability to be of professional assistance to clients, they avoid entering or immediately terminate a counseling relationship. Counselors are knowledgeable about referral resources and suggest appropriate alternatives. If clients decline the suggested referral, counselors should discontinue the relationship.

c. *Appropriate Termination.*

Counselors terminate a counseling relationship, securing client agreement when possible, when it is reasonably clear that the client is no longer benefiting, when services are no longer required, when counseling no longer serves the client's needs or interests, when clients do not pay fees charged, or when agency or institution limits do not allow provision of further counseling services. (See A.10.b. and C.2.g.)

A.12. Computer Technology

a. *Use of Computers.*

When computer applications are used in counseling services, counselors ensure that: (1) the client is intellectually, emotionally, and physically capable of using the computer application; (2) the computer application is appropriate for the needs of the client; (3) the client understands the purpose and operation of the computer applications; and (4) a follow-up of client use of a computer application is provided to correct possible misconceptions, discover inappropriate use, and assess subsequent needs.

b. *Explanation of Limitations.*

Counselors ensure that clients are provided information as a part of the counseling relationship that adequately explains the limitations of computer technology.

c. *Access to Computer Applications.*

Counselors provide for equal access to computer applications in counseling services. (See A.2.a.)

Section B: Confidentiality

B.1. Right to Privacy

a. *Respect for Privacy.*

Counselors respect their clients' right to privacy and avoid illegal and unwarranted disclosures of confidential information. (See A.3.a. and B.6.a.)

b. *Client Waiver.*

The right to privacy may be waived by the client or their legally recognized representative.

c. *Exceptions.*

The general requirement that counselors keep information confidential does not apply when disclosure is required to prevent clear and imminent danger to the client or others or when legal requirements demand that confidential information be revealed. Counselors consult with other professionals when in doubt as to the validity of an exception.

d. *Contagious, Fatal Diseases.*

A counselor who receives information confirming that a client has a disease commonly known to be both communicable and fatal is justified in disclosing information to an identifiable third party, who by his or her relationship with the client is at a high risk of contracting the disease. Prior to making a disclosure the counselor should ascertain that the client has not already informed the third party about his or her disease and that the client is not intending to inform the third party in the immediate future. (See B.1.c and B.1.f.)

e. *Court Ordered Disclosure.*

When court ordered to release confidential information without a client's permission, counselors request to the court that the disclosure not be required due to potential harm to the client or counseling relationship. (See B.1.c.)

f. *Minimal Disclosure.*

When circumstances require the disclosure of confidential information, only essential information is revealed. To the extent possible, clients are informed before confidential information is disclosed.

g. *Explanation of Limitations.*

When counseling is initiated and throughout the counseling process as necessary, counselors inform clients of the limitations of confidentiality and identify foreseeable situations in which confidentiality must be breached. (See G.2.a.)

h. *Subordinates.*

Counselors make every effort to ensure that privacy and confidentiality of clients are maintained by subordinates including employees, supervisees, clerical assistants, and volunteers. (See B.1.a.)

i. *Treatment Teams.*

If client treatment will involve a continued review by a treatment team, the client will be informed of the team's existence and composition.

B.2. Groups and Families

a. *Group Work.*

In group work, counselors clearly define confidentiality and the parameters for the specific group being entered, explain its importance, and discuss the difficulties related to confidentiality involved in group work. The fact that confidentiality cannot be guaranteed is clearly communicated to group members.

b. *Family Counseling.*

In family counseling, information about one family member cannot be disclosed to another member without permission. Counselors protect the privacy rights of each family member. (See A.8., B.3., and B.4.d.)

B.3. Minor or Incompetent Clients

When counseling clients who are minors or individuals who are unable to give voluntary, informed consent, parents or guardians may be included in the counseling process as appropriate. Counselors act in the best interests of clients and take measures to safeguard confidentiality. (See A.3.c.)

B.4. Records

a. *Requirement of Records.*

Counselors maintain records necessary for rendering professional services to their clients and as required by laws, regulations, or agency or institution procedures.

b. *Confidentiality of Records.*

Counselors are responsible for securing the safety and confidentiality of any counseling records they create, maintain, transfer, or destroy whether the records are written, taped, computerized, or stored in any other medium. (See B.1.a.)

c. *Permission to Record or Observe.*

Counselors obtain permission from clients prior to electronically recording or observing sessions. (See A.3.a.)

d. *Client Access.*

Counselors recognize that counseling records are kept for the benefit of clients, and therefore provide access to records and copies of records when requested by competent clients, unless the records contain information that may be misleading and detrimental to the client. In situations involving multiple clients, access to records is limited to those parts of records that do not include confidential information related to another client. (See A.8., B.1.a., and B.2.b.)

e. *Disclosure or Transfer.*

Counselors obtain written permission from clients to disclose or transfer records to legitimate third parties unless exceptions to confidentiality exist as listed in Section B.1. Steps are taken to ensure that receivers of counseling records are sensitive to their confidential nature.

B.5. Research and Training

a. *Data Disguise Required.*

Use of data derived from counseling relationships for purposes of training, research, or publication is confined to content that is disguised to ensure the anonymity of the individuals involved. (See B.1.g. and G.3.d.)

b. *Agreement for Identification.*

Identification of a client in a presentation or publication is permissible only when the client has reviewed the material and has agreed to its presentation or publication. (See G.3.d.)

B.6. Consultation

a. *Respect for Privacy.*

Information obtained in a consulting relationship is discussed for professional purposes only with persons clearly concerned with the case. Written and oral reports present data germane to the purposes of the consultation, and every effort is made to protect client identity and avoid undue invasion of privacy.

b. *Cooperating Agencies.*

Before sharing information, counselors make efforts to ensure that there are defined policies in other agencies serving the counselor's clients that effectively protect the confidentiality of information.

Section C: Professional Responsibility

C.1. Standards Knowledge

Counselors have a responsibility to read, understand, and follow the Code of Ethics and the Standards of Practice.

C.2. Professional Competence

a. *Boundaries of Competence.*

Counselors practice only within the boundaries of their competence, based on their education, training, supervised experience, state and national professional credentials, and appropriate professional experience. Counselors will demonstrate a commitment to gain knowledge, personal awareness, sensitivity, and skills pertinent to working with a diverse client population.

b. *New Specialty Areas of Practice.*

Counselors practice in specialty areas new to them only after appropriate education, training, and supervised experience. While developing skills in new specialty areas, counselors take steps to ensure the competence of their work and to protect others from possible harm.

c. *Qualified for Employment.*

Counselors accept employment only for positions for which they are qualified by education, training, supervised experience, state and national professional credentials, and appropriate professional experience. Counselors hire for professional counseling positions only individuals who are qualified and competent.

d. *Monitor Effectiveness.*

Counselors continually monitor their effectiveness as professionals and take steps to improve when necessary. Counselors in private practice take reasonable steps to seek out peer supervision to evaluate their efficacy as counselors.

e. *Ethical Issues Consultation.*

Counselors take reasonable steps to consult with other counselors or related professionals when they have questions regarding their ethical obligations or professional practice. (See H.1.)

f. *Continuing Education.*

Counselors recognize the need for continuing education to maintain a reasonable level of awareness of current scientific and professional information in their fields of activity. They take steps to maintain competence in the skills they use, are open to new procedures, and keep current with the diverse and/or special populations with whom they work.

g. *Impairment.*

Counselors refrain from offering or accepting professional services when their physical, mental, or emotional problems are likely to harm a client or others. They are alert to the signs of impairment, seek assistance for problems, and, if necessary, limit, suspend, or terminate their professional responsibilities. (See A.11.c.)

C.3. Advertising and Soliciting Clients

a. *Accurate Advertising.*

There are no restrictions on advertising by counselors except those that can be specifically justified to protect the public from deceptive practices. Counselors advertise or represent their services to the public by identifying their credentials in an accurate manner that is not false, misleading, deceptive, or fraudulent. Counselors may only advertise the highest degree earned which is in counseling or a closely related field from a college or university that was accredited when the degree was awarded by one of the regional accrediting bodies recognized by the Council on Postsecondary Accreditation.

b. *Testimonials.*

Counselors who use testimonials do not solicit them from clients or other persons who, because of their particular circumstances, may be vulnerable to undue influence.

c. *Statements by Others.*

Counselors make reasonable efforts to ensure that statements made by others about them or the profession of counseling are accurate.

d. *Recruiting through Employment.*

Counselors do not use their places of employment or institutional affiliation to recruit or gain clients, supervisees, or consultees for their private practices. (See C.5.e.)

e. *Products and Training Advertisements.*

Counselors who develop products related to their profession or conduct workshops or training events ensure that the advertisements concerning these products or events are accurate and disclose adequate information for consumers to make informed choices.

f. *Promoting to Those Served.*

Counselors do not use counseling, teaching, training, or supervisory relationships to promote their products or training events in a manner that is deceptive or would exert undue influence on individuals who may be vulnerable. Counselors may adopt textbooks they have authored for instruction purposes.

g. *Professional Association Involvement.*

Counselors actively participate in local, state, and national associations that foster the development and improvement of counseling.

C.4. Credentials

a. *Credentials Claimed.*

Counselors claim or imply only professional credentials possessed and are responsible for correcting any known misrepresentations of their credentials by others. Professional credentials include graduate degrees in counseling or closely related mental health fields, accreditation of graduate programs, national voluntary certifications, government issued certifications or licenses, ACA professional membership, or any other credential that might indicate to the public specialized knowledge or expertise in counseling.

b. *ACA Professional Membership.*

ACA professional members may announce to the public their membership status. Regular members may not announce their ACA membership in a manner that might imply they are credentialed counselors.

c. *Credential Guidelines.*

Counselors follow the guidelines for use of credentials that have been established by the entities that issue the credentials.

d. *Misrepresentation of Credentials.*

Counselors do not attribute more to their credentials than the credentials represent, and do not imply that other counselors are not qualified because they do not possess certain credentials.

e. *Doctoral Degrees from Other Fields.*
Counselors who hold a master's degree in counseling or a closely related mental health field, but hold a doctoral degree from other than counseling or a closely related field do not use the title "Dr." in their practices and do not announce to the public in relation to their practice or status as a counselor that they hold a doctorate.

C.5. Public Responsibility

a. *Nondiscrimination.*
Counselors do not discriminate against clients, students, or supervisees in a manner that has a negative impact based on their age, color, culture, disability, ethnic group, gender, race, religion, sexual orientation, or socioeconomic status, or for any other reason. (See A.2.a.)

b. *Sexual Harassment.*
Counselors do not engage in sexual harassment. Sexual harassment is defined as sexual solicitation, physical advances, or verbal or nonverbal conduct that is sexual in nature, that occurs in connection with professional activities or roles, and that either: (1) is unwelcome, is offensive, or creates a hostile workplace environment, and counselors know or are told this; or (2) is sufficiently severe or intense to be perceived as harassment to a reasonable person in the context. Sexual harassment can consist of a single intense or severe act or multiple persistent or pervasive acts.

c. *Reports to Third Parties.*
Counselors are accurate, honest, and unbiased in reporting their professional activities and judgments to appropriate third parties including courts, health insurance companies, those who are the recipients of evaluation reports, and others. (See B.1.g.)

d. *Media Presentations.*
When counselors provide advice or comment by means of public lectures, demonstrations, radio or television programs, prerecorded tapes, printed articles, mailed material, or other media, they take reasonable precautions to ensure that (1) the statements are based on appropriate professional counseling literature and practice; (2) the statements are otherwise consistent with the Code of Ethics and the Standards of Practice; and (3) the recipients of the information are not encouraged to infer that a professional counseling relationship has been established. (See C.6.b.)

e. *Unjustified Gains.*
Counselors do not use their professional positions to seek or receive unjustified personal gains, sexual favors, unfair advantage, or unearned goods or services. (See C.3.d.)

C.6. Responsibility to Other Professionals

a. *Different Approaches.*
Counselors are respectful of approaches to professional counseling that differ from their own. Counselors know and take into account the traditions and practices of other professional groups with which they work.

b. *Personal Public Statements.*
When making personal statements in a public context, counselors clarify that they are speaking from their personal perspectives and that they are not speaking on behalf of all counselors or the profession. (See C.5.d.)

c. *Clients Served by Others.*
When counselors learn that their clients are in a professional relationship with another mental health professional, they request release from clients to inform the other professionals and strive to establish positive and collaborative professional relationships. (See A.4.)

Section D: Relationships with Other Professionals

D.1. Relationships with Employers and Employees

a. *Role Definition.*
Counselors define and describe for their employers and employees the parameters and levels of their professional roles.

b. *Agreements.*

Counselors establish working agreements with supervisors, colleagues, and subordinates regarding counseling or clinical relationships, confidentiality, adherence to professional standards, distinction between public and private material, maintenance and dissemination of recorded information, workload, and accountability. Working agreements in each instance are specified and made known to those concerned.

c. *Negative Conditions.*

Counselors alert their employers to conditions that may be potentially disruptive or damaging to the counselor's professional responsibilities or that may limit their effectiveness.

d. *Evaluation.*

Counselors submit regularly to professional review and evaluation by their supervisor or the appropriate representative of the employer.

e. *In-Service.*

Counselors are responsible for in-service development of self and staff.

f. *Goals.*

Counselors inform their staff of goals and programs.

g. *Practices.*

Counselors provide personnel and agency practices that respect and enhance the rights and welfare of each employee and recipient of agency services. Counselors strive to maintain the highest levels of professional services.

h. *Personnel Selection and Assignment.*

Counselors select competent staff and assign responsibilities compatible with their skills and experiences.

i. *Discrimination.*

Counselors, as either employers or employees, do not engage in or condone practices that are inhumane, illegal, or unjustifiable (such as considerations based on age, color, culture, disability, ethnic group, gender, race, religion, sexual orientation, or socioeconomic status) in hiring, promotion, or training. (See A.2.a. and C.5.b.)

j. *Professional Conduct.*

Counselors have a responsibility both to clients and to the agency or institution within which services are performed to maintain high standards of professional conduct.

k. *Exploitive Relationships.*

Counselors do not engage in exploitive relationships with individuals over whom they have supervisory, evaluative, or instructional control or authority.

l. *Employer Policies.*

The acceptance of employment in an agency or institution implies that counselors are in agreement with its general policies and principles. Counselors strive to reach agreement with employers as to acceptable standards of conduct that allow for changes in institutional policy conducive to the growth and development of clients.

D.2. Consultation

(See B.6.)

a. *Consultation as an Option.*

Counselors may choose to consult with any other professionally competent persons about their clients. In choosing consultants, counselors avoid placing the consultant in a conflict of interest situation that would preclude the consultant being a proper party to the counselor's efforts to help the client. Should counselors be engaged in a work setting that compromises this consultation standard, they consult with other professionals whenever possible to consider justifiable alternatives.

b. *Consultant Competency.*

Counselors are reasonably certain that they have or the organization represented has the necessary competencies and resources for giving the kind of consulting services needed and that appropriate referral resources are available.

c. *Understanding with Clients.*

When providing consultation, counselors attempt to develop with their clients a clear understanding of problem definition, goals for change, and predicted consequences of interventions selected.

d. *Consultant Goals.*

The consulting relationship is one in which client adaptability and growth toward self-direction are consistently encouraged and cultivated. (See A.1.b.)

D.3. Fees for Referral

a. *Accepting Fees from Agency Clients.*

Counselors refuse a private fee or other remuneration for rendering services to persons who are entitled to such services through the counselor's employing agency or institution. The policies of a particular agency may make explicit provisions for agency clients to receive counseling services from members of its staff in private practice. In such instances, the clients must be informed of other options open to them should they seek private counseling services. (See A.10.a., A.11.b., and C.3.d.)

b. *Referral Fees.*

Counselors do not accept a referral fee from other professionals.

D.4. Subcontractor Arrangements

When counselors work as subcontractors for counseling services for a third party, they have a duty to inform clients of the limitations of confidentiality that the organization may place on counselors in providing counseling services to clients. The limits of such confidentiality ordinarily are discussed as part of the intake session. (See B.1.e. and B.1.f.)

Section E: Evaluation, Assessment, and Interpretation

E.1. General

a. *Appraisal Techniques.*

The primary purpose of educational and psychological assessment is to provide measures that are objective and interpretable in either comparative or absolute terms. Counselors recognize the need to interpret the statements in this section as applying to the whole range of appraisal techniques, including test and nontest data.

b. *Client Welfare.*

Counselors promote the welfare and best interests of the client in the development, publication, and utilization of educational and psychological assessment techniques. They do not misuse assessment results and interpretations and take reasonable steps to prevent others from misusing the information these techniques provide. They respect the client's right to know the results, the interpretations made, and the bases for their conclusions and recommendations.

E.2. Competence to Use and Interpret Tests

a. *Limits of Competence.*

Counselors recognize the limits of their competence and perform only those testing and assessment services for which they have been trained. They are familiar with reliability, validity, related standardization, error of measurement, and proper application of any technique utilized. Counselors using computer-based test interpretations are trained in the construct being measured and the specific instrument being used prior to using this type of computer application. Counselors take reasonable measures to ensure the proper use of psychological assessment techniques by persons under their supervision.

b. *Appropriate Use.*

Counselors are responsible for the appropriate application, scoring, interpretation, and use of assessment instruments, whether they score and interpret such tests themselves or use computerized or other services.

c. *Decisions Based on Results.*

Counselors responsible for decisions involving individuals or policies that are based on assessment results have a thorough understanding of educational and psychological measurement, including validation criteria, test research, and guidelines for test development and use.

    d. *Accurate Information.*

       Counselors provide accurate information and avoid false claims or misconceptions when making statements about assessment instruments or techniques. Special efforts are made to avoid unwarranted connotations of such terms as IQ and grade equivalent scores. (See C.5.c.)

E.3. Informed Consent

    a. *Explanation to Clients.*

       Prior to assessment, counselors explain the nature and purposes of assessment and the specific use of results in language the client (or other legally authorized person on behalf of the client) can understand, unless an explicit exception to this right has been agreed upon in advance. Regardless of whether scoring and interpretation are completed by counselors, by assistants, or by computer or other outside services, counselors take reasonable steps to ensure that appropriate explanations are given to the client.

    b. *Recipients of Results.*

       The examinee's welfare, explicit understanding, and prior agreement determine the recipients of test results. Counselors include accurate and appropriate interpretations with any release of individual or group test results. (See B.1.a. and C.5.c.)

E.4. Release of Information to Competent Professionals

    a. *Misuse of Results.*

       Counselors do not misuse assessment results, including test results, and interpretations, and take reasonable steps to prevent the misuse of such by others. (See C.5.c.)

    b. *Release of Raw Data.*

       Counselors ordinarily release data (e.g., protocols, counseling or interview notes, or questionnaires) in which the client is identified only with the consent of the client or the client's legal representative. Such data are usually released only to persons recognized by counselors as competent to interpret the data. (See B.1.a.)

E.5. Proper Diagnosis of Mental Disorders

    a. *Proper Diagnosis.*

       Counselors take special care to provide proper diagnosis of mental disorders. Assessment techniques (including personal interview) used to determine client care (e.g., locus of treatment, type of treatment, or recommended follow-up) are carefully selected and appropriately used. (See A.3.a. and C.5.c.)

    b. *Cultural Sensitivity.*

       Counselors recognize that culture affects the manner in which clients' problems are defined. Clients' socioeconomic and cultural experience is considered when diagnosing mental disorders.

E.6. Test Selection

    a. *Appropriateness of Instruments.*

       Counselors carefully consider the validity, reliability, psychometric limitations, and appropriateness of instruments when selecting tests for use in a given situation or with a particular client.

    b. *Culturally Diverse Populations.*

       Counselors are cautious when selecting tests for culturally diverse populations to avoid inappropriateness of testing that may be outside of socialized behavioral or cognitive patterns.

E.7. Conditions of Test Administration

    a. *Administration Conditions.*

       Counselors administer tests under the same conditions that were established in their standardization. When tests are not administered under standard conditions or when unusual behavior or irregularities occur during the testing session, those conditions are noted in interpretation, and the results may be designated as invalid or of questionable validity.

b. *Computer Administration.*
Counselors are responsible for ensuring that administration programs function properly to provide clients with accurate results when a computer or other electronic methods are used for test administration. (See A.12.b.)

c. *Unsupervised Test-Taking.*
Counselors do not permit unsupervised or inadequately supervised use of tests or assessments unless the tests or assessments are designed, intended, and validated for self-administration and/or scoring.

d. *Disclosure of Favorable Conditions.*
Prior to test administration, conditions that produce most favorable test results are made known to the examinee.

E.8. Diversity in Testing

Counselors are cautious in using assessment techniques, making evaluations, and interpreting the performance of populations not represented in the norm group on which an instrument was standardized. They recognize the effects of age, color, culture, disability, ethnic group, gender, race, religion, sexual orientation, and socioeconomic status on test administration and interpretation and place test results in proper perspective with other relevant factors. (See A.2.a.)

E.9. Test Scoring and Interpretation

a. *Reporting Reservations.*
In reporting assessment results, counselors indicate any reservations that exist regarding validity or reliability because of the circumstances of the assessment or the inappropriateness of the norms for the person tested.

b. *Research Instruments.*
Counselors exercise caution when interpreting the results of research instruments possessing insufficient technical data to support respondent results. The specific purposes for the use of such instruments are stated explicitly to the examinee.

c. *Testing Services.*
Counselors who provide test scoring and test interpretation services to support the assessment process confirm the validity of such interpretations. They accurately describe the purpose, norms, validity, reliability, and applications of the procedures and any special qualifications applicable to their use. The public offering of an automated test interpretations service is considered a professional-to-professional consultation. The formal responsibility of the consultant is to the consultee, but the ultimate and overriding responsibility is to the client.

E.10. Test Security

Counselors maintain the integrity and security of tests and other assessment techniques consistent with legal and contractual obligations. Counselors do not appropriate, reproduce, or modify published tests or parts thereof without acknowledgment and permission from the publisher.

E.11. Obsolete Tests and Outdated Test Results

Counselors do not use data or test results that are obsolete or outdated for the current purpose. Counselors make every effort to prevent the misuse of obsolete measures and test data by others.

E.12. Test Construction

Counselors use established scientific procedures, relevant standards, and current professional knowledge for test design in the development, publication, and utilization of educational and psychological assessment techniques.

Section F: Teaching, Training, and Supervision

F. 1. Counselor Educators and Trainers

a. *Educators as Teachers and Practitioners.*

Counselors who are responsible for developing, implementing, and supervising educational programs are skilled as teachers and practitioners. They are knowledgeable regarding the ethical, legal, and regulatory aspects of the profession, are skilled in applying that knowledge, and make students and supervisees aware of their responsibilities. Counselors conduct counselor education and training programs in an ethical manner and serve as role models for professional behavior. Counselor educators should make an effort to infuse material related to human diversity into all courses and/or workshops that are designed to promote the development of professional counselors.

b. *Relationship Boundaries with Students and Supervisees.*

Counselors clearly define and maintain ethical, professional, and social relationship boundaries with their students and supervisees. They are aware of the differential in power that exists and the student's or supervisee's possible incomprehension of that power differential. Counselors explain to students and supervisees the potential for the relationship to become exploitive.

c. *Sexual Relationships.*

Counselors do not engage in sexual relationships with students or supervisees and do not subject them to sexual harassment. (See A.6. and C.5.b.)

d. *Contributions to Research.*

Counselors give credit to students or supervisees for their contributions to research and scholarly projects. Credit is given through coauthorship, acknowledgment, footnote statement, or other appropriate means, in accordance with such contributions. (See G.4.b. and G.4.c.)

e. *Close Relatives.*

Counselors do not accept close relatives as students or supervisees.

f. *Supervision Preparation.*

Counselors who offer clinical supervision services are adequately prepared in supervision methods and techniques. Counselors who are doctoral students serving as practicum or internship supervisors to master's level students are adequately prepared and supervised by the training program.

g. *Responsibility for Services to Clients.*

Counselors who supervise the counseling services of others take reasonable measures to ensure that counseling services provided to clients are professional.

h. *Endorsement.*

Counselors do not endorse students or supervisees for certification, licensure, employment, or completion of an academic or training program if they believe students or supervisees are not qualified for the endorsement. Counselors take reasonable steps to assist students or supervisees who are not qualified for endorsement to become qualified.

F.2. Counselor Education and Training Programs

a. *Orientation.*

Prior to admission, counselors orient prospective students to the counselor education or training program's expectations, including but not limited to the following: (1) the type and level of skill acquisition required for successful completion of the training, (2) subject matter to be covered, (3) basis for evaluation, (4) training components that encourage self-growth or self-disclosure as part of the training process, (5) the type of supervision settings and requirements of the sites for required clinical field experiences, (6) student and supervisee evaluation and dismissal policies and procedures, and (7) up-to-date employment prospects for graduates.

b. *Integration of Study and Practice.*

Counselors establish counselor education and training programs that integrate academic study and supervised practice.

c. *Evaluation.*

Counselors clearly state to students and supervisees, in advance of training, the levels of competency expected, appraisal methods, and timing of evaluations for both didactic and experiential components. Counselors provide students and supervisees with periodic performance appraisal and evaluation feedback throughout the training program.

d. *Teaching Ethics.*

Counselors make students and supervisees aware of the ethical responsibilities and standards of the profession and the students' and supervisees' ethical responsibilities to the profession. (See C.1. and F.3.e.)

e. *Peer Relationships.*

When students or supervisees are assigned to lead counseling groups or provide clinical supervision for their peers, counselors take steps to ensure that students and supervisees placed in these roles do not have personal or adverse relationships with peers and that they understand they have the same ethical obligations as counselor educators, trainers, and supervisors. Counselors make every effort to ensure that the rights of peers are not compromised when students or supervisees are assigned to lead counseling groups or provide clinical supervision.

f. *Varied Theoretical Positions.*

Counselors present varied theoretical positions so that students and supervisees may make comparisons and have opportunities to develop their own positions. Counselors provide information concerning the scientific bases of professional practice. (See C.6.a.)

g. *Field Placements.*

Counselors develop clear policies within their training program regarding field placement and other clinical experiences. Counselors provide clearly stated roles and responsibilities for the student or supervisee, the site supervisor, and the program supervisor. They confirm that site supervisors are qualified to provide supervision and are informed of their professional and ethical responsibilities in this role.

h. *Dual Relationships as Supervisors.*

Counselors avoid dual relationships such as performing the role of site supervisor and training program supervisor in the student's or supervisee's training program. Counselors do not accept any form of professional services, fees, commissions, reimbursement, or remuneration from a site for student or supervisee placement.

i. *Diversity in Programs.*

Counselors are responsive to their institution's and program's recruitment and retention needs for training program administrators, faculty, and students with diverse backgrounds and special needs. (See A.2.a.)

F.3. Students and Supervisees

a. *Limitations.*

Counselors, through ongoing evaluation and appraisal, are aware of the academic and personal limitations of students and supervisees that might impede performance. Counselors assist students and supervisees in securing remedial assistance when needed, and dismiss from the training program supervisees who are unable to provide competent service due to academic or personal limitations. Counselors seek professional consultation and document their decision to dismiss or refer students or supervisees for assistance. Counselors assure that students and supervisees have recourse to address decisions made, to require them to seek assistance, or to dismiss them.

b. *Self-Growth Experiences.*

Counselors use professional judgment when designing training experiences conducted by the counselors themselves that require student and supervisee self-growth or self-disclosure. Safeguards are provided so that students and supervisees are aware of the ramifications their self-disclosure may have on counselors whose primary role as teacher, trainer, or supervisor requires acting on ethical obligations to the profession. Evaluative components of experiential training experiences explicitly delineate predetermined academic standards that are separate and not dependent on the student's level of self-disclosure. (See A.6.)

c. *Counseling for Students and Supervisees.*

If students or supervisees request counseling, supervisors or counselor educators provide them with acceptable referrals. Supervisors or counselor educators do not serve as counselor to students or supervisees over whom they hold administrative, teaching, or evaluative roles unless this is a brief role associated with a training experience. (See A.6.b.)

d. *Clients of Students and Supervisees.*

Counselors make every effort to ensure that the clients at field placements are aware of the services rendered and the qualifications of the students and supervisees rendering those services. Clients receive professional disclosure information and are informed of the limits of confidentiality. Client permission is obtained in order for the students and supervisees to use any information concerning the counseling relationship in the training process. (See B.1.e.)

e. *Standards for Students and Supervisees.*

Students and supervisees preparing to become counselors adhere to the Code of Ethics and the Standards of Practice. Students and supervisees have the same obligations to clients as those required of counselors. (See H.1.)

Section G: Research and Publication

G .1. Research Responsibilities

a. *Use of Human Subjects.*

Counselors plan, design, conduct, and report research in a manner consistent with pertinent ethical principles, federal and state laws, host institutional regulations, and scientific standards governing research with human subjects. Counselors design and conduct research that reflects cultural sensitivity appropriateness.

b. *Deviation from Standard Practices.*

Counselors seek consultation and observe stringent safeguards to protect the rights of research participants when a research problem suggests a deviation from standard acceptable practices. (See B.6.)

c. *Precautions to Avoid Injury.*

Counselors who conduct research with human subjects are responsible for the subjects' welfare throughout the experiment and take reasonable precautions to avoid causing injurious psychological, physical, or social effects to their subjects.

d. *Principal Researcher Responsibility.*

The ultimate responsibility for ethical research practice lies with the principal researcher. All others involved in the research activities share ethical obligations and full responsibility for their own actions.

e. *Minimal Interference.*

Counselors take reasonable precautions to avoid causing disruptions in subjects' lives due to participation in research.

f. *Diversity.*

Counselors are sensitive to diversity and research issues with special populations. They seek consultation when appropriate. (See A.2.a. and B.6.)

G.2. Informed Consent

a. *Topics Disclosed.*

In obtaining informed consent for research, counselors use language that is understandable to research participants and that: (1) accurately explains the purpose and procedures to be followed; (2) identifies any procedures that are experimental or relatively untried; (3) describes the attendant discomforts and risks; (4) describes the benefits or changes in individuals or organizations that might be reasonably expected; (5) discloses appropriate alternative procedures that would be advantageous for subjects; (6) offers to answer any inquiries concerning the procedures; (7) describes any limitations on confidentiality; and (8) instructs that subjects are free to withdraw their consent and to discontinue participation in the project at any time. (See B.1.f.)

b. *Deception.*

Counselors do not conduct research involving deception unless alternative procedures are not feasible and the prospective value of the research justifies the deception. When the methodological requirements of a study necessitate concealment or deception, the investigator is required to explain clearly the reasons for this action as soon as possible.

c. *Voluntary Participation.*

Participation in research is typically voluntary and without any penalty for refusal to participate. Involuntary participation is appropriate only when it can be demonstrated that participation will have no harmful effects on subjects and is essential to the investigation.

d. *Confidentiality of Information.*

Information obtained about research participants during the course of an investigation is confidential. When the possibility exists that others may obtain access to such information, ethical research practice requires that the possibility, together with the plans for protecting confidentiality, be explained to participants as a part of the procedure for obtaining informed consent. (See B.1.e.)

e. *Persons Incapable of Giving Informed Consent.*

When a person is incapable of giving informed consent, counselors provide an appropriate explanation, obtain agreement for participation, and obtain appropriate consent from a legally authorized person.

f. *Commitments to Participants.*

Counselors take reasonable measures to honor all commitments to research participants.

g. *Explanations After Data Collection.*

After data are collected, counselors provide participants with full clarification of the nature of the study to remove any misconceptions. Where scientific or human values justify delaying or withholding information, counselors take reasonable measures to avoid causing harm.

h. *Agreements to Cooperate.*

Counselors who agree to cooperate with another individual in research or publication incur an obligation to cooperate as promised in terms of punctuality of performance and with regard to the completeness and accuracy of the information required.

i. *Informed Consent for Sponsors.*

In the pursuit of research, counselors give sponsors, institutions, and publication channels the same respect and opportunity for giving informed consent that they accord to individual research participants. Counselors are aware of their obligation to future research workers and ensure that host institutions are given feedback information and proper acknowledgment.

G.3. Reporting Results

a. *Information Affecting Outcome.*

When reporting research results, counselors explicitly mention all variables and conditions known to the investigator that may have affected the outcome of a study or the interpretation of data.

b. *Accurate Results.*

Counselors plan, conduct, and report research accurately and in a manner that minimizes the possibility that results will be misleading. They provide thorough discussions of the limitations of their data and alternative hypotheses. Counselors do not engage in fraudulent research, distort data, misrepresent data, or deliberately bias their results.

c. *Obligation to Report Unfavorable Results.*

Counselors communicate to other counselors the results of any research judged to be of professional value. Results that reflect unfavorably on institutions, programs, services, prevailing opinions, or vested interests are not withheld.

d. *Identity of Subjects.*

Counselors who supply data, aid in the research of another person, report research results, or make original data available take due care to disguise the identity of respective subjects in the absence of specific authorization from the subjects to do otherwise. (See B.1.g. and B.5.a.)

e. *Replication Studies.*

Counselors are obligated to make available sufficient original research data to qualified professionals who may wish to replicate the study.

G.4. Publication

a. *Recognition of Others.*

When conducting and reporting research, counselors are familiar with and give recognition to previous work on the topic, observe copyright laws, and give full credit to those to whom credit is due. (See F.1.d. and G.4.c.)

b. *Contributors.*

Counselors give credit through joint authorship, acknowledgment, footnote statements, or other appropriate means to those who have contributed significantly to research or concept development in accordance with such contributions. The principal contributor is listed first and minor technical or professional contributions are acknowledged in notes or introductory statements.

c. *Student Research.*

For an article that is substantially based on a student's dissertation or thesis, the student is listed as the principal author. (See F.1.d. and G.4.a.)

d. *Duplicate Submission.*

Counselors submit manuscripts for consideration to only one journal at a time. Manuscripts that are published in whole or in substantial part in another journal or published work are not submitted for publication without acknowledgment and permission from the previous publication.

e. *Professional Review.*

Counselors who review material submitted for publication, research, or other scholarly purposes respect the confidentiality and proprietary rights of those who submitted it.

Section H: Resolving Ethical Issues

H.1. Knowledge of Standards

Counselors are familiar with the *Code of Ethics* and the *Standards of Practice* and other applicable ethics codes from other professional organizations of which they are members, or from certification and licensure bodies. Lack of knowledge or misunderstanding of an ethical responsibility is not a defense against a charge of unethical conduct. (See F.3.e.)

H.2. Suspected Violations

a. *Ethical Behavior Expected.*

Counselors expect professional associates to adhere to the *Code of Ethics.* When counselors possess reasonable cause that raises doubts as to whether a counselor is acting in an ethical manner, they take appropriate action. (See H.2.d. and H.2.e.)

b. *Consultation.*

When uncertain as to whether a particular situation or course of action may be in violation of the *Code of Ethics,* counselors consult with other counselors who are knowledgeable about ethics, with colleagues, or with appropriate authorities.

c. *Organization Conflicts.*

If the demands of an organization with which counselors are affiliated pose a conflict with the *Code of Ethics,* counselors specify the nature of such conflicts and express to their supervisors or other responsible officials their commitment to the *Code of Ethics.* When possible, counselors work toward change within the organization to allow full adherence to the *Code of Ethics.*

d. *Informal Resolution.*

When counselors have reasonable cause to believe that another counselor is violating an ethical standard, they attempt to first resolve the issue informally with the other counselor if feasible, providing that such action does not violate confidentiality rights that may be involved.

e. *Reporting Suspected Violations.*
   When an informal resolution is not appropriate or feasible, counselors, upon reasonable cause, take action such as reporting the suspected ethical violation to state or national ethics committees, unless this action conflicts with confidentiality rights that cannot be resolved.
f. *Unwarranted Complaints.*
   Counselors do not initiate, participate in, or encourage the filing of ethics complaints that are unwarranted or intend to harm a counselor rather than to protect clients or the public.

H.3. Cooperation with Ethics Committees

Counselors assist in the process of enforcing the *Code of Ethics*. Counselors cooperate with investigations, proceedings, and requirements of the ACA Ethics Committee or ethics committees of other duly constituted associations or boards having jurisdiction over those charged with a violation. Counselors are familiar with the ACA Policies and Procedures and use it as a reference in assisting the enforcement of the *Code of Ethics*.

STANDARDS OF PRACTICE (AMERICAN COUNSELING ASSOCIATION)

All members of the American Counseling Association (ACA) are required to adhere to the *Standards of Practice* and the *Code of Ethics*. The *Standards of Practice* represent minimal behavioral statements of the *Code of Ethics*. Members should refer to the applicable section of the *Code of Ethics* for further interpretation and amplification of the applicable Standard of Practice.

Section A: The Counseling Relationship

Standard of Practice One (SP-1)
Nondiscrimination

Counselors respect diversity and must not discriminate against clients because of age, color, culture, disability, ethnic group, gender, race, religion, sexual orientation, marital status, or socioeconomic status. (See A.2.a.)

Standard of Practice Two (SP-2)
Disclosure to Clients

Counselors must adequately inform clients, preferably in writing, regarding the counseling process and counseling relationship at or before the time it begins and throughout the relationship. (See A.3.a.)

Standard of Practice Three (SP-3)
Dual Relationships

Counselors must make every effort to avoid dual relationships with clients that could impair their professional judgment or increase the risk of harm to clients. When a dual relationship cannot be avoided, counselors must take appropriate steps to ensure that judgment is not impaired and that no exploitation occurs. (See A.6.a. and A.6.b.)

Standard of Practice Four (SP-4)
Sexual Intimacies with Clients

Counselors must not engage in any type of sexual intimacies with current clients and must not engage in sexual intimacies with former clients within a minimum of two years after terminating the counseling relationship. Counselors who engage in such relationship after two years following termination have the responsibility to thoroughly examine and document that such relations did not have an exploitative nature.

Standard of Practice Five (SP-5)
Protecting Clients During Group Work

Counselors must take steps to protect clients from physical or psychological trauma resulting from interactions during group work. (See A.9.b.)

Standard of Practice Six (SP-6)
Advance Understanding of Fees

Counselors must explain to clients, prior to their entering the counseling relationship, financial arrangements related to professional services. (See A.10. a.-d. and A.11.c.)

Standard of Practice Seven (SP-7)
Termination

Counselors must assist in making appropriate arrangements for the continuation of treatment of clients, when necessary, following termination of counseling relationships. (See A.11.a.)

Standard of Practice Eight (SP-8)
Inability to Assist Clients

Counselors must avoid entering or immediately terminate a counseling relationship if it is determined that they are unable to be of professional assistance to a client. The counselor may assist in making an appropriate referral for the client. (See A.11.b.)

Section B: Confidentiality

Standard of Practice Nine (SP-9)
Confidentiality Requirement

Counselors must keep information related to counseling services confidential unless disclosure is in the best interest of clients, is required for the welfare of others, or is required by law. When disclosure is required, only information that is essential is revealed and the client is informed of such disclosure. (See B.1. a.-f.)

Standard of Practice Ten (SP-10)
Confidentiality Requirements for Subordinates

Counselors must take measures to ensure that privacy and confidentiality of clients are maintained by subordinates. (See B.1.h.)

Standard of Practice Eleven (SP-11)
Confidentiality in Group Work

Counselors must clearly communicate to group members that confidentiality cannot be guaranteed in group work. (See B.2.a.)

Standard of Practice Twelve (SP-12)
Confidentiality in Family Counseling

Counselors must not disclose information about one family member in counseling to another family member without prior consent. (See B.2.b.)

Standard of Practice Thirteen (SP-13)
Confidentiality of Records

Counselors must maintain appropriate confidentiality in creating, storing, accessing, transferring, and disposing of counseling records. (See B.4.b.)

Standard of Practice Fourteen (SP-14)
Permission to Record or Observe

Counselors must obtain prior consent from clients in order to electronically record or observe sessions. (See B.4.c.)

Standard of Practice Fifteen (SP-15)
Disclosure or Transfer of Records

Counselors must obtain client consent to disclose or transfer records to third parties, unless exceptions listed in SP-9 exist. (See B.4.e.)

Standard of Practice Sixteen (SP-16)
Data Disguise Required

Counselors must disguise the identity of the client when using data for training, research, or publication. (See B.5.a.)

Section C: Professional Responsibility

Standard of Practice Seventeen (SP-17)
Boundaries of Competence

Counselors must practice only within the boundaries of their competence. (See C.2.a.)

Standard of Practice Eighteen (SP-18)
Continuing Education

Counselors must engage in continuing education to maintain their professional competence. (See C.2.f.)

Standard of Practice Nineteen (SP-19)
Impairment of Professionals

Counselors must refrain from offering professional services when their personal problems or conflicts may cause harm to a client or others. (See C.2.g.)

Standard of Practice Twenty (SP-20)
Accurate Advertising

Counselors must accurately represent their credentials and services when advertising. (See C.3.a.)

Standard of Practice Twenty-one (SP-21)
Recruiting Through Employment

Counselors must not use their place of employment or institutional affiliation to recruit clients for their private practices. (See C.3.d.)

Standard of Practice Twenty-two (SP-22)
Credentials Claimed

Counselors must claim or imply only professional credentials possessed and must correct any known misrepresentations of their credentials by others. (See C.4.a.)

Standard of Practice Twenty-three (SP-23)
Sexual Harassment

Counselors must not engage in sexual harassment. (See C.5.b.)

Standard of Practice Twenty-four (SP-24)
Unjustified Gains

Counselors must not use their professional positions to seek or receive unjustified personal gains, sexual favors, unfair advantage, or unearned goods or services. (See C.5.e.)

Standard of Practice Twenty-five (SP-25)
Clients Served by Others

With the consent of the client, counselors must inform other mental health professionals serving the same client that a counseling relationship between the counselor and client exists. (See C.6.c.)

Standard of Practice Twenty-six (SP-26)
Negative Employment Conditions

Counselors must alert their employers to institutional policy or conditions that may be potentially disruptive or damaging to the counselor's professional responsibilities, or that may limit their effectiveness or deny clients' rights. (See D.1.c.)

Standard of Practice Twenty-seven (SP-27)
Personnel Selection and Assignment

Counselors must select competent staff and must assign responsibilities compatible with staff skills and experiences. (See D.1.h.)

Standard of Practice Twenty-eight (SP-28)
Exploitive Relationships with Subordinates

Counselors must not engage in exploitive relationships with individuals over whom they have supervisory, evaluative, or instructional control or authority. (See D.1.k.)

Section D: Relationship with Other Professionals

Standard of Practice Twenty-nine (SP-29)
Accepting Fees from Agency Clients

Counselors must not accept fees or other remuneration for consultation with persons entitled to such services through the counselor's employing agency or institution. (See D.3.a.)

Standard of Practice Thirty (SP-30)
Referral Fees

Counselors must not accept referral fees. (See D.3.b.)

Section E: Evaluation, Assessment, and Interpretation

Standard of Practice Thirty-one (SP-31)
Limits of Competence

Counselors must perform only testing and assessment services for which they are competent. Counselors must not allow the use of psychological assessment techniques by unqualified persons under their supervision. (See E.2.a.)

Standard of Practice Thirty-two (SP-32)
Appropriate Use of Assessment Instruments

Counselors must use assessment instruments in the manner for which they were intended. (See E.2.b.)

Standard of Practice Thirty-three (SP-33)
Assessment Explanations to Clients

Counselors must provide explanations to clients prior to assessment about the nature and purposes of assessment and the specific uses of results. (See E.3.a.)

Standard of Practice Thirty-four (SP-34)
Recipients of Test Results

Counselors must ensure that accurate and appropriate interpretations accompany any release of testing and assessment information. (See E.3.b.)

Standard of Practice Thirty-five (SP-35)
Obsolete Tests and Outdated Test Results

Counselors must not base their assessment or intervention decisions or recommendations on data or test results that are obsolete or outdated for the current purpose. (See E.11.)

Section F: Teaching, Training, and Supervision

Standard of Practice Thirty-six (SP-36)
Sexual Relationships with Students or Supervisees

Counselors must not engage in sexual relationships with their students and supervisees. (See F.1.c.)

Standard of Practice Thirty-seven (SP-37)
Credit for Contributions to Research

Counselors must give credit to students or supervisees for their contributions to research and scholarly projects. (See F.1.d.)

Standard of Practice Thirty-eight (SP-38)
Supervision Preparation

Counselors who offer clinical supervision services must be trained and prepared in supervision methods and techniques. (See F.1.f.)

Standard of Practice Thirty-nine (SP-39)
Evaluation Information

Counselors must clearly state to students and supervisees in advance of training, the levels of competency expected, appraisal methods, and timing of evaluations. Counselors must provide students and supervisees with periodic performance appraisal and evaluation feedback throughout the training program. (See F.2.c.)

Standard of Practice Forty (SP-40)
Peer Relationships in Training

Counselors must make every effort to ensure that the rights of peers are not violated when students and supervisees are assigned to lead counseling groups or provide clinical supervision. (See F.2.e.)

Standard of Practice Forty-one (SP-41)
Limitations of Students and Supervisees

Counselors must assist students and supervisees in securing remedial assistance, when needed, and must dismiss from the training program students and supervisees who are unable to provide competent service due to academic or personal limitations. (See F.3.a.)

Standard of Practice Forty-two (SP-42)
Self-growth Experiences

Counselors who conduct experiences for students or supervisees that include self-growth or self-disclosure must inform participants of counselors' ethical obligations to the profession and must not grade participants based on their nonacademic performance. (See F.3.b.)

Standard of Practice Forty-three (SP-43)
Standards for Students and Supervisees

Students and supervisees preparing to become counselors must adhere to the Code of Ethics and the Standards of Practice of counselors. (See F.3.e.)

Section G: Research and Publication

Standard of Practice Forty-four (SP-44)
Precautions to Avoid Injury in Research

Counselors must avoid causing physical, social, or psychological harm or injury to subjects in research. (See G.1.c.)

Standard of Practice Forty-five (SP-45)
Confidentiality of Research Information

Counselors must keep confidential information obtained about research participants. (See G.2.d.)

Standard of Practice Forty-six (SP-46)
Information Affecting Research Outcome

Counselors must report all variables and conditions known to the investigator that may have affected research data or outcomes. (See G.3.a.)

Standard of Practice Forty-seven (SP-47)
Accurate Research Results

Counselors must not distort or misrepresent research data, nor fabricate or intentionally bias research results. (See G.3.b.)

Standard of Practice Forty-eight (SP-48)
Publication Contributors

Counselors must give appropriate credit to those who have contributed to research. (See G.4.a. and G.4.b.)

Section H: Resolving Ethical Issues

Standard of Practice Forty-nine (SP-49)
Ethical Behavior Expected

Counselors must take appropriate action when they possess reasonable cause that raises doubts as to whether counselors or other mental health professionals are acting in an ethical manner. (See H.2.a.)

Standard of Practice Fifty (SP-50)
Unwarranted Complaints

Counselors must not initiate, participate in, or encourage the filings of ethics complaints that are unwarranted or intended to harm a mental health professional rather than to protect clients or the public. (See H.2.f.)

Standard of Practice Fifty-one (SP-51)
Cooperation with Ethics Committees

Counselors must cooperate with investigations, proceedings, and requirements of the ACA Ethics Committee or ethics committees of other duly constituted associations or boards having jurisdiction over those charged with a violation. (See H.3.)

ETHICAL PRINCIPLES OF PSYCHOLOGISTS AND CODE OF CONDUCT (AMERICAN PSYCHOLOGICAL ASSOCIATION)

Contents

Introduction

The American Psychological Association's (APA's) Ethical Principles of Psychologists and Code of Conduct (hereinafter referred to as the Ethics Code) consists of an Introduction, a Preamble, six General Principles (A–F), and specific Ethical Standards. The Introduction discusses the intent, organization, procedural considerations, and scope of application of the Ethics Code. The Preamble and General Principles are *aspirational* goals to guide psychologists toward the highest ideals of psychology. Although the Preamble and General Principles are not themselves enforceable rules, they should be considered by psychologists in arriving at an ethical course of action and may be considered by ethics bodies in interpreting the Ethical Standards. The Ethical Standards set forth *enforceable* rules for conduct as psychologists. Most of the Ethical Standards are written broadly, in order to apply to psychologists in varied roles, although the application of an Ethical Standard may vary depending on the context. The Ethical Standards are not exhaustive. The fact that a given conduct is not specifically addressed by the Ethics Code does not mean that it is necessarily either ethical or unethical.

Membership in the APA commits members to adhere to the APA Ethics Code and to the rules and procedures used to implement it. Psychologists and students, whether or not they are APA members, should be aware that the Ethics Code may be applied to them by state psychology boards, courts, or other public bodies.

This Ethics Code applies only to psychologists' work-related activities, that is, activities that are part of the psychologists' scientific and professional functions or that are psychological in nature. It includes the clinical or counseling practice of psychology, research, teaching, supervision of trainees, development of assessment instruments, conducting assessments, educational counseling, organizational consulting, social intervention, administration, and other activities as well. These work-related activities can be distinguished from the purely private conduct of a psychologist, which ordinarily is not within the purview of the Ethics Code.

The Ethics Code is intended to provide standards of professional conduct that can be applied by the APA and by other bodies that choose to adopt them. Whether or not a psychologist has violated the Ethics Code does not by itself determine whether he or she is legally liable in a court action, whether a contract is enforceable, or whether other legal consequences occur. These results are based on legal rather than ethical rules. However, compliance with or violation of the Ethics Code may be admissible as evidence in some legal proceedings, depending on the circumstances.

In the process of making decisions regarding their professional behavior, psychologists must consider this Ethics Code, in addition to applicable laws and psychology board regulations. If the

Ethics Code establishes a higher standard of conduct than is required by law, psychologists must meet the higher ethical standard. If the Ethics Code standard appears to conflict with the requirements of law, then psychologists make known their commitment to the Ethics Code and take steps to resolve the conflict in a responsible manner. If neither law nor the Ethics Code resolves an issue, psychologists should consider other professional materials and the dictates of their own conscience, as well as seek consultation with others within the field when this is practical.

The procedures for filing, investigating, and resolving complaints of unethical conduct are described in the current Rules and Procedures of the APA Ethics Committee. The actions that APA may take for violations of the Ethics Code include actions such as reprimand, censure, termination of APA membership, and referral of the matter to other bodies. Complainants who seek remedies such as monetary damages in alleging ethical violations by psychologists must resort to private negotiations, administrative bodies, or the courts. Actions that violate the Ethics Code may lead to the imposition of sanctions on a psychologist by bodies other than APA, including state psychological associations, other professional groups, psychology boards, other state or federal agencies, and payors for health services. In addition to actions for violation of the Ethics Code, the APA Bylaws provide that APA may take action against a member after his or her conviction of a felony, expulsion or suspension from an affiliated state psychological association, or suspension or loss of licensure.

Preamble

Psychologists work to develop a valid and reliable body of scientific knowledge based on research. They may apply that knowledge to human behavior in a variety of contexts. In doing so, they perform many roles, such as researcher, educator, diagnostician, therapist, supervisor, consultant, administrator, social interventionist, and expert witness. Their goal is to broaden knowledge of behavior and, where appropriate, to apply it pragmatically to improve the condition of both the individual and society. Psychologists respect the central importance of freedom of inquiry and expression in research, teaching, and publication. They also strive to help the public in developing informed judgments and choices concerning human behavior. This Ethics Code provides a common set of values upon which psychologists build their professional and scientific work.

This Code is intended to provide both the general principles and the decision rules to cover most situations encountered by psychologists. It has as its primary goal the welfare and protection of the individuals and groups with whom psychologists work. It is the individual responsibility of each psychologist to aspire to the highest possible standards of conduct. Psychologists respect and protect human and civil rights, and do not knowingly participate in or condone unfair discriminatory practices.

The development of a dynamic set of ethical standards for a psychologist's work-related conduct requires a personal commitment to a lifelong effort to act ethically; to encourage ethical behavior by students, supervisees, employees, and colleagues, as appropriate; and to consult with others, as needed, concerning ethical problems. Each psychologist supplements, but does not violate, the Ethics Code's values and rules on the basis of guidance drawn from personal values, culture, and experience.

General Principles

Principle A: Competence

Psychologists strive to maintain high standards of competence in their work. They recognize the boundaries of their particular competencies and the limitations of their expertise. They provide only those services and use only those techniques for which they are qualified by education, training, or experience. Psychologists are cognizant of the fact that the competencies required in serving, teaching, and/or studying groups of people vary with the distinctive characteristics of those groups. In those areas in which recognized professional standards do not yet exist, psychologists exercise careful judgment and take appropriate precautions to protect the welfare of those with whom they work. They maintain knowledge of relevant scientific and professional information related to the services they render, and they recognize the need for ongoing education. Psychologists make appropriate use of scientific, professional, technical, and administrative resources.

Principle B: Integrity

Psychologists seek to promote integrity in the science, teaching, and practice of psychology. In these activities psychologists are honest, fair, and respectful of others. In describing or reporting their qualifications, services, products, fees, research, or teaching, they do not make statements that are false, misleading, or deceptive. Psychologists strive to be aware of their own belief systems, values, needs, and limitations and the effect of these on their work. To the extent feasible, they attempt to clarify for relevant parties the roles they are performing and to function appropriately in accordance with those roles. Psychologists avoid improper and potentially harmful dual relationships.

Principle C: Professional and Scientific Responsibility

Psychologists uphold professional standards of conduct, clarify their professional roles and obligations, accept appropriate responsibility for their behavior, and adapt their methods to the needs of different populations. Psychologists consult with, refer to, or cooperate with other professionals and institutions to the extent needed to serve the best interests of their patients, clients, or other recipients of their services. Psychologists' moral standards and conduct are personal matters to the same degree as is true for any other person, except as psychologists' conduct may compromise their professional responsibilities or reduce the public's trust in psychology and psychologists. Psychologists are concerned about the ethical compliance of their colleagues' scientific and professional conduct. When appropriate, they consult with colleagues in order to prevent or avoid unethical conduct.

Principle D: Respect for People's Rights and Dignity

Psychologists accord appropriate respect to the fundamental rights, dignity, and worth of all people. They respect the rights of individuals to privacy, confidentiality, self-determination, and autonomy, mindful that legal and other obligations may lead to inconsistency and conflict with the exercise of these rights. Psychologists are aware of cultural, individual, and role differences, including those due to age, gender, race, ethnicity, national origin, religion, sexual orientation, disability, language, and socioeconomic status. Psychologists try to eliminate the effect on their work of biases based on those factors, and they do not knowingly participate in or condone unfair discriminatory practices.

Principle E: Concern for Others' Welfare

Psychologists seek to contribute to the welfare of those with whom they interact professionally. In their professional actions, psychologists weigh the welfare and rights of their patients or clients, students, supervisees, human research participants, and other affected persons, and the welfare of animal subjects of research. When conflicts occur among psychologists' obligations or concerns, they attempt to resolve these conflicts and to perform their roles in a responsible fashion that avoids or minimizes harm. Psychologists are sensitive to real and ascribed differences in power between themselves and others, and they do not exploit or mislead other people during or after professional relationships.

Principle F: Social Responsibility

Psychologists are aware of their professional and scientific responsibilities to the community and the society in which they work and live. They apply and make public their knowledge of psychology in order to contribute to human welfare. Psychologists are concerned about and work to mitigate the causes of human suffering. When undertaking research, they strive to advance human welfare and the science of psychology. Psychologists try to avoid misuse of their work. Psychologists comply with the law and encourage the development of law and social policy that serve the interests of their patients and clients and the public. They are encouraged to contribute a portion of their professional time for little or no personal advantage.

Ethical Standards

1. General Standards

These General Standards are potentially applicable to the professional and scientific activities of all psychologists.

1.01 Applicability of the Ethics Code

The activity of a psychologist subject to the Ethics Code may be reviewed under these Ethical Standards only if the activity is part of his or her work-related functions or the activity is psychological in nature. Personal activities having no connection to or effect on psychological roles are not subject to the Ethics Code.

1.02 Relationship of Ethics and Law

If psychologists' ethical responsibilities conflict with law, psychologists make known their commitment to the Ethics Code and take steps to resolve the conflict in a responsible manner.

1.03 Professional and Scientific Relationship

Psychologists provide diagnostic, therapeutic, teaching, research, supervisory, consultative, or other psychological services only in the context of a defined professional or scientific relationship or role. (See also Standards 2.01, Evaluation, Diagnosis, and Interventions in Professional Context, and 7.02, Forensic Assessments.)

1.04 Boundaries of Competence

(a) Psychologists provide services, teach, and conduct research only within the boundaries of their competence, based on their education, training, supervised experience, or appropriate professional experience.

(b) Psychologists provide services, teach, or conduct research in new areas or involving new techniques only after first undertaking appropriate study, training, supervision, and/or consultation from persons who are competent in those areas or techniques.

(c) In those emerging areas in which generally recognized standards for preparatory training do not yet exist, psychologists nevertheless take reasonable steps to ensure the competence of their work and to protect patients, clients, students, research participants, and others from harm.

1.05 Maintaining Expertise

Psychologists who engage in assessment, therapy, teaching, research, organizational consulting, or other professional activities maintain a reasonable level of awareness of current scientific and professional information in their fields of activity, and undertake ongoing efforts to maintain competence in the skills they use.

1.06 Basis for Scientific and Professional Judgments

Psychologists rely on scientifically and professionally derived knowledge when making scientific or professional judgments or when engaging in scholarly or professional endeavors.

1.07 Describing the Nature and Results of Psychological Services

(a) When psychologists provide assessment, evaluation, treatment, counseling, supervision, teaching, consultation, research, or other psychological services to an individual, a group, or an organization, they provide, using language that is reasonably understandable to the recipient of those services, appropriate information beforehand about the nature of such services and appropriate information later about results and conclusions. (See also Standard 2.09, Explaining Assessment Results.)

(b) If psychologists will be precluded by law or by organizational roles from providing such information to particular individuals or groups, they so inform those individuals or groups at the outset of the service.

1.08 Human Differences

Where differences of age, gender, race, ethnicity, national origin, religion, sexual orientation, disability, language, or socioeconomic status significantly affect psychologists' work concerning particular individuals or groups, psychologists obtain the training, experience, consultation, or supervision necessary to ensure the competence of their services, or they make appropriate referrals.

1.09 Respecting Others

In their work-related activities, psychologists respect the rights of others to hold values, attitudes, and opinions that differ from their own.

1.10 Nondiscrimination

In their work-related activities, psychologists do not engage in unfair discrimination based on age, gender, race, ethnicity, national origin, religion, sexual orientation, disability, socioeconomic status, or any basis proscribed by law.

1.11 Sexual Harassment

(a) Psychologists do not engage in sexual harassment. Sexual harassment is sexual solicitation, physical advances, or verbal or nonverbal conduct that is sexual in nature, that occurs in connection with the psychologists' activities or roles as a psychologist, and that either: (1) is unwelcome, is offensive, or creates a hostile workplace environment, and the psychologist knows or is told this; or (2) is sufficiently severe or intense to be abusive to a reasonable person in the context. Sexual harassment can consist of a single intense or severe act or of multiple persistent or pervasive acts.

(b) Psychologists accord sexual-harassment complainants and respondents dignity and respect. Psychologists do not participate in denying a person academic admittance or advancement, employment, tenure, or promotion, based solely upon their having made, or their being the subject of, sexual-harassment charges. This does not preclude taking action based upon the outcome of such proceedings or consideration of other appropriate information.

1.12 Other Harassment

Psychologists do not knowingly engage in behavior that is harassing or demeaning to persons with whom they interact in their work based on factors such as those persons' age, gender, race, ethnicity, national origin, religion, sexual orientation, disability, language, or socioeconomic status.

1.13 Personal Problems and Conflicts

(a) Psychologists recognize that their personal problems and conflicts may interfere with their effectiveness. Accordingly, they refrain from undertaking an activity when they know or should know that their personal problems are likely to lead to harm to a patient, client, colleague, student, research participant, or other person to whom they may owe a professional or scientific obligation.

(b) In addition, psychologists have an obligation to be alert to signs of, and to obtain assistance for, their personal problems at an early stage, in order to prevent significantly impaired performance.

(c) When psychologists become aware of personal problems that may interfere with their performing work-related duties adequately, they take appropriate measures, such as obtaining professional consultation or assistance, and determine whether they should limit, suspend, or terminate their work-related duties.

1.14 Avoiding Harm

Psychologists take reasonable steps to avoid harming their patients or clients, research participants, students, and others with whom they work, and to minimize harm where it is foreseeable and unavoidable.

1.15 Misuse of Psychologists' Influence

Because psychologists' scientific and professional judgments and actions may affect the lives of others, they are alert to and guard against personal, financial, social, organizational, or political factors that might lead to misuse of their influence.

1.16 Misuse of Psychologists' Work

(a) Psychologists do not participate in activities in which it appears likely that their skills or data will be misused by others, unless corrective mechanisms are available. (See also Standard 7.04, Truthfulness and Candor.)

(b) If psychologists learn of misuse or misrepresentation of their work, they take reasonable steps to correct or minimize the misuse or misrepresentation.

1.17 Multiple Relationships

(a) In many communities and situations, it may not be feasible or reasonable for psychologists to avoid social or other nonprofessional contacts with persons such as patients, clients, students, supervisees, or research participants. Psychologists must always be sensitive to the potential harmful effects of other contacts on their work and on those persons with whom they deal. A psychologist refrains from entering into or promising another personal, scientific, professional, financial, or other relationship with such persons if it appears likely that such a relationship reasonably might impair the psychologist's objectivity or otherwise interfere with the psychologist's effectively performing his or her functions as a psychologist, or might harm or exploit the other party.

(b) Likewise, whenever feasible, a psychologist refrains from taking on professional or scientific obligations when preexisting relationships would create a risk of such harm.

(c) If a psychologist finds that, due to unforeseen factors, a potentially harmful multiple relationship has arisen, the psychologist attempts to resolve it with due regard for the best interests of the affected person and maximal compliance with the Ethics Code.

1.18 Barter (with Patients or Clients)

Psychologists ordinarily refrain from accepting goods, services, or other nonmonetary remuneration from patients or clients in return for psychological services because such arrangements create inherent potential for conflicts, exploitation, and distortion of the professional relationship. A psychologist may participate in bartering *only* if (1) it is not clinically contraindicated, *and* (2) the relationship is not exploitative. (See also Standards 1.17, Multiple Relationships, and 1.25, Fees and Financial Arrangements.)

1.19 Exploitative Relationships

(a) Psychologists do not exploit persons over whom they have supervisory, evaluative, or other authority such as students, supervisees, employees, research participants, and clients or patients. (See also Standards 4.05–4.07 regarding sexual involvement with clients or patients.)

(b) Psychologists do not engage in sexual relationships with students or supervisees in training over whom the psychologist has evaluative or direct authority, because such relationships are so likely to impair judgment or be exploitative.

1.20 Consultations and Referrals

(a) Psychologists arrange for appropriate consultations and referrals based principally on the best interests of their patients or clients, with appropriate consent, and subject to other relevant considerations, including applicable law and contractual obligations. (See also Standards 5.01, Discussing the Limits of Confidentiality, and 5.06, Consultations.)

(b) When indicated and professionally appropriate, psychologists cooperate with other professionals in order to serve their patients or clients effectively and appropriately.

(c) Psychologists' referral practices are consistent with law.

1.21 Third-Party Requests for Services

(a) When a psychologist agrees to provide services to a person or entity at the request of a third party, the psychologist clarifies to the extent feasible, at the outset of the service, the nature of the relationship with each party. This clarification includes the role of the psychologist (such as therapist, organizational consultant, diagnostician, or expert witness), the probable uses of the services provided or the information obtained, and the fact that there may be limits to confidentiality.

(b) If there is a foreseeable risk of the psychologist's being called upon to perform conflicting roles because of the involvement of a third party, the psychologist clarifies the nature and direction of his or her responsibilities, keeps all parties appropriately informed as matters develop, and resolves the situation in accordance with this Ethics Code.

1.22 Delegation to and Supervision of Subordinates

(a) Psychologists delegate to their employees, supervisees, and research assistants only those responsibilities that such persons can reasonably be expected to perform competently, on the basis of their education, training, or experience, either independently or with the level of supervision being provided.

(b) Psychologists provide proper training and supervision to their employees or supervisees and take reasonable steps to see that such persons perform services responsibly, competently, and ethically.

(c) If institutional policies, procedures, or practices prevent fulfillment of this obligation, psychologists attempt to modify their role or to correct the situation to the extent feasible.

1.23 Documentation of Professional and Scientific Work

(a) Psychologists appropriately document their professional and scientific work in order to facilitate provision of services later by them or by other professionals, to ensure accountability, and to meet other requirements of institutions or the law.

(b) When psychologists have reason to believe that records of their professional services will be used in legal proceedings involving recipients of or participants in their work, they have a responsibility to create and maintain documentation in the kind of detail and quality that would be consistent with reasonable scrutiny in an adjudicative forum. (See also Standard 7.01, Professionalism, under Forensic Activities.)

1.24 Records and Data

Psychologists create, maintain, disseminate, store, retain, and dispose of records and data relating to their research, practice, and other work in accordance with law and in a manner that permits compliance with the requirements of this Ethics Code. (See also Standard 5.04, Maintenance of Records.)

1.25 Fees and Financial Arrangements

(a) As early as is feasible in a professional or scientific relationship, the psychologist and the patient, client, or other appropriate recipient of psychological services reach an agreement specifying the compensation and the billing arrangements.

(b) Psychologists do not exploit recipients of services or payors with respect to fees.

(c) Psychologists' fee practices are consistent with law.

(d) Psychologists do not misrepresent their fees.

(e) If limitations to services can be anticipated because of limitations in financing, this is discussed with the patient, client, or other appropriate recipient of services as early as is feasible. (See also Standard 4.08, Interruption of Services.)

(f) If the patient, client, or other recipient of services does not pay for services as agreed, and if the psychologist wishes to use collection agencies or legal measures to collect the fees, the psychologist first informs the person that such measures will be taken and provides that person an opportunity to make prompt payment. (See also Standard 5.11, Withholding Records for Nonpayment.)

1.26 Accuracy in Reports to Payors and Funding Sources

In their reports to payors for services or sources of research funding, psychologists accurately state the nature of the research or service provided, the fees or charges, and where applicable, the identity of the provider, the findings, and the diagnosis. (See also Standard 5.05, Disclosures.)

1.27 Referrals and Fees

When a psychologist pays, receives payment from, or divides fees with another professional other than in an employer–employee relationship, the payment to each is based on the services (clinical, consultative, administrative, or other) provided and is not based on the referral itself.

2. Evaluation, Assessment, or Intervention

2.01 Evaluation, Diagnosis, and Interventions in Professional Context

(a) Psychologists perform evaluations, diagnostic services, or interventions only within the context of a defined professional relationship. (See also Standard 1.03, Professional and Scientific Relationship.)

(b) Psychologists' assessments, recommendations, reports, and psychological diagnostic or evaluative statements are based on information and techniques (including personal interviews of the individual when appropriate) sufficient to provide appropriate substantiation for their findings. (See also Standard 7.02, Forensic Assessments.)

2.02 Competence and Appropriate Use of Assessments and Interventions

(a) Psychologists who develop, administer, score, interpret, or use psychological assessment techniques, interviews, tests, or instruments do so in a manner and for purposes that are appropriate in light of the research on or evidence of the usefulness and proper application of the techniques.

(b) Psychologists refrain from misuse of assessment techniques, interventions, results, and interpretations and take reasonable steps to prevent others from misusing the information these techniques provide. This includes refraining from releasing raw test results or raw data to persons, other than to patients or clients as appropriate, who are not qualified to use such information. (See also Standards 1.02, Relationship of Ethics and Law, and 1.04, Boundaries of Competence.)

2.03 Test Construction

Psychologists who develop and conduct research with tests and other assessment techniques use scientific procedures and current professional knowledge for test design, standardization, validation, reduction or elimination of bias, and recommendations for use.

2.04 Use of Assessment in General and with Special Populations

(a) Psychologists who perform interventions or administer, score, interpret, or use assessment techniques are familiar with the reliability, validation, and related standardization or outcome studies of, and proper applications and uses of, the techniques they use.

(b) Psychologists recognize limits to the certainty with which diagnoses, judgments, or predictions can be made about individuals.

(c) Psychologists attempt to identify situations in which particular interventions or assessment techniques or norms may not be applicable or may require adjustment in administration or interpretation because of factors such as individuals' gender, age, race, ethnicity, national origin, religion, sexual orientation, disability, language, or socioeconomic status.

2.05 Interpreting Assessment Results

When interpreting assessment results, including automated interpretations, psychologists take into account the various test factors and characteristics of the person being assessed that might affect psychologists' judgments or reduce the accuracy of their interpretations. They indicate any significant reservations they have about the accuracy or limitations of their interpretations.

2.06 Unqualified Persons

Psychologists do not promote the use of psychological assessment techniques by unqualified persons. (See also Standard 1.22, Delegation to and Supervision of Subordinates.)

2.07 Obsolete Tests and Outdated Test Results

(a) Psychologists do not base their assessment or intervention decisions or recommendations on data or test results that are outdated for the current purpose.

(b) Similarly, psychologists do not base such decisions or recommendations on tests and measures that are obsolete and not useful for the current purpose.

2.08 Test Scoring and Interpretation Services

(a) Psychologists who offer assessment or scoring procedures to other professionals accurately describe the purpose, norms, validity, reliability, and applications of the procedures and any special qualifications applicable to their use.

(b) Psychologists select scoring and interpretation services (including automated services) on the basis of evidence of the validity of the program and procedures as well as on other appropriate considerations.

(c) Psychologists retain appropriate responsibility for the appropriate application, interpretation, and use of assessment instruments, whether they score and interpret such tests themselves or use automated or other services.

2.09 Explaining Assessment Results

Unless the nature of the relationship is clearly explained to the person being assessed in advance and precludes provision of an explanation of results (such as in some organizational consulting, preemployment or security screenings, and forensic evaluations), psychologists ensure that an explanation of the results is provided using language that is reasonably understandable to the person assessed or to another legally authorized person on behalf of the client. Regardless of whether the scoring and interpretation are done by the psychologist, by assistants, or by automated or other outside services, psychologists take reasonable steps to ensure that appropriate explanations of results are given.

2.10 Maintaining Test Security

Psychologists make reasonable efforts to maintain the integrity and security of tests and other assessment techniques consistent with law, contractual obligations, and in a manner that permits compliance with the requirements of this Ethics Code. (See also Standard 1.02, Relationship of Ethics and Law.)

3. Advertising and Other Public Statements

3.01 Definition of Public Statements

Psychologists comply with this Ethics Code in public statements relating to their professional services, products, or publications or to the field of psychology. Public statements include but are not limited to paid or unpaid advertising, brochures, printed matter, directory listings, personal resumes or curricula vitae, interviews or comments for use in media, statements in legal proceedings, lectures and public oral presentations, and published materials.

3.02 Statements by Others

(a) Psychologists who engage others to create or place public statements that promote their professional practice, products, or activities retain professional responsibility for such statements.

(b) In addition, psychologists make reasonable efforts to prevent others whom they do not control (such as employers, publishers, sponsors, organizational clients, and representatives of the print or broadcast media) from making deceptive statements concerning psychologists' practice or professional or scientific activities.

(c) If psychologists learn of deceptive statements about their work made by others, psychologists make reasonable efforts to correct such statements.

(d) Psychologists do not compensate employees of press, radio, television, or other communication media in return for publicity in a news item.

(e) A paid advertisement relating to the psychologist's activities must be identified as such, unless it is already apparent from the context.

3.03 Avoidance of False or Deceptive Statements

(a) Psychologists do not make public statements that are false, deceptive, misleading, or fraudulent, either because of what they state, convey, or suggest or because of what they omit, concerning their research, practice, or other work activities or those of persons or organizations with which they are affiliated. As examples (and not in limitation) of this standard, psychologists do not make false or deceptive statements concerning (1) their training, experience, or competence; (2) their academic degrees; (3) their credentials; (4) their institutional or association affiliations; (5) their services; (6) the scientific or clinical basis for, or results or degree of success of, their services; (7) their fees; or (8) their publications or research findings. (See also Standards 6.15, Deception in Research, and 6.18, Providing Participants with Information About the Study.)

(b) Psychologists claim as credentials for their psychological work, only degrees that (1) were earned from a regionally accredited educational institution or (2) were the basis for psychology licensure by the state in which they practice.

3.04 Media Presentations

When psychologists provide advice or comment by means of public lectures, demonstrations, radio or television programs, prerecorded tapes, printed articles, mailed material, or other media, they take reasonable precautions to ensure that (1) the statements are based on appropriate psychological literature and practice, (2) the statements are otherwise consistent with this Ethics Code, and (3) the recipients of the information are not encouraged to infer that a relationship has been established with them personally.

3.05 Testimonials

Psychologists do not solicit testimonials from current psychotherapy clients or patients or other persons who because of their particular circumstances are vulnerable to undue influence.

3.06 In-Person Solicitation

Psychologists do not engage, directly or through agents, in uninvited in-person solicitation of business from actual or potential psychotherapy patients or clients or other persons who because of their particular circumstances are vulnerable to undue influence. However, this does not preclude attempting to implement appropriate collateral contacts with significant others for the purpose of benefiting an already engaged therapy patient.

4. Therapy

4.01 Structuring the Relationship

(a) Psychologists discuss with clients or patients as early as is feasible in the therapeutic relationship appropriate issues, such as the nature and anticipated course of therapy, fees, and confidentiality. (See also Standards 1.25, Fees and Financial Arrangements, and 5.01, Discussing the Limits of Confidentiality.)

(b) When the psychologist's work with clients or patients will be supervised, the above discussion includes that fact, and the name of the supervisor, when the supervisor has legal responsibility for the case.

(c) When the therapist is a student intern, the client or patient is informed of that fact.

(d) Psychologists make reasonable efforts to answer patients' questions and to avoid apparent misunderstandings about therapy. Whenever possible, psychologists provide oral and/or written information, using language that is reasonably understandable to the patient or client.

4.02 Informed Consent to Therapy

(a) Psychologists obtain appropriate informed consent to therapy or related procedures, using language that is reasonably understandable to participants. The content of informed consent will vary depending on many circumstances; however, informed consent generally implies that the person (1) has the capacity to consent, (2) has been informed of significant information concerning the procedure, (3) has freely and without undue influence expressed consent, and (4) consent has been appropriately documented.

(b) When persons are legally incapable of giving informed consent, psychologists obtain informed permission from a legally authorized person, if such substitute consent is permitted by law.

(c) In addition, psychologists (1) inform those persons who are legally incapable of giving informed consent about the proposed interventions in a manner commensurate with the persons' psychological capacities, (2) seek their assent to those interventions, and (3) consider such persons' preferences and best interests.

4.03 Couple and Family Relationships

(a) When a psychologist agrees to provide services to several persons who have a relationship (such as husband and wife or parents and children), the psychologist attempts to clarify at the outset (1) which of the individuals are patients or clients and (2) the relationship the psychologist will have with each person. This clarification includes the role of the psychologist and the probable uses of the services provided or the information obtained. (See also Standard 5.01, Discussing the Limits of Confidentiality.)

(b) As soon as it becomes apparent that the psychologist may be called on to perform potentially conflicting roles (such as marital counselor to husband and wife, and then witness for one party in a divorce proceeding), the psychologist attempts to clarify and adjust, or withdraw from, roles appropriately. (See also Standard 7.03, Clarification of Role, under Forensic Activities.)

4.04 Providing Mental Health Services to Those Served by Others

In deciding whether to offer or provide services to those already receiving mental health services elsewhere, psychologists carefully consider the treatment issues and the potential patient's or client's welfare. The psychologist discusses these issues with the patient or client, or another legally authorized person on behalf of the client, in order to minimize the risk of confusion and conflict, consults with the other service providers when appropriate, and proceeds with caution and sensitivity to the therapeutic issues.

4.05 Sexual Intimacies with Current Patients or Clients

Psychologists do not engage in sexual intimacies with current patients or clients.

4.06 Therapy with Former Sexual Partners

Psychologists do not accept as therapy patients or clients persons with whom they have engaged in sexual intimacies.

4.07 Sexual Intimacies with Former Therapy Patients

(a) Psychologists do not engage in sexual intimacies with a former therapy patient or client for at least two years after cessation or termination of professional services.

(b) Because sexual intimacies with a former therapy patient or client are so frequently harmful to the patient or client, and because such intimacies undermine public confidence in the psychology profession and thereby deter the public's use of needed services, psychologists do not engage in sexual intimacies with former therapy patients and clients even after a two-year interval except in the most unusual circumstances. The psychologist who engages in such activity after the two years following cessation or termination of treatment bears the burden of demonstrating that there has been no exploitation, in light of all relevant factors, including (1) the amount of time that has passed since therapy terminated, (2) the nature and duration of the therapy, (3) the circumstances of termination, (4) the patient's or client's personal history, (5) the patient's or client's current mental status, (6) the likelihood of adverse impact on the patient or client and others, and (7) any statements or actions made by the therapist during the course of therapy suggesting or inviting the possibility of a posttermination sexual or romantic relationship with the patient or client. (See also Standard 1.17, Multiple Relationships.)

4.08 Interruption of Services

(a) Psychologists make reasonable efforts to plan for facilitating care in the event that psychological services are interrupted by factors such as the psychologist's illness, death, unavailability, or relocation or by the client's relocation or financial limitations. (See also Standard 5.09, Preserving Records and Data.)

(b) When entering into employment or contractual relationships, psychologists provide for orderly and appropriate resolution of responsibility for patient or client care in the event that the employment or contractual relationship ends, with paramount consideration given to the welfare of the patient or client.

4.09 Terminating the Professional Relationship

(a) Psychologists do not abandon patients or clients. (See also Standard 1.25e, under Fees and Financial Arrangements.)

(b) Psychologists terminate a professional relationship when it becomes reasonably clear that the patient or client no longer needs the service, is not benefiting, or is being harmed by continued service.

(c) Prior to termination for whatever reason, except where precluded by the patient's or client's conduct, the psychologist discusses the patient's or client's views and needs, provides appropriate pretermination counseling, suggests alternative service providers as appropriate, and takes other reasonable steps to facilitate transfer of responsibility to another provider if the patient or client needs one immediately.

5. Privacy and Confidentiality

These Standards are potentially applicable to the professional and scientific activities of all psychologists.

5.01 Discussing the Limits of Confidentiality

(a) Psychologists discuss with persons and organizations with whom they establish a scientific or professional relationship (including, to the extent feasible, minors and their legal representatives) (1) the relevant limitations on confidentiality, including limitations where applicable in group, marital, and family therapy or in organizational consulting, and (2) the foreseeable uses of the information generated through their services.

(b) Unless it is not feasible or is contraindicated, the discussion of confidentiality occurs at the outset of the relationship and thereafter as new circumstances may warrant.

(c) Permission for electronic recording of interviews is secured from clients and patients.

5.02 Maintaining Confidentiality

Psychologists have a primary obligation and take reasonable precautions to respect the confidentiality rights of those with whom they work or consult, recognizing that confidentiality may be established by law, institutional rules, or professional or scientific relationships. (See also Standard 6.26, Professional Reviewers.)

5.03 Minimizing Intrusions on Privacy

(a) In order to minimize intrusions on privacy, psychologists include in written and oral reports, consultations, and the like, only information germane to the purpose for which the communication is made.

(b) Psychologists discuss confidential information obtained in clinical or consulting relationships, or evaluative data concerning patients, individual or organizational clients, students, research participants, supervisees, and employees, only for appropriate scientific or professional purposes and only with persons clearly concerned with such matters.

5.04 Maintenance of Records

Psychologists maintain appropriate confidentiality in creating, storing, accessing, transferring, and disposing of records under their control, whether these are written, automated, or in any other medium. Psychologists maintain and dispose of records in accordance with law and in a manner that permits compliance with the requirements of this Ethics Code.

5.05 Disclosures

(a) Psychologists disclose confidential information without the consent of the individual only as mandated by law, or where permitted by law for a valid purpose, such as (1) to provide needed professional services to the patient or the individual or organizational client, (2) to obtain appropriate professional consultations, (3) to protect the patient or client or others from harm, or (4) to obtain payment for services, in which instance disclosure is limited to the minimum that is necessary to achieve the purpose.

(b) Psychologists also may disclose confidential information with the appropriate consent of the patient or the individual or organizational client (or of another legally authorized person on behalf of the patient or client), unless prohibited by law.

5.06 Consultations

When consulting with colleagues, (1) psychologists do not share confidential information that reasonably could lead to the identification of a patient, client, research participant, or other person or organization with whom they have a confidential relationship unless they have obtained the prior consent of the person or organization or the disclosure cannot be avoided, and (2) they share information only to the extent necessary to achieve the purposes of the consultation. (See also Standard 5.02, Maintaining Confidentiality.)

5.07 Confidential Information in Databases

(a) If confidential information concerning recipients of psychological services is to be entered into databases or systems of records available to persons whose access has not been consented to by the recipient, then psychologists use coding or other techniques to avoid the inclusion of personal identifiers.

(b) If a research protocol approved by an institutional review board or similar body requires the inclusion of personal identifiers, such identifiers are deleted before the information is made accessible to persons other than those of whom the subject was advised.

(c) If such deletion is not feasible, then before psychologists transfer such data to others or review such data collected by others, they take reasonable steps to determine that appropriate consent of personally identifiable individuals has been obtained.

5.08 Use of Confidential Information for Didactic or Other Purposes

(a) Psychologists do not disclose in their writings, lectures, or other public media, confidential, personally identifiable information concerning their patients, individual or organizational clients, students, research participants, or other recipients of their services that they obtained during the course of their work, unless the person or organization has consented in writing or unless there is other ethical or legal authorization for doing so.

(b) Ordinarily, in such scientific and professional presentations, psychologists disguise confidential information concerning such persons or organizations so that they are not individually identifiable to others and so that discussions do not cause harm to subjects who might identify themselves.

5.09 Preserving Records and Data

A psychologist makes plans in advance so that confidentiality of records and data is protected in the event of the psychologist's death, incapacity, or withdrawal from the position or practice.

5.10 Ownership of Records and Data

Recognizing that ownership of records and data is governed by legal principles, psychologists take reasonable and lawful steps so that records and data remain available to the extent needed to serve the best interests of patients, individual or organizational clients, research participants, or appropriate others.

5.11 Withholding Records for Nonpayment

Psychologists may not withhold records under their control that are requested and imminently needed for a patient's or client's treatment solely because payment has not been received, except as otherwise provided by law.

6. Teaching, Training Supervision, Research, and Publishing

6.01 Design of Education and Training Programs

Psychologists who are responsible for education and training programs seek to ensure that the programs are competently designed, provide the proper experiences, and meet the requirements for licensure, certification, or other goals for which claims are made by the program.

6.02 Descriptions of Education and Training Programs

(a) Psychologists responsible for education and training programs seek to ensure that there is a current and accurate description of the program content, training goals and objectives, and requirements that must be met for satisfactory completion of the program. This information must be made readily available to all interested parties.

(b) Psychologists seek to ensure that statements concerning their course outlines are accurate and not misleading, particularly regarding the subject matter to be covered, bases for evaluating progress, and the nature of course experiences. (See also Standard 3.03, Avoidance of False or Deceptive Statements.)

(c) To the degree to which they exercise control, psychologists responsible for announcements, catalogs, brochures, or advertisements describing workshops, seminars, or other non-degree-granting educational programs ensure that they accurately describe the audience for which the program is intended, the educational objectives, the presenters, and the fees involved.

6.03 Accuracy and Objectivity in Teaching

(a) When engaged in teaching or training, psychologists present psychological information accurately and with a reasonable degree of objectivity.

(b) When engaged in teaching or training, psychologists recognize the power they hold over students or supervisees and therefore make reasonable efforts to avoid engaging in conduct that is personally demeaning to students or supervisees. (See also Standards 1.09, Respecting Others, and 1.12, Other Harassment.)

6.04 Limitation on Teaching

Psychologists do not teach the use of techniques or procedures that require specialized training, licensure, or expertise, including but not limited to hypnosis, biofeedback, and projective techniques, to individuals who lack the prerequisite training, legal scope of practice, or expertise.

6.05 Assessing Student and Supervisee Performance

(a) In academic and supervisory relationships, psychologists establish an appropriate process for providing feedback to students and supervisees.

(b) Psychologists evaluate students and supervisees on the basis of their actual performance on relevant and established program requirements.

6.06 Planning Research

(a) Psychologists design, conduct, and report research in accordance with recognized standards of scientific competence and ethical research.

(b) Psychologists plan their research so as to minimize the possibility that results will be misleading.

(c) In planning research, psychologists consider its ethical acceptability under the Ethics Code. If an ethical issue is unclear, psychologists seek to resolve the issue through consultation with institutional review boards, animal care and use committees, peer consultations, or other proper mechanisms.

(d) Psychologists take reasonable steps to implement appropriate protections for the rights and welfare of human participants, other persons affected by the research, and the welfare of animal subjects.

6.07 Responsibility

(a) Psychologists conduct research competently and with due concern for the dignity and welfare of the participants.

(b) Psychologists are responsible for the ethical conduct of research conducted by them or by others under their supervision or control.

(c) Researchers and assistants are permitted to perform only those tasks for which they are appropriately trained and prepared.

(d) As part of the process of development and implementation of research projects, psychologists consult those with expertise concerning any special population under investigation or most likely to be affected.

6.08 Compliance with Law and Standards

Psychologists plan and conduct research in a manner consistent with federal and state law and regulations, as well as professional standards governing the conduct of research, and particularly those standards governing research with human participants and animal subjects.

6.09 Institutional Approval

Psychologists obtain from host institutions or organizations appropriate approval prior to conducting research, and they provide accurate information about their research proposals. They conduct the research in accordance with the approved research protocol.

6.10 Research Responsibilities

Prior to conducting research (except research involving only anonymous surveys, naturalistic observations, or similar research), psychologists enter into an agreement with participants that clarifies the nature of the research and the responsibilities of each party.

6.11 Informed Consent to Research

(a) Psychologists use language that is reasonably understandable to research participants in obtaining their appropriate informed consent (except as provided in Standard 6.12, Dispensing with Informed Consent). Such informed consent is appropriately documented.

(b) Using language that is reasonably understandable to participants, psychologists inform participants of the nature of the research; they inform participants that they are free to participate or to decline to participate or to withdraw from the research; they explain the foreseeable consequences of declining or withdrawing; they inform participants of significant factors that may be expected to influence their willingness to participate (such as risks, discomfort, adverse effects, or limitations on confidentiality, except as provided in Standard 6.15, Deception in Research); and they explain other aspects about which the prospective participants inquire.

(c) When psychologists conduct research with individuals such as students or subordinates, psychologists take special care to protect the prospective participants from adverse consequences of declining or withdrawing from participation.

(d) When research participation is a course requirement or opportunity for extra credit, the prospective participant is given the choice of equitable alternative activities.

(e) For persons who are legally incapable of giving informed consent, psychologists nevertheless (1) provide an appropriate explanation, (2) obtain the participant's assent, and (3) obtain appropriate permission from a legally authorized person, if such substitute consent is permitted by law.

6.12 Dispensing with Informed Consent

Before determining that planned research (such as research involving only anonymous questionnaires, naturalistic observations, or certain kinds of archival research) does not require the informed consent of research participants, psychologists consider applicable regulations and institutional review board requirements, and they consult with colleagues as appropriate.

6.13 Informed Consent in Research Filming or Recording

Psychologists obtain informed consent from research participants prior to filming or recording them in any form, unless the research involves simply naturalistic observations in public places and it is not anticipated that the recording will be used in a manner that could cause personal identification or harm.

6.14 Offering Inducements for Research Participants

(a) In offering professional services as an inducement to obtain research participants, psychologists make clear the nature of the services, as well as the risks, obligations, and limitations. (See also Standard 1.18, Barter [with Patients or Clients].)

(b) Psychologists do not offer excessive or inappropriate financial or other inducements to obtain research participants, particularly when it might tend to coerce participation.

6.15 Deception in Research

(a) Psychologists do not conduct a study involving deception unless they have determined that the use of deceptive techniques is justified by the study's prospective scientific, educational, or applied value and that equally effective alternative procedures that do not use deception are not feasible.

(b) Psychologists never deceive research participants about significant aspects that would affect their willingness to participate, such as physical risks, discomfort, or unpleasant emotional experiences.

(c) Any other deception that is an integral feature of the design and conduct of an experiment must be explained to participants as early as is feasible, preferably at the conclusion of their participation, but no later than at the conclusion of the research. (See also Standard 6.18, Providing Participants with Information About the Study.)

6.16 Sharing and Utilizing Data

Psychologists inform research participants of their anticipated sharing or further use of personally identifiable research data and of the possibility of unanticipated future uses.

6.17 Minimizing Invasiveness

In conducting research, psychologists interfere with the participants or milieu from which data are collected only in a manner that is warranted by an appropriate research design and that is consistent with psychologists' roles as scientific investigators.

6.18 Providing Participants with Information About the Study

(a) Psychologists provide a prompt opportunity for participants to obtain appropriate information about the nature, results, and conclusions of the research, and psychologists attempt to correct any misconceptions that participants may have.

(b) If scientific or humane values justify delaying or withholding this information, psychologists take reasonable measures to reduce the risk of harm.

6.19 Honoring Commitments

Psychologists take reasonable measures to honor all commitments they have made to research participants.

6.20 Care and Use of Animals in Research

(a) Psychologists who conduct research involving animals treat them humanely.

(b) Psychologists acquire, care for, use, and dispose of animals in compliance with current federal, state, and local laws and regulations, and with professional standards.

(c) Psychologists trained in research methods and experienced in the care of laboratory animals supervise all procedures involving animals and are responsible for ensuring appropriate consideration of their comfort, health, and humane treatment.

(d) Psychologists ensure that all individuals using animals under their supervision have received instruction in research methods and in the care, maintenance, and handling of the species being used, to the extent appropriate to their role.

(e) Responsibilities and activities of individuals assisting in a research project are consistent with their respective competencies.

(f) Psychologists make reasonable efforts to minimize the discomfort, infection, illness, and pain of animal subjects.

(g) A procedure subjecting animals to pain, stress, or privation is used only when an alternative procedure is unavailable and the goal is justified by its prospective scientific, educational, or applied value.

(h) Surgical procedures are performed under appropriate anesthesia; techniques to avoid infection and minimize pain are followed during and after surgery.

(i) When it is appropriate that the animal's life be terminated, it is done rapidly, with an effort to minimize pain, and in accordance with accepted procedures.

6.21 Reporting of Results

(a) Psychologists do not fabricate data or falsify results in their publications.

(b) If psychologists discover significant errors in their published data, they take reasonable steps to correct such errors in a correction, retraction, erratum, or other appropriate publication means.

6.22 Plagiarism

Psychologists do not present substantial portions or elements of another's work or data as their own, even if the other work or data source is cited occasionally.

6.23 Publication Credit

(a) Psychologists take responsibility and credit, including authorship credit, only for work they have actually performed or to which they have contributed.

(b) Principal authorship and other publication credits accurately reflect the relative scientific or professional contributions of the individuals involved, regardless of their relative status. Mere possession of an institutional position, such as Department Chair, does not justify authorship credit. Minor contributions to the research or to the writing for publications are appropriately acknowledged, such as in footnotes or in an introductory statement.

(c) A student is usually listed as principal author on any multiple-authored article that is substantially based on the student's dissertation or thesis.

6.24 Duplicate Publication of Data

Psychologists do not publish, as original data, data that have been previously published. This does not preclude republishing data when they are accompanied by proper acknowledgment.

6.25 Sharing Data

After research results are published, psychologists do not withhold the data on which their conclusions are based from other competent professionals who seek to verify the substantive claims through reanalysis and who intend to use such data only for that purpose, provided that the confidentiality of the participants can be protected and unless legal rights concerning proprietary data preclude their release.

6.26 Professional Reviewers

Psychologists who review material submitted for publication, grant, or other research proposal review respect the confidentiality of and the proprietary rights in such information of those who submitted it.

7. Forensic Activities

7.01 Professionalism

Psychologists who perform forensic functions, such as assessments, interviews, consultations, reports, or expert testimony, must comply with all other provisions of this Ethics Code to the extent that they apply to such activities. In addition, psychologists base their forensic work on appropriate knowledge of and competence in the areas underlying such work, including specialized knowledge concerning special populations. (See also Standards 1.06, Basis for Scientific and Professional Judgments; 1.08, Human Differences; 1.15, Misuse of Psychologists' Influence; and 1.23, Documentation of Professional and Scientific Work.)

7.02 Forensic Assessments

(a) Psychologists' forensic assessments, recommendations, and reports are based on information and techniques (including personal interviews of the individual, when appropriate) sufficient to provide appropriate substantiation for their findings. (See also Standards 1.03, Professional and Scientific Relationship; 1.23, Documentation of Professional and Scientific Work; 2.01, Evaluation, Diagnosis, and Interventions in Professional Context; and 2.05, Interpreting Assessment Results.)

(b) Except as noted in (c), below, psychologists provide written or oral forensic reports or testimony of the psychological characteristics of an individual only after they have conducted an examination of the individual adequate to support their statements or conclusions.

(c) When, despite reasonable efforts, such an examination is not feasible, psychologists clarify the impact of their limited information on the reliability and validity of their reports and testimony, and they appropriately limit the nature and extent of their conclusions or recommendations.

7.03 Clarification of Role

In most circumstances, psychologists avoid performing multiple and potentially conflicting roles in forensic matters. When psychologists may be called on to serve in more than one role in a legal proceeding—for example, as consultant or expert for one party or for the court and as a fact witness—they clarify role expectations and the extent of confidentiality in advance to the extent feasible, and thereafter as changes occur, in order to avoid compromising their professional judgment and objectivity and in order to avoid misleading others regarding their role.

7.04 Truthfulness and Candor

(a) In forensic testimony and reports, psychologists testify truthfully, honestly, and candidly and, consistent with applicable legal procedures, describe fairly the bases for their testimony and conclusions.

(b) Whenever necessary to avoid misleading, psychologists acknowledge the limits of their data or conclusions.

7.05 Prior Relationships

A prior professional relationship with a party does not preclude psychologists from testifying as fact witnesses or from testifying to their services to the extent permitted by applicable law. Psychologists appropriately take into account ways in which the prior relationship might affect their professional objectivity or opinions and disclose the potential conflict to the relevant parties.

7.06 Compliance with Law and Rules

In performing forensic roles, psychologists are reasonably familiar with the rules governing their roles. Psychologists are aware of the occasionally competing demands placed upon them by these principles and the requirements of the court system, and attempt to resolve these conflicts by making known their commitment to this Ethics Code and taking steps to resolve the conflict in a responsible manner. (See also Standard 1.02, Relationship of Ethics and Law.)

8. Resolving Ethical Issues

8.01 Familiarity with Ethics Code

Psychologists have an obligation to be familiar with this Ethics Code, other applicable ethics codes, and their application to psychologists' work. Lack of awareness or misunderstanding of an ethical standard is not itself a defense to a charge of unethical conduct.

8.02 Confronting Ethical Issues

When a psychologist is uncertain whether a particular situation or course of action would violate this Ethics Code, the psychologist ordinarily consults with other psychologists knowledgeable about ethical issues, with state or national psychology ethics committees, or with other appropriate authorities in order to choose a proper response.

8.03 Conflicts Between Ethics and Organizational Demands

If the demands of an organization with which psychologists are affiliated conflict with this Ethics Code, psychologists clarify the nature of the conflict, make known their commitment to the Ethics Code, and to the extent feasible, seek to resolve the conflict in a way that permits the fullest adherence to the Ethics Code.

8.04 Informal Resolution of Ethical Violations

When psychologists believe that there may have been an ethical violation by another psychologist, they attempt to resolve the issue by bringing it to the attention of that individual if an informal resolution appears appropriate and the intervention does not violate any confidentiality rights that may be involved.

8.05 Reporting Ethical Violations

If an apparent ethical violation is not appropriate for informal resolution under Standard 8.04 or is not resolved properly in that fashion, psychologists take further action appropriate to the situation, unless such action conflicts with confidentiality rights in ways that cannot be resolved. Such action might include referral to state or national committees on professional ethics or to state licensing boards.

8.06 Cooperating with Ethics Committees

Psychologists cooperate in ethics investigations, proceedings, and resulting requirements of the APA or any affiliated state psychological association to which they belong. In doing so, they make reasonable efforts to resolve any issues as to confidentiality. Failure to cooperate is itself an ethics violation.

8.07 Improper Complaints

Psychologists do not file or encourage the filing of ethics complaints that are frivolous and are intended to harm the respondent rather than to protect the public.

NASW CODE OF ETHICS (NATIONAL ASSOCIATION OF SOCIAL WORKERS)

Preamble

The primary mission of the social work profession is to enhance human well-being and help meet basic human needs, with particular attention to the needs of people who are vulnerable, oppressed, and living in poverty. A historic and defining feature of social work is the profession's focus on individual well-being in a social context and the well-being of society. Fundamental to social work is attention to the environmental forces that create, contribute to, and address problems in living.

The mission of the social work profession is rooted in a set of core values. These core values, embraced by social workers throughout the profession's history, are the foundation of social work's unique purpose and perspective. Core values, and the ethical principles that flow from them, must be balanced within the context and complexity of the human experience.

Core Values and Ethical Principles

Value: *Service*
Ethical Principle: *Social workers' primary goal is to help people in need and to address social problems.*

Value: *Social Justice*
Ethical Principle: *Social workers challenge social injustice.*

Value: *Dignity and Worth of the Person*
Ethical Principle: *Social workers respect the inherent dignity and worth of the person.*

Value: *Importance of Human Relationships*
Ethical Principle: *Social workers recognize the central importance of human relationships.*

Value: *Integrity*
Ethical Principle: *Social workers behave in a trustworthy manner.*

Value: *Competence*
Ethical Principle: *Social workers practice within their areas of competence and develop and enhance their professional expertise.*

The above is an extract of the *NASW Code of Ethics* approved by the 1996 Delegate Assembly. The complete text is available from the National Association of Social Workers, 750 First Street, NE, Suite 700, Washington, DC 20002-4241, or on-line at http://www.naswdc.org/code.htm.

Appendix B

Professional Organizations in Human Services

This appendix expands on information presented in the text about the two organizations in the U.S. that focus on the human service profession and education for the profession. This information is adapted from the membership brochures of the two organizations.

NATIONAL ORGANIZATION FOR HUMAN SERVICE EDUCATION (NOHSE)

History and purposes. The National Organization for Human Service Education (NOHSE) was founded in 1975 at the 5th Annual Faculty Development Conference of the Southern Regional Education Board (SREB). Growing out of the need for improved methods of service delivery, NOHSE strives to promote excellence in human service delivery. Through the professional efforts of NOHSE members, many human service programs have been developed to address unique social, behavioral, and educational issues in society. NOHSE supports and promotes improvements in direct service, public education, program development, planning and evaluation, administration, and public policy. NOHSE's purposes are to:

- Provide opportunities for cooperation and communication among human service organizations, practitioners, faculty, and students.
- Foster excellence in teaching, research, curriculum development and service delivery.
- Sponsor conferences, publications, and research that foster creative approaches to meeting human service needs.

Membership and benefits. Members of NOHSE are drawn from diverse educational and professional backgrounds—for example, corrections, mental health, child care, social services, human resource management, gerontology, developmental disabilities, addictions, recreation, and education. Since NOHSE's founding, the organization has grown to include members from the United States, Canada, Israel, and Australia. (See Appendix C, page 275, for contact information.) Members include educators, students, direct care professionals, administrators, and organizations. Benefits of membership include:

- *Human Service Education*—NOHSE's peer-reviewed journal
- *The Link*—NOHSE's newsletter
- Workshops and conferences
- Scholarships
- Research grants

- Professional development grants
- Membership handbook
- Networking opportunities
- Recognition awards

Web site. The latest information about the organization, membership, upcoming events, and officers, plus an on-line issues forum and related links, is posted regularly on NOHSE's Web location: http://www.nohse.com

COUNCIL FOR STANDARDS IN HUMAN SERVICE EDUCATION (CSHSE)

History and purposes. Founded in 1979 to improve the quality, consistency, and relevance of human service training programs, the Council for Standards in Human Service Education (CSHSE) is the national organization that sets standards and provides assistance to programs to accomplish these goals. CSHSE achieves its purposes by:

- Applying national standards for training programs at the associate and baccalaureate degree levels
- Reviewing and recognizing programs that meet established standards
- Sponsoring faculty development workshops in curriculum design, program policy making, resource development, program evaluation, and other areas
- Offering vital technical and informational assistance to programs seeking to improve the quality and relevance of their training
- Publishing a *Bulletin* to keep programs informed of CSHSE activities, training information and resources, and issues and trends in human service education

During the past 20 years, the number of certificate, associate degree, baccalaureate degree, and graduate-level human service programs in the nation has grown to more than 400. Nearly 85,000 workers have graduated from these programs, and at least 5,000 more graduates are expected each year. Several factors set the stage for the emergence of these programs: a growing need for services and a resulting manpower crisis, the effectiveness of beginning professionals working in human service settings, the widespread popularity of community college education, and local needs.

Many of these programs are generalist in nature, preparing practitioners to help clients meet a range of needs. The focus is on interdisciplinary training with development of practical skills and self-awareness.

Over three-fourths of the graduates of these programs are employed in human service settings—for example, community mental health, mental retardation, and drug and alcohol treatment centers; programs that serve older adults; and a variety of residential treatment programs. These practitioners perform a variety of functions, including screening and evaluation, direct treatment, crisis intervention, client advocacy, community consultation, research, and supervision.

Membership. Membership is open to educational programs, both undergraduate programs in human services and training programs not affiliated with colleges or universities. (See Appendix C, page 274, for contact information.) Benefits of membership include:

- CSHSE publications and newsletter
- Access to program approval and approval applications materials
- Access to technical assistance, consultation, and CSHSE-sponsored workshops

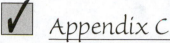

Appendix C

Organizations in Human Services and Selected Related Professions: Contact Information

There are many professional organizations in the human services and related professions. Some of the better-known ones are listed here. They can provide you with information about their membership, activities, ethical standards, and publications. Many can be found electronically on the World Wide Web or via e-mail. If you use e-mail to request information, don't forget to include your street or post office address!

American Association of Family and Consumer Sciences (AAFCS)
1555 King St.
Alexandria, VA 22314
Phone: 703-706-4600
Fax: 703-706-4663
Ethics publication: *Code of Professional Responsibility* and *Statement of Principles of Professional Practice*

American Counseling Association (ACA)
5999 Stevenson Ave.
Alexandria, VA 22304
Phone: 703-823-9800
Toll-free: 1-800-347-6647
Fax: 703-823-0252
Web site: http://www.counseling.org
Ethics publication: *Code of Ethics* and *Standards of Practice*

American Nurses Association (ANA)
600 Maryland Ave., SW, Ste. 100W
Washington, DC 20024-2571
Phone: 202-651-7000
Toll-free (orders): 1-800-637-0323
Fax: 202-651-7001
Web site: http://www.ana.org
Ethics publication: *Code for Nurses*

American Psychological Association (APA)
750 First St., NE
Washington, DC 20002-4242
Phone: 202-336-5500

Phone (Ethics Office): 202-336-5930
Web site: http://www.apa.org
Ethics publication: *Ethical Principles of Psychologists*

American School Counselor Association (ASCA)
801 N. Fairfax St., Ste. 301
Alexandria, VA 22314
Phone: 703-683-2722
Toll-free: 1-800-306-4722
Fax: 703-683-1619
e-mail: ascaoffice@aol.com
Web site: http://www.edge.net/asca
Ethics publication: *Ethical Standards for School Counselors*

Canadian Association of Social Workers (CASW)
383 Parkdale Ave., Ste. 402
Ottawa, ON, Canada K1Y 4R4
Phone: 613-729-6668
e-mail: casw@casw-acts.ca
Web site: http://www.intranet.ca/~casw-acts
Ethics publication: *Code of Ethics*

Commission on Rehabilitation Counselor Certification (CRCC)
1835 Rohlwing Rd., Ste. E
Rolling Meadows, IL 60008
Phone: 708-394-2104
Fax: 708-394-2108
Ethics publication: *Ethical Standards for Rehabilitation Counselors*

Council for Standards in Human Service Education (CSHSE)
Mary DiGiovanni
Northern Essex Community College
Mental Health Technology Program
Elliott Way
Haverhill, MA 01830

National Association of Alcoholism and Drug Abuse Counselors (NAADAC)
1911 N. Fort Myer Dr., Ste. 900
Arlington, VA 22209
Phone: 703-741-7686
Toll-free: 1-800-548-0497
Fax: 703-741-7698
Toll-free fax: 1-800-377-1136
Web site: http://www.naadac.org
Ethics publication: *Ethical Standards of Alcoholism and Drug Abuse Counselors*

National Association of Social Workers (NASW)
750 First St., NE, Ste. 700
Washington DC 20002-4241
Phone: 202-408-8600
Toll-free: 1-800-638-8799
Fax: 202-336-8310
TTD: 202-408-8396
Web site: http://www.naswdc.org
Ethics publication: *Code of Ethics* and *Standards for the Practice of Clinical Social Work*

National Board for Certified Counselors (NBCC)
3 Terrace Way, Ste. D
Greensboro, NC 27403-3660
Phone: 910-547-0607
Toll-free: 1-800-398-5389
Fax: 910-547-0017

National Education Association (NEA)
1201 16th St., NW
Washington, DC 20036
Phone: 202-822-7346
Fax: 202-822-7974
Web site: http://www.nea.org
Ethics publication: *Code of Ethics of the Education Profession*

National Federation of Societies for Clinical Social Work (NFSCSW)
P.O. Box 3740
Arlington, VA 22203
Phone: 703-522-3866
Fax: 703-522-9441
Web site: http://www.nfscsw.org
Ethics publication: *Code of Ethics*

National Organization for Human Service Education (NOHSE)
James F. Carroll, President 96–98
Tacoma Community College
6501 S. 19th St.
Tacoma, WA 98466-6100
Phone: 206-566-5214
Fax: 206-566-5365
e-mail: jcarroll@tcc.tacoma.ctc.edu
Web site: http://www.nohse.com
Ethics publication: *Ethical Standards of Human Service Professionals*

National Rehabilitation Counseling Association (NRCA)
8807 Sudley Rd., Ste. 102
Manassas, VA 22110-4719
Phone: 703-361-2077
Fax: 703-361-2489
Ethics publication: *Code of Ethics*

Appendix D

Questionnaires Used in Collecting Reports of Ethical Experiences

The questionnaires that follow were used to collect reports of ethical experiences from human service students, practitioners, and faculty for this workbook.

ETHICAL ISSUES AND DILEMMAS: EXPERIENCES OF STUDENTS AND ENTRY-LEVEL PROFESSIONALS IN HUMAN SERVICES[1]

Explanation: I'm asking you to contribute your experiences to an upcoming ethical issue workbook—I am convinced that students and entry-level professionals will find the workbook most meaningful if it features real case anecdotes from you and others already in human services. Below and on the back of this page are definitions of the terms "ethical issue" and "ethical dilemma," followed by some questions pertaining to your own experiences with ethical problems. Please answer the questions and return the questionnaire to me by May 9, 1996. (My address is on the back.) Include enough detail so I will understand the issue and the choices from your point of view. Your name is optional; if you include it, I will plan to give you credit in the book.

Pat Kenyon, March 1996

A Common Ethical Issue

Ethical Issue   A matter which involves morality, rules or standards by which one judges right and wrong. Ethical issues affect our decisions about what we will do (our actions, conduct or behavior).

Describe one common ethical issue which you have faced as a human services student or professional.

What choices did you have?

How did you resolve this issue?

An Ethical Dilemma

Ethical Dilemma   An ethical issue which is especially complex because every option for action will result in some degree of harm or wrong-doing. Our ethical duties are in conflict and we can see no totally "right" actions. Even taking no action is "wrong."

Describe one ethical dilemma which you have found to be particularly troubling in your role as a student or professional in human services.

What choices did you have?

Was there a resolution to the dilemma? **What** was it?

Your name (optional) _____

Position (optional) _____

Thank you for your participation.

Return the completed questionnaire to:
   Patricia Kenyon, NOHSE Education Committee
   Arizona Western College
   PO Box 929
   Yuma, AZ 85366-0929

ETHICAL DILEMMAS[2]

Directions: Please complete the following questionnaire and return it in the enclosed self-addressed, stamped envelope. To maintain your anonymity we are not requesting your name on this form.

1. As a professional or a student, have you ever faced a serious ethical dilemma (a situation which caused you internal conflict in considering what was the "right" thing to do) relative to your role?   Yes _____   No _____

   (If no, go on to Item 7)

2. Using the scale below, circle the number that indicates how influential each factor has been in resolving ethical dilemmas you have faced.

Not at all influential			Very influential	
1	2	3	4	5

1 2 3 4 5 spiritual background	1 2 3 4 5 past experience
1 2 3 4 5 college courses	1 2 3 4 5 social context
1 2 3 4 5 media	1 2 3 4 5 emotional bias ("feels" right)
1 2 3 4 5 literature	1 2 3 4 5 colleagues
1 2 3 4 5 workshop(s)	1 2 3 4 5 professor(s)
1 2 3 4 5 code of ethics	1 2 3 4 5 parental influence
1 2 3 4 5 cultural influences and traditions	
1 2 3 4 5 other (please list: _____)	

3. How adequately did your undergraduate or graduate course work prepare you for the professional ethical dilemmas you have faced? (Circle the number which best represents your educational preparation.)

Very inadequately			Very adequately	
1	2	3	4	5

4. As a professional, what ethical dilemmas have you encountered? Using the scale below, circle the number that indicates how commonly you have encountered each type of dilemma.

Very uncommon			Very common	
1	2	3	4	5

1 2 3 4 5 current social issues	1 2 3 4 5 sexual misconduct
1 2 3 4 5 academic issues	1 2 3 4 5 confidentiality
1 2 3 4 5 research issues	1 2 3 4 5 job-related issues
1 2 3 4 5 lack of professionalism in students	
1 2 3 4 5 lack of professionalism in colleagues	
1 2 3 4 5 other (please list:_____)	

5. As a student, what ethical dilemmas did you encounter or are you encountering? Using the scale below, circle the number that indicates how commonly you have encountered each type of dilemma.

Very uncommon			Very common	
1	2	3	4	5

1 2 3 4 5 current social issues	1 2 3 4 5 sexual misconduct
1 2 3 4 5 academic issues	1 2 3 4 5 confidentiality

1 2 3 4 5   research issues   1 2 3 4 5   job-related issues
1 2 3 4 5   lack of professionalism in students
1 2 3 4 5   lack of professionalism in colleagues
1 2 3 4 5   other (please list:_____)

6. In the next six sections, we are asking you about one of the ethical problems listed above that illustrates the kind of dilemma you have found to be particularly troubling in your role as a student or professional.

   6a. Please describe the problem.

   6b. Please discuss the reasons why this dilemma was difficult from both a personal and professional perspective. (If not enough room, include an additional sheet of paper.)

   6c. Was there a resolution to this dilemma?   Yes ____   No ____

   6d. If yes, how was the dilemma resolved?

   6e. Was this resolution to your satisfaction?   Yes ____   No ____

   6f. Did your educational preparation help you
       in the resolution of this dilemma?   Yes ____   No ____

Please give us some information about you:

7. What is your primary professional position?

8. Gender: Male ____   Female ____

9. Age: _____

10. Are you a member of any of these organizations? (please check all that apply)

National Organization for Human Service Education ____
Council for Standards in Human Service Education ____
National Association of Social Workers ____
American Psychological Association ____
American Nurses Association ____
American Association for Counseling and Development ____
Another professional organization ____
        Please list: _____

11. Are you familiar with the new Statement on
    Standards for Human Service Professionals?   Yes ____   No ____

Thank you for your participation.

Patricia Kenyon
Education Committee, NOHSE

ETHICAL DILEMMAS[3]
(OPTIONAL)

Are you interested in further collaboration with members of the NOHSE Education Committee in developing a manual of case studies which reflect current ethical issues in human services? If so, please send us information about your interest and how to contact you.

Name _____

Home address _____

_____

Home phone _____

Work address _____

_____

Work phone _____

The best time to reach me is _____

Below is a description of my interest in this project:

Return this to:
    Patricia Kenyon
    Human Service Program
    Arizona Western College
    PO Box 929
    Yuma, AZ 85366-0929

NOTES

1. This questionnaire was distributed to participants in workshops at regional human service conferences during the spring of 1996.
2. This mail survey—adapted from Knaub, Weber, and Russ (1994)—was distributed to members of the National Organization for Human Service Education during the spring of 1995.
3. This form was included in the mail survey to NOHSE members in 1995.

Glossary

absolute confidentiality The type of confidentiality that guards information against access by anyone, even courts of law. The professions that generally are granted absolute confidentiality by the courts are lawyers and clergy.

anecdote A succinct description of an event or interaction.

attitude A mental perspective or stance, usually assumed in relation to others or the environment.

autonomy The ethical principle that humans have a duty to maximize the individual's right to make his or her own decisions.

beneficence The ethical principle that humans have a duty to do good.

burnout A state of physical and mental exhaustion, usually considered to be a result of unresolved stress.

capacity See *competence*.

case study A description, based on a real situation, that contains critical aspects of an issue or problem to be considered. Case studies are used in education to aid students in applying concepts to the real world.

client The recipient (an individual, group, or community) of human services. This term is in disfavor in some parts of the United States because it seems to imply a passive role. *Consumer* is a preferred term in those areas.

clinical An issue faced by a human service professional in which the professional must decide the best approach to use, but that is not primarily an ethical or legal decision. A clinical issue usually involves the application of theories and concepts pertaining to the helping process itself and/or the needs and problems of special populations.

code of ethics A system of principles about right and wrong conduct, on which decisions can be based.

competence A legal term that indicates an individual is mentally capable of making his or her own decisions.

comprehension of information See *knowledge*.

confidentiality An ethical principle that says that humans have a duty to respect privacy of information. This concept is related to the legal concept of privacy, a person's freedom from undesired intrusions by others. In human services, practitioners are committed to keeping to themselves the information that clients share in the course of being helped. Confidentiality can be absolute (even a court of law cannot force the revelation of the information), but in human services is usually relative (in certain situations the information can be revealed without the client's consent).

conflict An interpersonal situation or an internal condition in which opposing or mutually exclusive preferences create a discordant state.

consumer The recipient (an individual, group, or community) of human services. This term is being substituted for the term *client* in some parts of the United States.

criteria Benchmarks or principles that guide decision making and evaluations of actions.

critical thinking An intellectually disciplined approach to decision making that progresses in a step-by-step fashion and that ensures all important elements are considered before a decision is made. The term *decision making* is often used interchangeably with the term *critical thinking*.

decision The act of reaching a conclusion or resolution to a matter of concern.

decision-making process A step-by-step process that promotes consideration of all aspects of an issue or problem prior to reaching a judgment or making a decision. The term *critical thinking* is also used to refer to this process.

dilemma A situation that requires a choice among options that are equally unfavorable or mutually exclusive.

dual relationship A relationship in which a professional and a client are associated in an additional way. Examples: The faculty member may also be the student's personal counselor. The client may pay for services by providing goods or another service. The practitioner and the client may be involved in the social activities of the same synagogue.

entry-level professional A helper who has prepared for the responsibilities of providing direct service through a formal educational program or through broad service experience. Increasingly, this beginning professional has earned an associate or baccalaureate degree. Entry-level professionals may assume high levels of service responsibility but are unlikely to assume leadership roles in management, policy making, or research without further education or experience. In some parts of the U.S., the term *paraprofessional* is preferred.

ethical Conforming to recognized standards for governing conduct.

ethical dilemma An issue that is especially complex because every option for action—including taking no action—will result in some degree of harm or wrongdoing. One is forced, therefore, to make a choice among conflicting ethical duties or obligations.

ethical duty An obligation for one's conduct imposed by one's personal or professional ethics—or both.

ethical issue A matter that involves morality, rules, or standards by which one judges right and wrong.

ethical principles Generally accepted statements of humans' obligations or duties.

ethical standards Guidelines or criteria by which one decides the rightness or wrongness of specific conduct.

ethics The rules, standards, or moral principles adopted by an individual or group to govern conduct. It is expected that following these standards will lead to what is best for human life collectively. Often this term is used in the more specialized sense of being the set of standards followed by the members of a profession.

external conflict A state of disharmony that involves the individual and others—for example, other people, the environment, or sociocultural norms.

fidelity The ethical principle that humans have a duty to keep their promise or word.

finality The ethical principle that one's ethical duty may require action that overrides the demands of law and social customs.

gratitude The ethical principle that humans have a duty to make up for a good.

informed consent A legal concept—based on the ethical principle of autonomy—that holds that before an individual agrees to a procedure, he or she must understand all aspects of the procedure and agree voluntarily.

internal conflict A state of disharmony within an individual, involving his or her beliefs, values, ideas, or preferences.

justice The ethical principle that risks and benefits should be distributed among people equitably.

knowledge A legal term that describes the level of understanding of an individual who makes a decision to accept an intervention by a professional. He or she must understand the procedure, benefits, risks, alternatives, and potential consequences.

liability Accountability or responsibility for something.

liability insurance Insurance that offers protection against the financial costs of being found guilty of failure to meet one's professional or personal responsibilities or obligations.

malpractice Negligence by a professional in fulfilling the responsibilities of his or her profession.

malpractice insurance Liability insurance that specifically covers situations in which one is found responsible for improper conduct as a professional.

morality An evaluation of one's conduct on the basis of some broad cultural context or religious standard.

multiple relationship An expansion of the concept of dual relationship. A relationship in which the professional and the client are associated in more than one other way. Examples: The residential worker at the domestic violence shelter may be a member of a support group together with some of the residents at the shelter and also volunteer with them at a local food cooperative. Members in a therapy group may be part of a group of friends outside the group and also work together in a local school.

negligence Failure to fulfill one's duty. Negligence is often used in a specific legal sense. See also *malpractice*.

nonmaleficence The ethical principle that humans have a duty to cause no harm.

ordering The ethical principle that ethical principles must be ranked in order of priority and that humans have a duty to follow that ranking in resolving ethical problems.

paraprofessional See *entry-level professional*.

paternalism An ethical approach in which a responsible person, group, or agency provides for others without giving them rights and responsibilities. Paternalism is often considered antithetical to the principle of autonomy.

plagiarism Reproduction or presentation of another person's written work as one's own.

policy A statement or rule, usually written, that expresses a guiding principle for an organization. Policies are set by the governing board or its equivalent.

pragmatism The quality of being practical in one's approach. A human service professional who is pragmatic seeks solutions which are possible and effective.

principle A fundamental legal or ethical guideline or criterion.

privacy A legal concept that protects citizens against unwarranted intrusions into their persons, property, or information about them. The concept of confidentiality is tied to the concept of privacy.

procedure A step-by-step process for accomplishing something. In organizations, procedures direct the staff and volunteers in performing aspects of the work.

profession An occupation requiring considerable educational preparation. Also, the members of that occupation, when considered together.

professional practice standards The guidelines or criteria that are used to judge the professional's level of conduct.

publicity The ethical principle that ethical standards must be known and recognized by all who are involved.

quality An essential or identifying attribute; a trait.

relative confidentiality The type of confidentiality that guards information against access by most others, but in certain situations the information can be revealed without the client's consent. Human service professionals generally practice relative confidentiality and can be required to divulge information by a court of law.

reparation The ethical principle that humans have a duty to make up for a wrong.

respect for persons An ethical principle that humans have a duty to honor other people and their rights and responsibilities. It involves esteem felt and shown to other people.

right to refuse treatment A legal concept that guarantees that the informed individual can refuse interventions offered to him or her.

scenario A short description of a situation or incident. See *anecdote*.

socialization The process in and by which the individual learns the ways, ideas, beliefs, values, patterns, and norms of a particular culture and adapts them as part of his or her own character.

standard A point of reference against which individuals and their conduct are compared and evaluated.

universality The ethical principle that ethical standards must hold for everyone, regardless of time, place, or people involved.

utility The ethical principle that humans have a duty to provide the greatest good or the least harm for the greatest number of people.

value A belief about what is right, beneficial, or commendable. Values, because they are based on one's choice and are considered important, guide one's conduct.

value system A set of values adopted by an individual or society, governing the behavior of the individual or the members of the society, often without the conscious awareness of the individual or the members of the society.

veracity The ethical principle that humans have a duty to tell the truth.

whistle blower A person who publicly exposes illegal or improper actions. This term is applied to individuals who seek to correct organizational malfeasance through exposure of the misconduct to powerful individuals or groups within or outside the organization.

written consent A client's permission, in writing, to release information, obtained prior to the release of that information about the client to another practitioner or agency. The written consent is filed in the client's permanent record.

Bibliography

American Nurses Association. (1985). *Code for nurses*. Washington, DC: American Nurses Publishing, 600 Maryland Avenue SW, Suite 100W, 20024-2571.

American Psychological Association. (1992). Ethical principles of psychologists and code of conduct. *American Psychologist, 47*, 1597–1611.

Berrenberg, J. L. (1987). *The belief in personal control scale: A revised, short form*. ERIC–Educational Resources Information Center, ED# 325 488, TM# 015 697.

Bissell, L., & Royce, J. E. (1987). *Ethics for addiction professionals*. Center City, MN: Hazelden Educational Materials.

Bond, T. (1993). *Standards and ethics for counselling in action*. Thousand Oaks, CA: Sage Publications.

Bronowski, J. (1973). *The ascent of man*. Boston: Little, Brown.

Callahan, J. C. (1988). *Ethical issues in professional life*. New York: Oxford University Press.

Clifton, R. L., & Dahms, A. M. (1993). *Grassroots organizations: A resource book for directors, staff, and volunteers of small, community-based nonprofit agencies* (2nd ed.). Prospect Heights, IL: Waveland Press.

Corey, G. (1996). *Theory and practice of counseling and psychotherapy* (5th ed.). Pacific Grove, CA: Brooks/Cole.

Corey, G., & Corey, M. S. (1993). *Becoming a helper* (2nd ed.). Pacific Grove, CA: Brooks/Cole.

Corey, G., Corey, M. S., & Callanan, P. (1993). *Issues and ethics in the helping professions* (4th ed.). Pacific Grove, CA: Brooks/Cole.

Corey, G., Corey, M. S., & Callanan, P. (1998). *Issues and ethics in the helping professions* (5th ed.). Pacific Grove, CA: Brooks/Cole.

Edelstein, L. (1987). *Ancient medicine: Selected papers* (O. Temkin & C. L. Temkin, Eds.; C. L. Temkin, Trans.). Baltimore: Johns Hopkins University Press. (Original work published 1943)

Egan, G. (1994). *The skilled helper: A problem-management approach to helping* (5th ed.). Pacific Grove, CA: Brooks/Cole.

Fulghum, R. (1988). *All I really need to know I learned in kindergarten: Uncommon thoughts on common things*. New York: Ivy Books.

Gilligan, C. (1982). *In a different voice*. Cambridge, MA: Harvard University Press.

Herlihy, B., & Corey, G. (1996). *ACA ethical standards casebook* (5th ed.). Alexandria, VA: American Counseling Association.

Herlihy, B., & Corey, G. (1997). Codes of ethics as catalysts for improving practice. In *The Hatherleigh guide to ethics in therapy*. New York: Hatherleigh Press.

Holmes, T. H., & Masuda, M. (1973). Life change and illness susceptibility. In J. P. Scott & E. C. Senay (Eds.), *Publication No. 94 of the American Association for the Advancement of Science. Separation and depression: Clinical and research aspects* (pp. 161–186). Washington, D.C.: American Association for the Advancement of Science. A report of a symposium presented at the Chicago meeting of the American Association for the Advancement of Science on December 27, 1970.

Holmes, T. H., & Rahe, R. H. (1967). The social readjustment scale. *Journal of Psychosomatic Research, 11*, 213–218.

Hughes, L. (1996). *Expanding your experience: Exercises and activities*. Pacific Grove, CA: Brooks/Cole.

Kalisch, P. A., & Kalisch, B. J. (1986). *The advance of American nursing* (2nd ed.). Boston: Little, Brown.

Kane, R. A., & Caplan, A. L. (Eds.). (1993). *Ethical conflicts in the management of home care: The case manager's dilemma*. New York: Springer.

Kentsmith, D. K., Salladay, S. A., & Miya, P. A. (Eds.). (1986). *Ethics in mental health practice*. Orlando, FL: Grune & Stratton.

Kinnier, R. T. (1987). Development of a values conflict resolution assessment. *Journal of Counseling Psychology, 34* (1), 31–37.

Knaub, P. K., Weber, M. J., & Russ, R. R. (Fall 1994). Ethical dilemmas encountered in human environmental sciences: Implications for ethics education. *Journal of Family and Consumer Sciences, 86*, 23–30.

Lee, C. L., Weber, M. J., & Knaub, P. K. (Winter 1994). Ethical dilemmas of human science professionals: Developing case studies for ethics education. *Journal of Family and Consumer Sciences, 86*, 23–29.

Levy, C. S. (1993). *Social work ethics on the line*. New York: Haworth Press.

Lichtman, J. (1996). *The Lone Ranger's code of the west: An action-packed adventure in values and ethics with the legendary champion of justice.* Palm Desert, CA: Scribbler's Ink, 42-335 Washington Street, Suite F #328, 92211.

Linzer, N. (1990). Ethics and human service practice. *Human Service Education, 10* (1), 15–21.

Loewenberg, F. M., & Dolgoff, R. (1996). *Ethical decisions for social work practice* (5th ed.). Itasca, IL: F. E. Peacock.

McClam, T., & Woodside, M. (1993). Human services: Keys to the future. In I. Heckman, Ed., *Human services: Visions for the future.* Council for Standards in Human Services Monograph Series, No. 8. Available from H. S. Harris, Publication and Technical Assistance, Bronx Community College, University Avenue and West 181st Street, Bronx, NY 10453.

Mehr, J. (1995). *Human services: Concepts and intervention strategies* (6th ed.). Boston: Allyn & Bacon.

National Organization for Human Service Education. (1996). Ethical standards of human service professionals. *Human Service Education, 16* (1), 11–17.

New York State Commission on Quality of Care. (1994). *Choice and responsibility: Legal and ethical dilemmas in services for persons with mental disabilities.* Albany, NY: Author.

Nugent, W. R., & Thomas, J. W. (1993). Validation of a clinical measure of self-esteem. *Research on Social Work Practice, 3* (2), 191–207.

Penslar, R. L. (Ed.). (1995). *Research ethics: Cases and materials.* Bloomington, IN: Indiana University Press.

Rahe, R. H. (1968). Life-change measurement as a predictor of illness. *Proceedings of the Royal Society of Medicine, 61,* 1124–1126.

Rahe, R. H. (1974). Life changes and subsequent illness reports. In E. K. E. Gunderson & R. H. Rahe (Eds.), *Life stress and illness* (pp. 58–78). Springfield, IL: Charles C Thomas.

Reamer, F. G. (1990). *Ethical dilemmas in social service* (2nd ed.). New York: Columbia University Press.

Reamer, F. G. (1995). *Social work values and ethics.* New York: Columbia University Press.

Rinas, J., & Clyne-Jackson, S. (1988). *Professional conduct and legal concerns in mental health practice.* Norwalk, CT: Appleton & Lange.

Saltzman, A., & Proch, K. (1990). *Law in social work practice.* Chicago: Nelson-Hall.

Special feature: Ethical standards of human service professionals. (1996). *Human Service Education, 16* (1), 11–17.

Stadler, H. A. (1986). Making hard choices: Clarifying controversial ethical issues. *Counseling and Human Development, 19* (1), 1–10.

Stein, R. H. (1990). *Ethical issues in counseling.* Buffalo, NY: Prometheus Books.

Tec, L. (1980). *Targets: How to set goals for yourself and reach them!* New York: Harper & Row.

Uustal, D. B. (1993). *Clinical ethics and values: Issues and insights in a changing healthcare environment.* East Greenwich, RI: Educational Resources in Healthcare.

Van Hoose, W. H., & Paradise, L. V. (1979). *Ethics in counseling and psychotherapy.* Cranston, RI: Carroll Press.

Woodside, M., & McClam, T. (1994). *An introduction to human services* (2nd ed.). Pacific Grove, CA: Brooks/Cole.

Subject and Author Index

Decision-making process
  (continued)
  ethical decision-making
    process, 15–20
  legal and ethical approaches
    to, 13
Deontologists, 7
Describe the issue, 16
  applied in case study, 80
Dilemma(s). *See also* Conflict(s);
    Ethical dilemma(s)
  defined, 284
  and welfare reform, 84
Dolgoff, R., 7, 16, 18, 19
Dual relationship, 175–190
  defined, 284
Duty, ethical
  defined, 285
  and ethical principles, 7–8

Edelstein, L., 9
Egan, G., 6
Egoism, 7
Egoists, 7
Enforcement of ethical guidelines
    and standards, 9, 60
Entry-level professional
  and agency wrong doing, 206,
    209–210
  defined, 285
  and typical work environment,
    191
  and unethical research
    practices, 211
Ethical, defined, 285
Ethical choices, 4
Ethical code(s), 8. *See also* Code(s)
    of ethics
  functions of professional ethical
    codes, 8–9
Ethical decision-making, 4–20
  practice and experience
    necessary to develop skill
    in, 14–15
Ethical decision-making model,
    16–20
  applied in case study, 78–84
  describe issue, 16
  consider ethical guidelines, 16
  evaluate outcome, 19
  examine and evaluate action
    alternatives, 18–19
  examine conflicts, 17–18
  examine implications, 20
  generate action alternatives, 18
  plan action, 19
  resolve conflicts, 18
  select and evaluate preferred
    action, 19
Ethical decision-making process,
    15–20
  in a dilemma when multiple
    ethical standards apply, 14
  applied in case study, 78–85
Ethical dilemma(s), 14. *See also*
    Conflict(s); Dilemma(s)
  as a source of burnout, 15, 162

defined, 215, 285
  preventing, 15
  and sense of isolation, 163
Ethical duty (duties)
  defined, 285
  and ethical principles, 7–8
Ethical guidelines for profession-
    als. *See* Professional ethical
    guidelines
Ethical issue(s)
  defined, 215, 285
  in college, 86
Ethical obligations, 13
  and ethical principles, 7–8
Ethical principles, 7–8
  defined, 285
  autonomy, 8, 80, 81, 284
  beneficence, 8, 13, 80, 284
  confidentiality, 9, 13, 136–147,
    284
  common breaches of, 145–146
  relative, 136, 286
  fidelity, 8, 13, 285
  finality, 8, 13, 285
  gratitude, 8, 285
  justice, 8, 19, 285
  justice applied in case study,
    82–83
  nonmaleficence, 8, 13, 285
  ordering, 8, 285
  publicity, 8, 19, 286
  publicity applied in case study,
    82–83
  reparation, 8, 286
  respect for persons, 8, 286
  universality, 8, 19, 286
  universality applied in case
    study, 82–83
  utility, 8, 286
  veracity, 8, 286
*Ethical Principles of Psychologists and
    Code of Conduct,* 250–269
Ethical standards. *See also Code of
    Ethics and Standards of Practice,*
    American Counseling Asso-
    ciation, *Code of Ethics,* Na-
    tional Association of Social
    Workers, *Ethical Principles of
    Psychologists and Code of Con-
    duct, Ethical Standards of Alco-
    holism and Drug Abuse Counse-
    lors, Ethical Standards of
    Human Service Professionals*
  defined, 285
  development of, 60
*Ethical Standards of Alcoholism
    and Drug Abuse Counselors,*
    223–226
*Ethical Standards of Human
    Service Professionals,* 10–12,
    61–77
Ethical theories, 7
  absolutism, 7
  relativism, 7
Ethical thinking
  developing your, 15–16

Ethics, 6–7
  defined, 285
  difference between law and
    ethics, 12–14
  systems of, 7
Evaluate outcome, 19
  applied in case study, 83
Examine conflicts, 17–18
  applied in case study, 81
Examine and evaluate action
    alternatives, 18–19
  applied in case study, 82–83
Examine implications, 20
  applied in case study, 84

Fidelity, 13
  defined, 8, 285
Finality, 13
  defined, 8, 285
Florence Nightingale Pledge, 9
Functions of professional ethical
    guidelines, 8–9

Generate action alternatives, 18
  applied in case study, 81–82
Glossary, 284–286
Golden Rule, 7
Gratitude, defined, 8, 285
Guidelines, ethical. *See* Profes-
    sional ethical guidelines

Herlihy, B., 8, 16, 60
Human Service Professionals
  Ethical Standards of, 10–12
Human Service Professional's
    Responsibility
  to Clients, 10–11
  to Colleagues, 11–12
  to Community and Society, 11
  to Employers, 12
  to Profession, 12
  to Self, 12
Human service values, 5–6

Immigration
  and reporting of clients who
    are undocumented aliens, 13
Informed consent
  and criteria for, 155–156
  defined, 285
Invasion of privacy, 13
Isolation, sense of
  and ethical dilemmas, 163

Justice, 19
  applied in case study, 82–83
  defined, 8, 285

Kalisch, B. J., 9
Kalisch, P. A., 9
Kentsmith, D. K., 16
Knowledge
  defined, 285
  and informed consent, 155–156

Law
   difference between law and
      ethics, 12–14
Legal approaches to decision-
      making, 13
   considered in case study, 81
Levy, C. S., 8, 16
Liability
   concern about legal liability, 13
   defined, 285
Liability insurance, defined, 285
Loewenberg, F. M., 7, 16, 18, 19

Malpractice, defined, 285
Malpractice insurance, defined,
      285
McClam, T., 6, 61, 206
Mehr, J., 61
Miya, P. A., 16
Morality, 4
   conventional, 4
   defined, 285
   reflective, 4
Multiple relationship(s), 106, 175
   defined, 285

National Association of Alcohol-
      ism and Drug Abuse Counse-
      lors, 274
   Ethical Standards of, 223–226
National Association of Social
      Workers, 274
   Code of Ethics, 270
National Board for Certified
      Counselors, 275
National Education Association,
      275
National Federation of Societies
      for Clinical Social Work, 275
National Organization for Human
      Service Education, 60, 271–
      272, 275
National Rehabilitation Counsel-
      ing Association, 275
Nonmaleficence, 13
   defined, 8, 285

Oath of Hippocrates, 9
Obligations, ethical, 13
   and ethical principles, 7–8
Ordering, defined, 8, 285

Paraprofessional, defined, 285
Paternalism
   and autonomy, 172
   defined, 285
Personal values, 21–59, 80
   and internal conflict, 14, 18
   and match with professional
      values, 6, 9
   and societal values in ethical
      decision making, 18
Plagiarism, defined, 286

Plan action, 19
   applied in case study, 83
Policy, 13
   defined, 286
   social policy, 14
Principle(s)
   defined, 286
   ethical, 7–8, 8
Privacy
   defined, 286
   invasion of, 13
Procedure(s), defined, 286
Profession, defined, 286
Professional ethical guidelines, 8–
      12, 60
   applied in case study, 80–81
   development of, 60
   enforcement of, 60
   precedence over personal value
      system, 18
   three primary functions of, 8–9
   violations of, 60
Professional practice standards,
      defined, 286
Psychologists
   Ethical Principles and Code of
      Conduct, 250–269
Publicity, 19
   applied in case study, 82–83
   defined, 8, 286

Quality, defined, 286

Reamer, F. G., 14
Relative confidentiality, 136
   defined, 286
Reparation, defined, 8, 286
Resolve conflicts, 18
   applied in case study, 81
Respect for persons, defined, 8,
      286
Responsibilities of human service
      professionals, 13
   to promote change in laws,
      social policy, and societal
      values, 14
   to keep abreast of changes in
      law, ethics, and social policy,
      14
   to respond to agency wrong-
      doing, 206
Right to refuse treatment
   and criteria for informed
      consent, 155–156
   defined, 286

Salladay, S. A., 16
Scenario, defined, 286
Select and evaluate preferred
      action, 19
   applied in case study, 83
Sense of isolation
   and ethical dilemmas, 163

Socialization, 191
   defined, 286
Social workers
   Code of Ethics, 270
Societal values
   applied in case study, 80
   and internal conflicts, 18
   and personal issues, 104
   and personal values in ethical
      decision making, 18
   provide guidance in ethical
      decision-making, 14
Southern Regional Education
      Board, 10 (footnote), 62
Standard(s). *See also* Ethical guide-
      lines for professionals; Ethi-
      cal standards.
   defined, 286
Standards of Practice, American
      Counseling Association,
      244–249

Teamwork
   to promote success in agency,
      191
Teleologists, 7
Theories, ethical, 7

Undocumented aliens, 13
Unethical research practices
   and entry-level professional,
      211
Universality, 19
   applied in case study, 82–83
   defined, 8, 286
Utilitarianism, 7
Utilitarians, 7
Utility, defined, 8, 286
Uustal, D. B., 4, 5, 16

Value(s), 4–5. *See also* Personal
      values; Societal values
   aesthetics-based, 5
   defined, 286
   development of, 4–5
   human service, 5–6
   knowledge-based, 5
   morals-based, 5
Value system, 21
   defined, 286
Veracity, defined, 8, 286

Welfare reform
   case study, 78–85
   and implications for human
      service professionals, 84
Whistle blower, 206
   defined, 286
Woodside, M., 6, 61, 206
Work environment
   of entry-level professional, 191
Workbook approach, 3
Written consent, defined, 286

Exercise and Anecdote Index

Credits

This page constitutes an extension of the copyright page. We have made every effort to trace the ownership of all copyrighted material and to secure permission from copyright holders. In the event of any question arising as to the use of any material, we will be pleased to make the necessary corrections in future printings. Thanks are due to the following authors, publishers, and agents for permission to use the material indicated.

Chapter 1:17: Table 1.2 from *The Ethical Standards of Human Services Professionals, Human Service Education, 16*, pp. 11–17. Copyright ©1996. Reprinted with permission.

Chapter 2:25: Exercise from *Clinical ethics and values: Issues and insights in a changing healthcare environment* by D. B. Uustal, pp. 25, 46–47. Copyright ©1993 by Educational Resources in Healthcare, Inc. Reprinted with permission. **29:** Exercise from "Validation of a clinical measure of self-esteem" from *Research on Social Work Practice, 3*, No. 2, by Nugent, W. R. and J. W. Thomas, pp. 191–207. Copyright ©1993 Sage Publications, Inc. Reprinted with permission. **31:** Exercise "The Belief in Personal Control Scale: A Revised, Short Form" by J. L. Berrenberg. Copyright ©1987 Educational Resources Information Center (ERIC) ED#325 488, TM# 015 697. Adapted with permission. **37:** Exercise "Social Readjustment Rating Scale" from *Journal of Psychosomatic Research 11*(2), by T. H. Holmes and R. H. Rahe, pp. 213–218. Copyright ©1967 Elsevier Science Inc. Reprinted with permission. **43:** Exercise "Rate Your Goal-setting ability" from *Targets: How to Set Goals for Yourself and Reach Them!* by L. Tec., pp. 8–9. Copyright ©1980 Harper & Row. Adapted by permission of Leon Tec. **47–50:** Exercise from "Development of a Values Conflict Resolution Asessment," *Journal of Counseling Psychology, 34*, No. 1 by Richard T. Kinnier, pp. 31–37. Copyright ©1987 American Psychological Association. Adapted with permission.

Chapter 14:219: Exercise from *Clinical ethics and values: Issues and insights in a changing healthcare environment* by D. B. Uustal, pp. 25, 46–47. Copyright ©1993 by Educational Resources in Healthcare, Inc. Reprinted with permission.

Appendix A:223–226: "Ethical Standards of Alcoholism and Drug Abuse Counselors" reprinted by permission from National Association of Alcoholism and Drug Abuse Counselors (NAADAC). **227–249:** "Code of Ethics" from *ACA Ethical Standards Casebook,* fifth edition, by B. Herlihy and G. Corey, pp. 27–59. Copyright ©1996 American Counseling Association. Reprinted with permission. **250–269:** "Ethical Principles of Psychologists and Code of Conduct" from *American Psychologist, 47*, pp. 1597–1611. Copyright ©1992 American Psychological Association. Reprinted with permission. **270:** "NASW Code of Ethics." Copyright ©1996 National Association of Social Workers, Inc. Reprinted with permission.

ETHICAL STANDARDS OF HUMAN SERVICE PROFESSIONALS

To the reader:

This is your opportunity to have input into the review of the *Ethical Standards of Human Service Professionals*. As described in chapter 3, the Education Committee of the National Organization of Human Service Education is responsible for reviewing the standards and suggesting revisions. Most of the revisions will come from you and others like you—students and practitioners who are using the Standards as a resource in work with clients.

To keep your workbook intact, you are welcome to make a copy of this form, rather than tearing it out. Use another page if you need more space. Include your name and address if you want. We will contact you for clarification as needed.

Consider your experiences so far with the Standards. What are your thoughts?

Standard   *Comments*

Preface   _____

_____

_____

_____

_____

Number (note in the space provided)

_____   _____

_____

_____

_____

_____   _____

_____

_____

_____

_____   _____

_____

_____

_____

_____ _____

_____

_____

_____

_____

_____

_____

_____ _____

_____

_____

_____

_____

_____

_____

Suggestions for additional standards: _____

_____

_____

_____

_____

_____

_____

_____

Please check one of the following. Which best describes your current status in human services?

student _____   practitioner _____   faculty member _____

Send your response to the NOHSE Education Committee, in care of the author:

Patricia Kenyon
Arizona Western College
P.O. Box 929
Yuma, AZ 85366-0929

EVALUATION OF THIS WORKBOOK

To the owner of this workbook:

    I hope you have enjoyed *What Would* You *Do?* I would like to hear from you about your experiences with it and your reactions to it. I will use your comments and those of others to improve it for future readers.

In what course or courses was this workbook assigned? _____

_____

_____

What did you like best about this workbook? _____

_____

_____

_____

What did you like least about it? _____

_____

_____

_____

Please consider each chapter. What other comments do you have?

_____

_____

_____

_____

College or university name: _____

_____

Your instructor's name: _____

_____

To keep your workbook intact, you are welcome to make a copy of this form, rather than tearing it out. Send it to me at the following address:

Patricia Kenyon
Arizona Western College
P.O. Box 929
Yuma, AZ 85366-0929

Thank you for your time, effort, and comments!
Patricia Kenyon